Praise for *Playing the Game*

Playing the Game is a provocative pastoral theological study that weaves together social theoretical insights, Black and womanist theologies, neuroscience, and personal experience in a narration of Black athletic life as representative of life in these United States of America. In this intriguing satire Gary Green gives us much food for thought and great spiritual counsel for navigating the political game of life. This book is for all people, for we are all athletes in mind, heart, and body.

      Emmanuel Y. Lartey, Charles Howard Candler Professor of Pastoral Theology and Spiritual Care, Emory University

Playing the Game is a raw and unapologetic dive into the relationship between Black embodiment, its brilliance, and the absurd. The import of its reading can be found in the way it unpacks the funny but true aspects of American culture that point to the hidden nature of Black divinity.

      Philip Butler, assistant professor of theology and Black posthuman artificial intelligence systems, Iliff School of Theology

Gary Green provides a unique window into the lives of Black men under the shadow of white supremacy. Through the metaphor of "beast," Green exposes the absurd dynamics of race in the context of everyday life. Honest, unflinching, and powerful, Green draws the parallels between racism as enacted in quotidian experience and in sport. A must-read for those of us who want to understand better the limitations and the binds that racism creates for the human beings it targets.

      Barbara J. McClure, associate professor of pastoral theology and practice, Brite Divinity School at Texas Christian University

Playing the Game is a masterful interrogation of the moral landscapes in which race, sport, and society collide. Gary F. Green II lays bare the ethical contradictions that Black athletes navigate, exposing the systemic forces that shape their embodied experiences. As a scholar of theological ethics and sports chaplaincy, I find Green's work to be a compelling moral critique, one that not only names the injustices but also calls for a deeper reckoning with the theological and ethical obligations of our shared humanity. Green's book is a crucial resource for those who serve athletes with integrity and care, so that ministers see sport as a site of both harm and hope—a place where prophetic truth-telling must accompany pastoral presence.

John B. White, Riley Professor of Practical Theology and Ethics, and director of Truett Seminary's Sport Chaplaincy/Ministry Program, Baylor University

PLAYING THE GAME

PLAYING THE GAME

EMBODIED BRILLIANCE BEYOND THE MORAL LIMITS OF RACE IN SPORT

GARY F. GREEN II

FORTRESS PRESS
Minneapolis

PLAYING THE GAME
Embodied Brilliance Beyond the Moral Limits of Race in Sport

Copyright © 2025 Fortress Press. All rights reserved. Except for brief quotations in critical articles or reviews, no part of this book may be reproduced in any manner without prior written permission from the publisher. Email copyright@fortresspress.com or write to Permissions, Fortress Press, PO Box 1209, Minneapolis, MN 55440-1209.

31 30 29 28 27 26 25   1 2 3 4 5 6 7 8 9

Library of Congress Control Number: 2024061412 (print)

Cover image: Profile of runner - stock photo from Digital Vision via Getty Images
Cover design: Kris E. Miller

Print ISBN: 979-8-8898-3358-1
eBook ISBN: 979-8-8898-3359-8

For all the Black athletes in the world who have had to carry the weight of white supremacy in our bodies, consciously and unconsciously

To the brothers I have made along the way, from teammates on the Southeast Apaches to my boys at KU

And for the Wrecking Crew

This is our story

CONTENTS

Acknowledgments ix
Preface xi

1. The Myth of Level Playing Fields — 1
2. Marshawn Lynch — 29
   "Beast" and the Historical Play on "Human"
3. Steph Curry — 59
   Range Beyond the Ploy of Neoliberal Rationality
4. Deion Sanders — 91
   Presence Beyond the Pull of Respectability
5. Embodied Brilliance Beyond the Myth — 133

Notes 173
Bibliography 195
Index 205

ACKNOWLEDGMENTS

This book is the result of conversations I have had and been held by all my life. It would not exist without the wisdom of people who have provided me space to think freely in community. I am grateful for collaborative conversations with my colleagues at United Theological Seminary, which have been fertile soil from which my theological perspective has blossomed. I am also grateful to my students, for challenging me and trusting me. The intellectual alchemy of the classroom is a magic that this book is indebted to, and that I am grateful for. I am also grateful for the collegial conversations I had with mentors while a PhD student at Brite Divinity School. I deeply appreciate Barbara McClure and Nancy Ramsay for the ways they both shaped me as a critical thinking pastoral theologian, and for affirming the uniqueness of my voice during a fragile time of transition in my life as a thinker. I am also grateful to Keri Day, who provided me a safe space where I could bring my Blackness to the conversation without dressing it up. I am also indebted to Dr. Day for introducing me to womanist theology. And to Molly Marshall, who saw a theologian in me long before I did, and who created a space for me to begin my theological journey of discovery. Thank you.

I have also been shaped by the conversations I've had with the brothers I made while playing football. To my KU brothers especially, all I will say is this: the Burge. The culture we created came in clutch during some of the most difficult times we dealt with. But they were some of the most enjoyable times too. Whether we were roasting each other in the Burge, or talking more deeply about shared pain, this book is a direct result of the space we gave each other to process. And laugh our asses off. And of course, the Green family, because laughing together with loved ones is a foundational piece of the person I am, and it continues to do my heart well. Thank you to my siblings and my cousins for loving me and laughing with me during my most formative years. And thank you for the ways we still do.

To Monica, my wife, my lover, and my best friend. I mean it when I tell Monica that I could not have done this without her, whether I was talking about pursuing a PhD, writing a dissertation, or now, publishing my first book. She has believed in me and supported me as I have pursued a calling that continues to unfold. And she has trusted the process with me while keeping our family afloat during the financial crisis that is graduate school. I am deeply grateful to you, Mimo, and I love you. I am also grateful to our children, and the beautiful chaos of our lives. My family is my heart and the lifeblood behind my intellectual energy. I am also grateful for Brandon Logan, my right hand. Our bond growing up has been bedrock for me, and our brotherhood continues to give me life in all directions. And to Carey Newman, my coach, who pushed me to take off the training wheels of my dissertation and take on the theological story I really wanted to tell. Thank you for cutting me loose.

The person I am today is the result of the ongoing conversations I have had with my parents, Gary Sr. and Mary Green-Lee. All the words in this book cannot fully capture my gratitude for having had two parents that loved me and were always present in my life growing up. I am grateful for the perspectives they both shaped me with, and for my dad's wisdom as a Black athlete, and coach, who could give me the game in ways that many young Black men never experience. I am grateful. But especially to my mom, who was the first conversation partner I ever had. My mom literally shaped me into the thinker I am today. During my most precious years, she talked to me. With me. She listened to my ideas and gave me space to work them out. The conversations she and I had during those long-ass road trips from Texas to Missouri sustained me, when I wasn't asleep. And my intellectual connection with my mom continues to sustain me, even though her grandchildren tend to dominate our conversations now. Thank you, Mom, for everything.

And of course, to Black athletes, who continue to inspire me. I am because we are.

PREFACE

Act I

I grew up watching BET's *Comic View*. This was a cutthroat stand-up comedy show akin to *Showtime at the Apollo* that featured some of the most brilliant up-and-coming Black comedians before they became household names. It was like the PG-13 version of *Def Comedy Jam*, which was the reason it aired on BET, rather than HBO, every Tuesday and Friday night at 9 p.m. EST, 8 p.m. Central. I grew up in Central time, and I remember every detail about the show because that is how much I loved it. This was the only show I looked forward to watching more than BET's *Uncut*, because what can I say? I was a young Black teenager who was just starting to feel himself (out) while trying to cultivate an identity called "man," which was even more overdetermined by hypermasculine sexuality then than it is now. Oh, how I would watch intently as these young Black stand-up comedians told jokes that ranged from sexuality to spirituality, back when I assumed the two were opposites. I was enamored with the different ways these brilliant minds embodied comedic sensibilities, and how they created worlds of alternative meaning that gave me a break from the reality I was living.

Whether it was Bruce Bruce telling a story about talking shit to an old Black churchwoman in the middle of service when he was a kid; or Sommore breaking open the sexual dynamics of Black intimate relationships; or Tyler Craig's fake drunk routine, where he would draw out these elaborate stories, giving glimpses of hilarity along the way before offering the real punchline, which was always preceded by, "The moral of the story is . . .," Black comedians gave me a peek behind the curtain of my own cultural reality, but in a much more unfiltered way than the sitcoms available at the time. I loved it, because I was raised in a family that loved to talk shit, playfully. Playing the Dozens was a love language for us. So, it makes sense that Black comedians would become the first social commentators to provoke my curiosity across a range of topics related to my masculinity. But as varied as their jokes were, poking holes in the problem of race as it played out in the context of everyday life was a common theme among them.

Black comedians gave me so many "morals of the story" about race that I began to question the relational rules by which we govern ourselves in society. Not only did Black comedians offer some of the best critiques of white supremacy I had heard, but they did so in a way that laid bare the absurdity of race in the first place. I appreciated how they brought attention to the subtle power dynamics of racial interactions, and how they did it creatively in ways that opened up windows into alternative realities that simultaneously shed light and shit on the racial reality I had to live. It looked increasingly stupid to me that I had to change the way I walked or talked around certain people just because I was Black. It made no sense that I had to downplay my personality so as not to draw too much attention to myself. And I hated the fact that I always had to say "yes sir" or "no sir" to the disrespectful cop who decided to exercise his state-sanctioned ability to harass me behind some bullshit. Really? I would think to myself, "Really, I have to play this game?" It made no sense but made all the sense in the world. I knew I had to play along, because I knew what could happen if I didn't. I was well aware of how easily the narrative of Black male criminality could converge on my circumstances, on my body, whether I was engaged in criminal activity or not. So, I never questioned it.

Each time my dad reminded me, "Son, you have to know how to play the game," I never questioned it. I conceded, every time. I downloaded that double consciousness in ways that would have made W. E. B. DuBois proud. And if you knew "Coach Green," you knew my dad prided himself on *thorough* communication—he lectured me all the damn time about this need to move with a kind of racial elusiveness that was always one step ahead of even the possibility of racialized mistreatment. No wonder I could make people miss on the field—all of us translates. I couldn't translate it at the time, but I was being trained to see life as a political game. My attention was being attuned to the subtleties of my own embodied performance as if I was an actor on a stage every day, caught up in a production with an all-white cast, tasked to play a part that I did not write, or else. Between Black comedians and two single parents who trained their son to live strategically, I was gifted with the curse of a comedic sensibility, which meant I couldn't help but pay attention to the relational dynamics of race before I knew how to say that academically, not to mention to see the charade of it all.

Of all the schooling I received, it was Black comedians who planted in my consciousness a curiosity about the politics of race that both warned me and left me wanting, needing to understand more deeply how a concocted myth about Black men, a caricature, could materialize in myriad forms of mistreatment despite society's best attempts to be "post-racial." This cursed gift of paying attention caused my curiosity to grow into frustration every time I watched news reports about Black men being racially targeted by white people who didn't mean to be racist, especially when there was no mention of the caricature. Never mind the psychological trauma I experienced from seeing Black men murdered and then blamed for their own untimely deaths behind portrayals of criminality. Sadly, I was accustomed to this same old song sung for so long in the United States, even while it *does* feel like a little piece of me dies every time I see it happen—I learned pretty quickly not to watch Fox News for that reason.

But what really frustrated me was how the caricature was never named on CNN or MSNBC either, when these were the more "progressive" attempts to critique white supremacy. Certainly, there is still the need to call out the "racist" in the white hood, especially given the ways our president has emboldened such blatancy. But watching coverage that leans to the left also tends to leave people lost, because they can't help but moralize white supremacy. This tendency to moralize complex racial interactions reduces the real culprit to a lone "racist" who is assumed to be acting independently, and willfully, as if locating guilt guarantees that justice has been served. Sometimes the conversation goes deeper, such as when George Floyd was murdered. This blatant act caught on camera proved again the plotline that Black people have been talking about for decades, and a whole new group of white people saw it this time too. But there was still that suspicious sigh when Derek Chauvin was convicted because, once again, we found the "racist." Usually when that happens, people relax. Society feels a little better about itself, so there is no real need to recalibrate. But finding the "racist" misses the mark because it allows the caricature behind the assumptions of Black male criminality to remain hidden, which makes it easier to maintain the (white) lie that keeps enlivening these circumstances in the first place.

Act II

Sport was supposed to be different, and in many respects it was. It offered me a different game to play, in a world where I thought I could create my own character away from the wiles of the caricature. From the time I was a young boy to the time I hung up my cleats after my tenure at the University of Kansas, people knew me as an athlete. I knew myself this way too. Sport provided a space that allowed me the freedom to explore and express my being more than any other social context, especially growing up in South Texas. This was the other game I felt I had to play, the game that seemingly chose me. My dad and uncle played at the highest levels, as did our cousins Jim and David Hill, and each of the "Green Boys" in my generation accepted scholarships to play in college, including myself. Plus, playing the game of football was always what got me recognized in a positive light growing up. This meant a lot to a Black kid in Texas. In some ways, sport was an escape from the stigma of my Blackness—from the caricature—because being an "athlete" meant I had an excuse for showing up in places I otherwise would not have been allowed into. But even then, athleticism was always more than just a meal ticket to me.

Sport was the language I spoke. Outside of comedy, it was the mother tongue I made sense of my world with. And athleticism always felt like my greatest gift, so naturally I put a lot of stock into my identity as an "athlete." Perhaps this is why one of my high school coaches, Ron Rittimann, would sometimes sarcastically say to me, "Be an athlete," anytime he wanted to motivate me to do better. His playful nudge would usually come when I had tripped over my own feet or made some other silly misstep that revealed a lackadaisical demeanor, to which he would offer this reminder. He was a coach that cared about me, and he believed in me. And similarly to my dad's reminders to "play the game," I knew exactly what Coach Rittimann meant each time he offered this loving critique: Pay attention, because we both know you are better than that.

And he was right, because athleticism was my craft. It was embodied art to me. I poured myself into developing my craft and used it as a tool because sport felt like my best chance at "making it" in life, even though I was a straight-A student. It simply made more sense when I looked at the images of successful Black men that populated my world, whether in my familial network or on ESPN. I studied sport every day, rep after rep, until all the conditioning I had done was second nature, and the once mindful movements that made me excel became muscle memory. I still find myself dishing out dead legs and spinning around corners—or the kids—in my home, because my brain simply cannot forget what has been downloaded, and what worked so well for so long. Being an athlete was always for me another way of paying a deeper kind of attention to life, a full-bodied attention. And it always registered in my brain as much as it did my body.

But no matter how far I went, that damn caricature kept showing up. Twice within the first week as a freshman at KU, he reared his ugly head to remind me that I couldn't escape—that no matter how much intellectual energy I put into my craft, most people would still only see me for what my Black athletic body could "uniquely" do. Navigating the world of sport always felt more intellectual than people made it out to be. And to be honest, I always felt more nuanced than I knew people were conditioned to think of me, *because* I was a Black athlete. To be "Black" and an "athlete" was like living with a double whammy of being dumbed down twice, fetishized for what my body could do on the field, but feared for what it might do off it. At least this is the story the caricature tells.

In the first interaction, he showed up in his usual (uni)form based on the cultural fear associated with my body. I was driving back to the Jayhawk Towers from the grocery store with one of my homegirls from the track team when I got pulled over by a police officer who was attending to people who had apparently just gotten into a car accident. If that sounds strange it is because it was. How could I have gotten "pulled over" by a cop who wasn't driving, but assisting people who might have been hurt? Well, because he left the scene of the accident to walk out into the middle of the street, raised his hand as if to tell me to stop, then walked over to the driver side window and told me, "I'm gonna write you a ticket because your music is too loud." Already having turned my music down, I said to him, "I'm sorry officer, I didn't know that was a law." I was from Texas where having beats in the trunk was a way of life. I didn't know it was a problem in Lawrence, Kansas. And I was a conscientious kid, my music really wasn't *that* loud to begin with. But my Black Hyundai Sonata with rims was, as was my lack of tint on the front window, which allowed him to see clearly who was driving. It was clear that I wasn't from around there, and probably feeling myself (out) a little too much.

He proceeded to flex, telling me repeatedly to turn my music down until it was on zero—I had turned it down as soon as I saw him, then again once he started talking, then I twisted the knob all the way to zero once it was clear what he was trying to do. He had to make a point. And it was clear to my homegirl as well, who immediately blurted out "this is bullshit," to which I quickly shushed her because growing up in Texas taught me not to talk back to the police. "Yes sir" and "no sir" only. She was Black but grew up in Iowa and had never experienced this firsthand before. It felt familiar to me. He took my driver's license, verified that I had insurance—and no warrants—then came back to the car and said, "I've decided I'm going to let you off with a warning this time." He then gave my belongings back and walked *back* over to the people who were still sitting in shock while waiting for tow trucks and EMS.

The caricature has a more slippery side though, suave even. Whereas he sows hate based on the cultural assumption that Black men are criminals—played out in the first interaction—he preys on softer sensibilities in this second interaction. Me and some of my teammates were walking out of the Jayhawk Towers when a group of white girls in a blue Volkswagen Beetle drove by, and one of them leaned out of the window and yelled my name, in her most excited, endearing way. It was like she was celebrating me as if I had already scored a touchdown. I was heavily recruited coming out of high school, so she probably had already heard my name. But to have developed the wherewithal to remember what I looked like well enough to recognize me walking out of the Jayhawk Towers suggests that she had done some research, which blew my mind.

I remember having two thoughts in that moment. One was definitely, "Ooooo weee it's finna be lit!"—or whatever version of that phrase we used in 2004. One cannot expect any college kid to get that kind of ego stroke and not at least be curious. I wasn't *that* curious though, because it was the second thought I had that reigned supreme: "Man, you don't even know me." I think I said it under my breath though, because I didn't want to reveal the emotional complexity young Black men were taught to hide in that culture. But it struck me in that moment that I was essentially, and potentially, a pricey piece of meat, fetishized because I was Black and I played football. For all I know, all she saw was "BBC" when she looked at me. Who knows, the imagination is expansive. But it is also socially linked, and there was already a market for America's masturbatory excitement about Black men, especially athletes. What I do know, and what I quickly found out, was that none of that flattening flattery happens when you get hurt.

Act III

I was trained as a pastoral theologian, yet another field that prides itself on paying attention.[1] The name of the disciplinary game, at least as I played it, was to figure out what "care" looked like for young Black men living in a racist society. The question itself seemed asinine to me, but I was the one asking it. I knew intuitively, from the first day, that even the best therapeutic models of care could only go so far when my literal life could be on the line, much less address the psychological complexity of having to live with that awareness. Fortunately, I had gone to a program that already had a sense of the politics surrounding practices (and theories) of care—that the therapeutic models themselves were caught up in social and political systems given to Eurocentric thinking, which meant they did little to address the politically complicated lives of racialized people. They were not designed to. This programmatic sensibility was born from an even deeper study of "human being," with a theological bent. Theological anthropology became the perfect playground for a curious mind that never got to ask these kinds of questions in the Black Church, at least not with the breadth that Black comedians had given me—or the raw honesty.

The program itself was built on the recognition that being human means being relational—that whether we like it or not, we exist in webs of interrelatedness that form, and deform, us as people. Pastoral theology taught me to recognize the complexity of our existence, how we live in relation to constructed categories that are laden with power. And how we reproduce them. But what I appreciated most about pastoral theology was how interdisciplinary it allowed me to be. By nature of trying to understand the "human" from all angles in service to constructing more adequate models of care for marginalized people, pastoral theology left the analytical door wide open for the "comedian" and the "athlete" to return. In hindsight, they had been with me the whole time just waiting to be let in.

The comedian reminded me that life is a charade, a political game we play that has material consequences. This caused me to see the tragedy of white supremacy more deeply. The despair. The fact that George Floyd didn't *have* to die. Nor did Trayvon Martin. Or Emmitt Till. And the comedian is relentless. He continues to show me the absurdity of men who murder Black boys because they are sanctioned by a State (of being) that makes this behavior culturally acceptable, because of a caricature; or women that fear, or fancy, Black men because of the same caricature; not to mention those of us Black men who buy into its seduction. The comedian sees the slippage in political life, stresses it even. He understands how a situation could go sideways or stay on track based solely on how we act in concert with whatever lies we believe, then embody in relation to each other. Refusing to let me look away, the comedian is hell-bent on revealing to me the relational science of racism in a way that would haunt me if it were not for the athlete, who looks deeper. He comes to the conversation with an optimism that is based in a deep knowledge of the body and its interworking.

The athlete reminds me how important laughter is for the body; for the brain; the heart. But the comedian, being the cynic he is, always chimes in, "Sheeeiit, imagine how bad white supremacy is then, for the body; the brain; the heart." I laugh. Remembering his training, the athlete retorts, "But what about the possibility of our bodies? Let's not forget about the neurophysiological changes that *could* happen if people took the comedian's insights seriously, not to mention how this might translate into embodied action to the contrary." After all, the athlete is an incurable optimist. The comedian, not so much: "But what about *probability* based on political design, or the fact that people embody white supremacy in ways they don't even realize?" Touché. The athlete, beginning to feel witty himself, says sarcastically, "Yea, but remember that political slippage you were talking about? How a situation *could* go either way based on what we believe, then embody in relation to each other?" Beginning to retreat, the comedian asks, "But how do you get people to believe something about Black men when they can't even see how the caricature has convinced them that we are not human?" The athlete smirks, "You show them how none of us are."

This book is born from the witty banter within me, informed by the fields on which I have played in service to telling a different story about Black men, by way of Black athletes. It is a story about Black athletes, told from the perspective of a Black athlete who found his voice only after reclaiming parts of himself that colonized thinking caused him to assume were not welcome, or legitimate, in the "academic" world—because the caricature is an imposter too. It was only after I learned to trust the comedian in me, and the athlete, that I realized Black athletes have a theological story to tell that goes much deeper than I could have ever imagined. The book demonstrates how Black athleticism possesses, and is possessed by, an embodied intellectual depth, a brilliance, that has eluded our cultural ability to recognize it as such. We simply cannot see it because the caricature has created a lens that is designed to protect the architect, the writer of the script, who uses "post-raciality" as a form of plausible deniability. As a result, we have all been recruited into a language game that forecloses our capacity to recognize the deeply embodied handle Black athletes have always had on the very "humanity" that (white) supremacist *(hi)stories* suggest we don't possess. And yet, without the technological brilliance of Black athleticism, this country would not know which way is up when it comes to the capitalist ideal that colonial whiteness created.

Playing the Game is a provocation. It is a work of theological satire that invites us to take seriously a hidden dimension of white supremacy as it plays out in plain sight. The story moves at the same level of subtlety with which white supremacy operates, breaking open its cultural logic across three dimensions that move from the surface of Black athletes' bodies down to the *crux* of our being. The narrative begins as a cultural criticism that develops into a conversation with Marshawn Lynch, illustrating how he exposes the *cultural* dimension of white supremacy. It proceeds with an exposé that Steph Curry provides, by disrupting the *embodied* dimensions of white supremacy's economic logic. It then gets into the finer details of the way Deion Sanders, a.k.a. "Prime Time," disrupts the *psychospiritual* dimensions of white supremacy. And it culminates by bringing the theological message of Black athletes close enough to home that we can feel the anthropological significance of Black athleticism. Hence, the theology of this book is sensual, but it only shows up as such after clearing the colonizing dross of doctrinal thinking. I am not concerned with finding the "racist," but rather calling us all to account and inviting a deeper attention to be paid.

Thus, *Playing the Game* weaves together the insights of social theory, Black and womanist theologies, and neuroscience to tell a story that renders the caricature laughable as a way to make legible a new language by which we can begin to recognize the ways Black athleticism already bleeds the categories and cultural logics of white supremacy, and how this illustrates the embodied brilliance of Black athletes.

CHAPTER ONE

The Myth of Level Playing Fields

We have to talk about liberating minds as well as liberating society.
—Angela Davis

THE COLONIAL UNITED States has always had a flattening fascination with Black men's bodies. Born from the space between fear and fetish, it is an exploitative fascination bound by the need to control. This fascination reflects an intuitive awareness of something more, but by capitalist necessity that "more" has been mythologized as something less, something "lower," akin to the animals. "Other" without the concession. Black men are rendered "other" without any recognition that their difference could be divine—a signal toward a deeper, darker dimension of *imago Dei*. And yet, at another level, this fascination reflects a tacit awareness of the possibility that the suspected divinity of Black men is central to the whole enterprise, and perhaps to human existence itself. But it is reticent to explore or admit as much, because that would be too costly. The stark reality is that this country has always needed a way to simultaneously extract vitality from Black men while somehow preventing them from using it for their own benefit, from realizing it and running out of bounds, from enfleshing their freedom and exposing it all as a charade.

Antebellum slavery was the first iteration of this colonizing game, where boundaries based on racialized myths were drawn and enforced with violence, legally. Eventually those boundaries became blurry, and there became the need to fold in new mechanisms of control. With lynching came more explicit articulations of the inscribed inhumanity used to justify the first iteration, but now blown into the kind of sexual proportions that could convince the public that they too should be afraid of these divine animals, which effectively justified the same dynamics of power amid changing rules to the game. Alongside lynching came incarceration, yet another political shoot that sprang from the same web of lies similarly spun toward the assumption of inherent criminality.

In many respects, the complex of sport is the next iteration of America's flattening fascination with the suspected divinity of Black men. To the degree that the Black male body can still function as the central prop while white men remain protagonists, sport is the perfect stage for this play of racial politics in the United States. It is both a microcosm and a microphone in relation to the insidious racism that visits Black men. Yet, by nature of its participation in neoliberal capitalism, the complex of sport has provided contemporary cover for the continued extraction of Black vitality. Only this time it is spun positively in a way that pays, which plays (to) a disillusioned public for whom "post-raciality" is a priority. It is a seductive space that allows Black men a level and regularity of free expression that is unique, but only insofar as such "freedom" can be contained and framed as inconsequential entertainment—where superhumanity can be dished out in subhuman doses and displays of divinity snapshot as mere spectacle. Operating alongside the continued legacies of lynching and incarcerating, sport is the ideal container where the veneration of Black men can remain couched in commodification based on the concocted belief that they are "beasts" at best.[1]

Marshawn Lynch is the perfect pin to place here. Lynch epitomizes the racializing way in which the embodied brilliance of Black athletes is flattened into a caricature able to be commodified and consumed by the public. Perhaps nothing illustrates this flattening better than the racial commentary surrounding his infamous game-winning touchdown during the NFC Wild Card Playoffs in 2010. In what future Hall of Fame defensive end Robert Mathis called the greatest run he has ever seen, and certainly the play that made "beast mode" go viral, Lynch took a handoff that should have merely gained a few yards to keep the clock running and turned it into one of the most brilliant displays of strength, power, speed, agility, acuity, elusiveness, and situational awareness ever embodied in a single play. And he did it with style.

Marshawn Lynch's game-winning touchdown has since been remembered as the "beast quake" because it sent fans into such a frenzy that nearby seismographs registered the stomping stadium activity as an earthquake. Clearly, it was not completely lost on fans that they had just witnessed something spectacular. That much was demonstrated by the decibels of their excitement. What was lost on them, however, and where viewing audiences often need help, is in knowing how to make technical sense of these dazzling displays of athleticism. Hence, sports commentary is a primary feature of the athletic industrial *complex*[2] that fans rely on to follow the movements of a game. Certainly, most people can surmise the significance of a sixty-seven-yard touchdown in which someone they call "beast mode" breaks half a dozen tackles and secures victory for the team they happen to be cheering for. But beyond this surface-level celebration, sports commentators are the narrators who fill in the conceptual gaps for the millions of television viewers and listeners on the radio. And when "beast quake" happened, legendary commentator Steve Raible stepped in:

> Matthew under center, Obamanu goes in motion right to left. Turn and hand to Lynch, left side. Finds a little bit of a hole, keeps his legs moving! He's across the 40!! Midfield!! 45, he's on the run, Lynch! 40, pushes a man, 35!! Look at him go!! He's down to the 20, 15!! He could go, he is gonna go! TOUCHDOWN SEAHAWKS!! OH MY WORD!! A 67-yard run!! Marshawn Lynch!! UNBELIEVABLE!! He must've knocked five guys down on the way to the endzone! THE BEAST IS ALIVE AND WELL!!![3]

And in that moment the historical association between Black men and "beast" was resuscitated. Good intentions notwithstanding, Raible's commentary contributes to the cultural tendency to interpret Black athleticism as a physical gift grounded by brutish sensibilities. To call a Black athlete a "beast"—even in a celebratory way—is to flatten an expression of embodied brilliance into an innate physicality that (presumably) exists independent of cognitive capabilities. In other words, it signifies the idea that Black athleticism is uniquely capable, but only in a carnal sense—but that cognition, according to cultural assumptions, is lacking. And insofar as these flattening references draw on the historical marriage between *cognition* and "human," yet another Black man is rendered inhuman.

The normalcy of "beast" in sport

Although this may seem like a leap to the untrained eye, particularly when considering the cultural capital that has been built up around this caricature, it is commonplace to associate Black athletic success with innate physical ability. Sports commentators regularly draw from the same script when filling in gaps for millions of fans who need help making sense of what they are watching. In a study that analyzed depictions of Black and white quarterbacks in college and professional football, researchers tested hypotheses occasioned by previous studies that demonstrated marked differences in the ways Black and white athletes were represented to the public. Given the recent uptick in Black quarterbacks in college and the NFL—a position previously reserved for white players due to its association with cognitive intelligence—researchers followed the logic of what seemed to be racial progress to discover if the content of on-air commentary was also changing with the times. The findings were not surprising. Despite increased numbers of Black quarterbacks across collegiate and professional football, commentators consistently depicted their success as the result of innate athletic (read: physical) skill over and against qualities such as composure, concentration, or commitment. Meanwhile, failures among white quarterbacks were attributed to a lack of athletic skill.[4] In other words, success among Black quarterbacks and failure among white quarterbacks were both assumed to be the result of genetic factors outside of their rational control, the difference of innate physical ability.

Similar studies have been conducted in the NBA, and the data testifies to the same trend: success among Black players is overwhelmingly attributed to innate physical ability, while failures are believed to result from a lack of qualities associated with intelligence.[5] Since these examples only represent sports commentary in the United States, one might wonder how this data bears out globally across sports with much larger viewerships and less specificity to American politics. In an analysis of match-day commentary at the men's 2018 FIFA World Cup, researchers analyzed the language and racial framing of commentators. The findings are as follows:

> The overall results indicated that praise comments differed for players of visibly different racial backgrounds with regard to their focus and frequency. The highest percentage of the 448 praise comments aimed at white players was directed at learned abilities (47.9%). This was followed by praise given for their physical (18.3%), character (13.8%), cognition (11.4%) and lastly natural (8.6%) attributes. The highest percentage of the 281 positive praise comments given to visibly black players centred on physicality (69.8%). Then natural (10.7%), learned (10.3%), character (5%) and cognition (4%).[6]

The data testifies to the ubiquity of the belief that Black athletic success is best attributed to innate physical ability—that Black men are just built differently. Perhaps the anecdotal evidence of this cultural tendency is even more telling. There is an abiding hesitancy among many of my own former teammates and current NFL athletes to associate players like Tom Brady with the same script. When asked if they would consider Tom Brady a "beast," there is often an initial pause, then either an allowance made or preference given to another phrase that similarly signifies the kind of dominance that "beast" is meant to register: G.O.A.T.[7] Tom Brady does not register as a "beast," but rather is celebrated as the Greatest Of All Time.[8] As legitimate as this accolade may be, the point here is that it requires intellectual effort to register Tom Brady in terms of a trope that is by default reserved for Black men.

The currency of "beast"

"Beast" has become cultural currency. And its popularity can be seen clearly in the ways this historically racist association has taken on a celebratory nature. All iterations of the phrase, "he's a beast," represent an arrival of sorts, especially in sports. To be deemed a "beast" is to be celebrated as one who has topped their respective field. It has been so popular that the NFL Network created a segment devoted to highlighting exceptional performances entitled, "He's a BEAST," wherein Hall of Fame players and coaches—now analysts—muster up their most aggressive, absurd tones and facial expressions to overlay (read: undercut) the most brilliant performances each week with this flattening phrase.[9] And they do so with the best intentions.

The celebratory nature of "beast" is common parlance in the NBA as well. In a podcast episode of *Jalen & Jacoby*, Jalen Rose, former NBA star, responded to his cohost David Jacoby about an elite performance on the part of NBA star Giannis Antetokounmpo. When describing what he liked most about Antetokounmpo's performance, Rose stated:

> Now when he dunks, he does it angrily. It's one thing to get the bucket, because you're the biggest, tallest dude out there. It's another thing to do it with ferocity. And that's what I saw from him, a "beast" out there! He's taking it personal on every possession. That's what I appreciate.[10]

While Rose made his final comments, Jacoby cosigned his statements with interjections of, "yep, yep," and "I like it." He then responded to Rose's "beast" comment by saying, "He's snarling, snarling, lifting up the knees while he hangs on the rim. I like it a lot, what I saw from the Greek Freak."[11] If this language is not obvious enough to illustrate both the regularity and celebratory weight of this term—and its racial association—the fact that Antetokounmpo has been given the nickname "The Greek Freak," which suggests that he is a "freak of nature," demonstrates how "beast" functions as a celebration of Black athleticism flattened to innate, animalistic talent.[12] Hence, even if Tom Brady is a "beast," the term lands in a sense much different than the "savagery" inscribed onto the bodies of his Black male counterparts.

"Beast" has become so popular that it has bled into other industries in similar celebratory fashion. In a BBC interview about his film *Black KKKlansman*, famed director Spike Lee is asked about the film's cast members. After describing the immense talent of John David Washington,[13] Spike Lee shares with movie critic Ali Plumb his assessment of Washington's co-star, Adam Driver:

Lee: And then let's talk about Adam Driver.
Plumb: He is, I mean astonishing. He's got so much work to do.
Lee: He ... he's a beast.[14]

After the interviewer laughs at the statement, aware of different cultural and linguistic norms in the United Kingdom, Lee clarifies his comments by stating explicitly that his reference to "beast" is a good thing. He then cites Driver's exceptional talent and unusually broad range as an actor as the rationale for his referring to him in this way. Beyond film and other cultural spaces where "beast" has become a signifier for mastery of one's craft, the top workout playlist on Spotify is entitled "Beast Mode," which itself is an ode to the nickname Marshawn Lynch himself has carried since high school. Despite its racist origins, but in keeping with its racial association to Black men, "beast" has become a cultural phenomenon. It is celebrated as an accolade that has been adopted by people across races and a variety of industries.

The political play of "beast"

The racial picture gets more complex, however, when considering the embrace of "beast" among Black athletes themselves. "I'm a beast" has become a mantra for many who claim this trope as a positive affirmation of athletic prowess. And its lure is connected to its lore, which is to acknowledge that the currency of "beast" is understandably attractive to young Black athletes, particularly when they see the ways Lynch has built up such a lucrative brand around it. He has a clothing line and a website that features apparel that any Black kid would covet, not to mention his viral popularity on talk shows and television series that have nothing to do with football.[15] Marshawn Lynch is a household name now, and "beast mode" is what got him there. However, it is important to note that Lynch's consent to be called a "beast" reflects a longstanding subculture among young Black athletes. It is the same subculture that has allowed young Black men to (re)claim words like "nigga" or "boy" for themselves as part of a wider reclamation of dignity in the face of denigration—a subculture that defangs the master's tools as a strategy to beat him at his own game.[16]

Lynch's embrace of "beast mode" was born from a well-established wellspring of Black men who have strategically agreed to the racial rules of a societal game set against them. What's more, much of the cultural popularity around "beast" has come from Black athletes' embrace of it. They have taken it and made it popular despite the disdain of its subtext. Black athletes know they are being exploited but they've bought into the mantra because of its monetary promise. They rightfully want a cut of the billions of dollars trafficked based on (the brilliance of) their bodies. And to be sure, it is about more than just the money, but rather doing what one has to do to secure the kind of life that money buys in a capitalist society co-constructed by white supremacy. *Playing* the game, as it were. But playing (along with) the game works in problematic directions as well. Its participatory function simultaneously *reflects* historical fictions while *reproducing* the political dynamics that give them rise.

On one level, the willingness of Black athletes to embrace this trope *reflects* and *reproduces* the cultural trauma that Black men endure vis-à-vis racist caricatures. In the same way that Lynch's consent to be called "beast" reflects a subculture of survival, his fame around it reproduces its broader cultural appeal. This can be particularly harmful for young Black athletes who have not yet become conscious of the collateral damage of trafficking a trope like "beast" onto their own bodies. That Black men and boys have been seduced into an embrace of their own commodification testifies to the way in which racial trauma has been normalized in our lives. However, the embrace of "beast" also testifies to its economic allure, which has an appeal that is hard to resist when trying to meet more immediate needs. Hence, when buying into the performance of "beast" offers the possibility of freedom from its consequences, many oblige.

On a broader level, the embrace of "beast" *reflects* and *reproduces* racial scripts that have been used to justify the dehumanization of Black men culturally. "Beast" has been constructed at the intersections of race, gender, and sexuality in ways that cast Black men as imminent threats to the social order. It plays on the historical fear of Black men violently pursuing white women, which was already a tacit aspect of its antebellum fiction, rearticulated during Jim Crow as a justification for lynching. Theologian Dwight Hopkins has conceived of this construct as a triangle of erotic desire. He notes how the fetishization of Black men was married to the fear of them, casting the Black male as a sexualized beast in pursuit of white women, requiring white men to step in as saviors to protect them.[17] Inasmuch as the presumed purity of white women was constructed as an idea that extended from the supremacy of whiteness, white men's pursuit of, and violence toward, Black men was believed to be necessary in order to protect society from the menacing of Black masculinity.

The legibility of Black male inhumanity

Tropes like "beast" register as normal because there is already a legibility to Black male inhumanity, and it plays out whether Black men are being criminalized or fetishized for their athletic prowess. This is not to suggest that Black men are not human, at least not in a way that takes that category—"human"—at its word. To the contrary, this project explores the ways Black being transcends the (political) category of "human" altogether. It reveals anthropological insights and anti-racist implications that come as a result of learning to recognize the brilliance of Black embodiment. What is important to note at this point is how racist depictions of Black athletes vis-à-vis "beast" contribute to a broader cultural incapacity to *see* Black men *as human*, which materializes suffering in ways that are largely mundane. This ongoing incapacity is born from the feedback loop of performing the assumptions of this trope as if they were true—a productive ritual which makes them real.

A central claim in this story is that Black men are seen through *scripts* of inhumanity, as represented in the stereotypical image "beast," with attention to two functions of *scripts* in relation to the problem of race. On one hand, the language of *scripts* points to the way "beast"—and race more broadly—is socially constructed based on mythic inscriptions that have become material reality. For something to be inscribed, there must be external markings. It is written upon or engraved—branded, as it were. The marks do not represent an essence, but rather a label determined by the one who decides what is written. Often this label is meant to signal ownership. In other instances, it is meant to determine how something will be categorized. In the case of Blackness, historically, it was meant to do both. On the other hand, *scripts* point to performance. Movies, television shows, and other forms of theater all rely on scripts to determine the roles to be played by the characters involved. These scripts have to do with writing as well but are more concerned with determining the behavior of a character rather than their essence. It provides the instruction an actor must follow if they are to participate in the production. Held together, these two understandings of scripts point to the problem of legibility.

Legibility denotes the level to which something is recognizable. For instance, a person's handwriting is deemed legible if someone else can understand it. This suggests that understanding itself is an interactive process which points more deeply to a linguistic agreement shared by both parties. Without this agreement, neither the writer nor the reader—or speaker and listener—will know the rules of their exchange, the grounds on which they can communicate. Hence, legibility is never a neutral process. It imposes a norm that reinforces itself by requiring communicators to adhere to its rules of interpretation. Legibility, then, should be understood as a political process by which one's sight (or sensibility) is *continually adjusted*. And this adjustment does not happen in a vacuum. Rather, it is always performed in relation to a political norm that must be maintained. In this sense, scripts function like policies in that they determine the performances that bring imagined futures to fruition, reinforcing their own norms and presumed truths in the process.

Legibility is born from the ongoing performance of said "truths." Considering the mutuality of scripts and legibility can shed light on the interworking of society's inability to see the humanities of Black men. The process is iterative in that the incapacity is produced, and reproduced, continually adjusted into place by the ritualized performance of the inhumanity it assumes. Consider the cover of *Vogue* magazine from April 2008 as an illustration. NBA star LeBron James is pictured dressed in all black, bouncing a basketball with the expression of a snarl on his face. In the embrace of his other arm is model Giselle Bündchen, featured in a flowy green dress with a look of joy on her face. While the obvious King Kong imagery drew some criticism, it did not offend James himself, at least publicly, who chalked it up to an honest show of "a little emotion."[18] Perhaps the honor of being the first Black man ever featured on the cover of *Vogue* blunted the edges of "beast" with the same seductiveness that the accolade enjoys in sport. Even if he did want to offer a critique, the celebratory circumstance would make it difficult for anyone to disrupt a potentially lucrative relationship, particularly for a young Black athlete trying to secure a future for his family. Regardless, millions saw the cover, and with it a stylized representation of one of the most popular athletes in the world cast as an animal with superhuman physical capabilities.

But James is not the first Black male athlete to be depicted this way. There is historical cadence to this kind of cover art that reveals an abiding cultural tendency to nurture the association between Black men and animals. Shortly after being drafted by the New York Knicks as the first pick in the 1986 NBA draft, Hall of Fame center Patrick Ewing, nicknamed "The *Beast* of the East," agreed to a sneaker deal with Adidas wherein the same thing happened. In one of the first publicized advertisements for the Adidas Conductor, a new shoe being released to the public, Ewing is shown, larger than life (and the Empire State Building), stepping into a New York street and towering above the skyline as ominous music plays against a backdrop of dark thunderous clouds, with a sky lit up by lightning.[19] To make matters worse, this was the revised version. In the first marketing ad for the Conductor, Ewing was shown *scaling* the Empire State Building in a way that is similarly suggestive, to say the least.[20]

The historical trajectory of these depictions reveals the productive interplay of scripts and legibility as it relates to the dehumanization of Black men. Regardless of good intentions, these scenes would have certainly called to mind the menacing monkey the world knows as King Kong.[21] And while their participation can be seen as "success," on the surface, James and Ewing illustrate how even the most successful Black athletes are centered as the main caricatures in a cultural story they did not write. The interplay highlights the way in which society's inability to see the humanity of Black men is produced based on cultural performances rooted in a history of presumed inhumanity. The lenses through which Black men are seen are continually adjusted to reflect norms, laws, and patterns of relating (read: scripts) that reflect this historical rendering. Hence, "beast" continues to be one of the most legible interpretations of Black men in the United States because it reflects the racist scripts that society continues to play out publicly. And the preeminence of bodies in sport allows for such scripts to be performed in ways that are hidden in plain sight.

Other scholars have highlighted similar concerns regarding legibility and Black men in the United States. In *Looking for Leroy*, cultural critic Mark Anthony Neal addresses the connections between the politics of legibility and presumptions of criminality in Black men. Neal presents the character Leroy from the 1980s film *Fame,* noting how the confluence of Leroy's suspected gayness and passion for dancing, his flamboyant irreverence and erotic appeal to (white) women, and

The Myth of Level Playing Fields

Neal's own difficulty locating Leroy in terms of existing images, present an alternative picture of a Black man that disrupts the historical fiction of Black men cast as hyper-heterosexual predators given to criminality. Neal argues that (re)reading Leroy—and Black men more broadly—can provide a basis for a "radical rescripting of the accepted performances of a heteronormative black masculinity."[22] Ultimately, Neal wants to disrupt the ways Black men are bound to, and by, a "legibility" based on existing stereotypes that reproduce historical fictions about Black men and their bodies. He writes:

> In contrast to Leroy and other illegible black males, the "legible" black male body is continually recycled to serve the historical fictions of American culture (as the state rolls tenuously into a future of continued globalization, terrorism, and privatization). Here black male bodies continue to function as tried and tested props, whether justifying the lynching of black male bodies after emancipation or the maintenance of antimiscegenation laws and Black Codes (well into the twentieth century) to discourage race mixing and limit black mobility. In the contemporary moment we witness the prison industrial complex (where privatization looms large), which warehouses black (and brown) male bodies for nonviolent offenses as part of some preemptive attack on the presumed criminality of those bodies, while simultaneously exploiting the labor of those bodies for the profit of private prisons, a form of mass incarceration that the legal scholar Michelle Alexander has described as the "new Jim Crow."[23]

The consequences of (il)legibility are clear. Failing to recognize Black masculinity in its complexity contributes to historical fictions that justify societal mistreatment of Black men. Neal is thus "looking for Leroy" in an attempt to "challenge prevailing logics about black male bodies," while simultaneously "rendering so-called illegible black male bodies—those black male bodies we can't believe are real—legible."[24]

While Neal's engagement with legibility addresses the criminalization of Black men publicly, pastoral theologian Greg Ellison addresses the psycho-emotional effects of it in their subjective experience. He argues that young Black men in the United States are regularly muted and rendered invisible to the point of being psychologically, emotionally, and spiritually snubbed altogether—"cut dead" by routine misrecognition based on racial stereotypes.[25] For Ellison, the failure to recognize the humanities of young Black men engenders a social psychological trauma that finds expression in one of two ways: (1) imploding as a self-destructive psychological retreat; or (2) exploding (socially) as a demand for attention.[26] Ellison's attention to the psychological, emotional, and spiritual suffering wrought by illegibility adds depth to Neal's cultural attention to the sociopolitical consequences of such illegibility. Not only does failing to recognize Black men's humanity inform cycles of imprisonment and death, but it also contributes to a depth of suffering that can only be fully appreciated by acknowledging the humanity of the one suffering, even if inadvertently.

Neal and Ellison address important themes related to the politics of legibility. Ellison's connection of illegibility to psycho-emotional and spiritual trauma is helpful in that it disrupts cultural interpretations of young Black men as emotionless and inherently threatening. He (re)humanizes young Black men by highlighting the relational pain that ensues from society's failure to recognize them. While Ellison's treatment of misrecognition is connected to society's failure to see, my argument is rooted in assumptions of familiarity. It is not so much that young Black men are unseen, but rather that they are seen in ways that are presumably known all too well. In other words, the legibility of "beast" references the hypervisibility of a stereotypical image that funds society's mistreatment of Black men. Missing from Neal's analysis are the deeper anthropological foundations on which these prevailing racial logics have been constructed. While his attention to issues of legibility reveal rigid cultural logics about the construction of Black masculinity, it is outside the scope of his project to connect his analysis to cultural scripts. Consequently, the underlying anthropological assumptions that underpin scripts of inhumanity remain hidden from view. Recognizing the performative interplay of scripts and legibility not only highlights the mythic political origins of "beast," but, more importantly, it brings attention to the way its legibility relies on ritualized cultural performances that first presume the inhumanity of Black men.

Casting Black men as "beast" has material consequences, despite good intentions or Black men's participation. Such portrayals are never just fixed images in time. They are iterations that simultaneously *reflect and reproduce* historical fictions about Black men—fictions that inform and incarnate rituals of (mis)interpretation that shape the ways people within social and political systems relate to Black men. And to the degree that performing "beast" functions as a means of security or survival, the fiction also informs the ways Black men relate to themselves and each other. It contributes to a muscle memory of mistreatment based on the belief that Black men are worthy of such.

The consequences of "beast"

Many contemporary examples play into and out of this historical narrative, but two events that took place on May 25, 2020, illustrate the death-dealing complexities of "beast" most explicitly. It was on this day that Amy Cooper, a white woman living in New York at the time, called the police on a Black man named Christian Cooper—no relation—because he was filming her with his phone in Central Park. Apparently, Amy Cooper was walking her dog off the leash in a portion of the park where dogs are supposed to be leashed. Christian Cooper took notice while birdwatching and proceeded to ask her to leash her dog. Then a verbal confrontation ensued wherein Amy Cooper called 911 and was captured on a viral video saying:

> I'm sorry, I'm in the Ramble, and there is a man—African American—he has a bicycle helmet on. He is recording me and threatening me and my dog.

With growing intensity in her voice, she continued:

> There is an African American man—I am in Central Park—he is recording me and threatening myself and my dog!

And then again, escalating into what sounded like a full-blown panic:

> I am being threatened by a man in the Ramble, please send the cops immediately![27]

Reports note that there was a second 911 call after this initial one, wherein Amy Cooper said outright that this "African American man tried to assault me," a claim that she later recanted when the police officers arrived. Perhaps the most troubling aspect of this encounter was Amy's preemptive announcement to Christian that she was going to call the cops and tell them, "There is an African American man threatening my life," to which Christian Cooper, while recording the whole interaction on his phone—and with a voice trembling like Amy's—said, "Please call the cops." This incident occurred on the same day that George Floyd was murdered by police officer Derek Chauvin. In another viral video caught on a bystander's cell phone, Chauvin in shown kneeling on Floyd's neck for nearly nine minutes. Despite Floyd's pleas for mercy—and his mother—Chauvin remained on his neck until Floyd stopped breathing and went unconscious. George Floyd was pronounced dead later that morning after paramedics administered CPR to no avail.

These examples illustrate the asphyxiating weight and contemporary impact of "beast" on Black men in the United States. In both cases, Black men were caught in the crosshairs of a cultural myth that materialized in their mistreatment. There is a reason Amy Cooper knew she could call the police and say a Black man was "threatening her life" in Central Park. Derek Chauvin would not have kneeled on George Floyd's neck for nearly nine minutes unless he believed him to be an animal. And Steve Raible, like the many other sports commentators around the world, would not have celebrated Lynch's historic run in this way if "beast" did not play so well in a society already accustomed to reading inhumanity onto Black men's bodies, even in celebratory ways.

Sport and the myth of level playing fields

The legibility of "beast" does not just affect Black men's lives directly, however. The real tragedy of racism can be seen in the ways "beast" contributes to the creation and maintenance of a broader racial myth within which the legacy of white supremacy can continue under the radar. It is in this sense that sport acts as a liminal space where competing racial myths play out in service to broader cultural realities that implicate everyone, whether they are sports fans or not. As a complex, sport functions as a microcosm where racial politics converge on the bodies of Black athletes in ways that reflect the exploitative relationship that white America enjoys in relation to Black people more generally. Not only are Black athletes not immune to racial exploitation, but they are also uniquely set up for it. However, the normalcy of this exploitation is cloaked by Black athletes' participation in mainstream sports *and* the *technical possibility* of Black athletic success. As a stage, sport functions like a microphone that is used to project the "success" of Black athletes, and which communicates the myth of racial progress in ways that shape public sensibilities accordingly. The subtle productivity cannot be overstated.

The complex of sport provides the perfect cover for the continued extraction of Black vitality. But it does so insidiously in a way that renders racism benign. It is in this sense that "beast" performs double duty. At the same time that this trope reinscribes racist assumptions onto Black men's bodies, the success it represents bolsters the cultural myth that the racial playing fields in the United States are finally level. In other words, if Black athletes like Marshawn Lynch, LeBron James, or Patrick Ewing can achieve this level of success, when previously their participation would have been prevented on account of their Blackness, then America must no longer be racist. It follows the same logic used in appeals to former president Barack Obama's election. If the United States can elect a Black president, then it must have finally crossed the threshold into a post-racial existence where any critique of structural racism, especially in sports, is understood to be asinine. This is the reason for the controversy surrounding Bill Rhoden's *New York Times* bestseller, *Forty Million Dollar Slaves*. Despite the fact that the title itself stemmed from a racial epithet hurled at then NBA star Larry Johnson by a white heckler—"Johnson, you're nothing but a $40 million slave!"—some could simply not get over the audacious association between any (Black) millionaire and "slave."[28] Rhoden's critique was not off base, however. Despite the discomfort of his insights, his exposé of the racial politics in and around sport does reveal racial imbalances that resemble the asymmetrical power dynamics of enslavement in the United States. The NFL draft process is one among many examples that clearly illustrate the exploitation he exposes.

The draft marks the time of year when each of the NFL's thirty-two teams makes their selections from the pool of collegiate players vying for a spot on an NFL roster. For many of these athletes, the draft is like a portal into a reality that, before passing through, would seem only a fantasy. And depending on their circumstances, this may be their best chance for a better life, despite the improbability of making it to the professional leagues.[29] Once drafted, they pick up and relocate to the destination of whatever organization has paid (for) them. They then begin a series of training regimens that span from just after the draft in February until training camp, which begins every year in July. At this point, if they are lucky enough to make the active roster, they are on lockdown for the duration of the season—July through (at least) December, with hopes of playing until February, in either the Pro Bowl or the Super Bowl.[30] The players themselves are some of the best athletes who have successfully navigated the collegiate, high school, middle school, and in many cases "pee wee" levels of participation. They are the lifeblood and labor force of their organizations, exercising expertise that is extracted until their bodies can no longer function. Then they retire and are replaced by someone of a similar stature and specialization. More often than not, their replacements arrive long before their retirement, selected from a pool of younger, fresher talent, ever ready to take over the previously established positions of those who came before them. And the cycle continues.

If this reading seems crass, consider more specifically the politics of the NFL Combine within the draft cycle. The combine is an invitation-only gathering among the best players in the country, draft hopefuls whom it behooves to participate because it maximizes their chances of being drafted. At the combine, players compete in a series of drills and aptitude tests in front of coaches, front-office managers, and owners of the thirty-two NFL teams. For players who are not invited to the combine, "Pro Days" act as a secondary opportunity for them to be measured and perform the same tests that take place at the combine, in the hope that interested NFL scouts and coaches will show up to their colleges where Pro Days are held to watch and take notes. This is all based on the probability that good performances will raise their draft status, but players are also aware of the possibility that bad performances can plummet their chances altogether. In front of everyone in attendance, players strip down to their underwear and subject themselves to a series of tests akin to the auction blocks of an antebellum past. They are poked, prodded, examined, measured, questioned, assessed, and then valued based on how well they perform in position-specific drills. And most of them are happy to do it because the promise of prestige and payment exceeds what any other profession would offer them as a base salary for someone their age.

Many of the same sports commentators who call NFL games throughout the season are also present at the combine. Those among them who are employed by the NFL Network add commentary for viewers as the players put their talents on public display. The normalcy of exploitation is clearly illustrated by the commentary of Mike Mayock, a former front-office executive for the Raiders and expert analyst for the NFL Network and NBC. After being prompted by another announcer's introduction of the next player up to run the forty-yard dash during the 2015 combine, Mayock commented as follows:

(He's) Six foot seven, 313, extremely long arms, underclassmen, still 20 years old. He flashes ... look at the lower body, just huge. He's got dancing feet, with that lower body. It's unbelievable. Look at the body. Look at that bubble butt. And thighs. I mean that's ... those are power generators right there.[31]

There are many other occasions during the combine where Mayock has used similar language to talk about other draft hopefuls. In fact, his regular use of "bubble butts" is a feature of social media—Black Twitter in particular—that has been the subject of much comedic ridicule. And while Mayock may be unique in his use of this particular phrase, the commodification and exploitation of Black athletes and their bodies is a normalcy throughout the life of the NFL, as well as other sports where the majority of participants happen to be Black men.[32] Moreover, if Mayock's commentary is any indication of the kinds of conversations that take place behind the closed doors of draft deliberation, then it is clear what matters most to the mostly white decision makers who are drafting and directing the mostly Black bodies that makeup the talent pool. Ironically, the fact that Andrus Peat, the player Mayock was referring to in this instance, played for Stanford mattered little in his draft stock. It was the utility of his body that got him selected.

The political play (space) of sport

Sport is unique among cultural spaces where this level of exploitation can play so positively to a public that prides itself on being post-racial. And to a certain degree, the post-raciality of sport bears some truth— enough to make it believable to those who want it to be true. Sports historian Louis Moore is right in noting the ways sport has functioned historically as a unique space within which to enact civil rights. He acknowledges the post–World War II significance of Black athletes being integrated into mainstream sports alongside, and in some cases ahead of, other cultural spaces that previously held to segregation.[33] In *We Will Win the Day*, Moore demonstrates how Black communities all over the country utilized the space that sport provided to advance civil rights causes in ways that (hopefully) contributed to racial justice off the field. In this sense, sport did provide a more level playing field that allowed Black athletes to compete across racial lines, at least from the standpoint of head-to-head competition. Moore's work is helpful in that it illustrates how sport provided a public domain for racial solidarity among Blacks and white allies to explore previously unseen democratic possibilities.[34]

However, one must acknowledge the insidious ways in which the integration of sports also functioned to support a broader cultural myth that was meant to undercut the advances of the very civil rights progress that Black athletic success seemed to be contributing to. There was always a political agenda underneath integration that was predicated on benefitting from Black bodies in sport while maintaining the very power dynamics that previously prevented Black participation. In other words, Blacks could participate, but only on the terms set by white power-brokers, and only insofar as their participation contributed to a new narrative of post-raciality that could be sold to the public. This is why acts of Black protest within sport have always been met with hostility, even if they took place within the rules as articulated. Examples of this abound: Tommie Smith and John Carlos were stripped of their medals for raising the Black Power fist in racial solidarity during the 1968 Summer Olympics; Colin Kaepernick was blackballed and many of his peers were referred to as "sons of bitches" by then president Donald Trump for kneeling during the National Anthem to protest police brutality; LeBron James was told to "shut up and dribble" by Fox News anchor Laura Ingraham in response to his critique of Donald Trump's leadership as president. And this is to name just a few examples. Hence, the integration of sport presented an opportunity to tell a different story that diverted attention away from the continued normalcy of systems and structures that maintain exploitative power dynamics on the basis of race. For this to make sense, however, sport should be placed and read in light of the socioeconomic and cultural shift toward neoliberal capitalism.

Whereas previous iterations of capitalism prioritized (more equal) exchange with an economic floor in place via social programs, neoliberal capitalism centers unfettered competition as its prevailing norm. It is a system predicated on a survival of the fittest—or richest—state of relations, where the economic floor has been methodically removed while the public's attention is averted to (the myth of) an ever-raising ceiling.[35] Neoliberalism has been sold to the public as a "fresh" economic start for previously marginalized communities, on the basis of claims that the field is now wide open, and (technically) fair—despite the convenience of being occasioned after centuries of racialized dehumanization and disempowerment, with no reparative actions to fill in the gaps. Neoliberalism signals a shift toward a society where inequality is rendered normal by nature of everyone's recruitment into an all-out competition that is now—all of a sudden—deemed fair. On a deeper level, however, neoliberalism also functions as a cultural project designed to (re)shape human sensibilities to reflect a social order where even the most intimate human relations are subject to the rationality of self-interest. Whether corporate culture, social media, or marriage and family life, human systems and sensibilities are becoming increasingly market-oriented, by design.[36] To justify this shift ideologically—or morally for that matter—the cultural messaging needs to convince the public of a few cultural myths around which this broader system can function.

First is the myth that human beings are **individuals**, autonomous and free to compete (read: capitalize) in every interaction without relational guilt. As long as one can justifiably say they did not intend harm, then virtually any relational fallout from their participation in competition is plausibly deniable. Suffering is thus rendered the fault of the one who suffers; a result of simply not competing hard enough.[37] Second is the myth of **meritocracy**, which signifies the belief that any person anywhere can "pull themselves up by their bootstraps" and pursue whatever life they want in the land of the free. The *myth of meritocracy*[38] purports the possibility that anyone can "make it," technically. However, it does not acknowledge probability based on political design. Rather, it denies that such a design exists. In fact, the interplay of individualism and meritocracy is meant to throw off any scent of a political design in favor of a feeling of freedom based on the popularized falsehood that the field is now wide open, and level. It subjects everyone to the machinations of the market without acknowledging the collusion between government officials and corporate elites to privatize and deregulate, which represent the primary political shifts that allow the market to govern in place of governments. In other words, political governments become market actors in much the same way as citizens. All are invited to play the game in service to the (freedom of the) market.

These shifts did not happen in a vacuum, however. Pastoral theologian Cedric Johnson rightly contextualizes the cultural and political shift toward neoliberal governance as a racialized response to the perceived loss of white political control during the 1960s and 1970s.[39] In much the same way that Reconstruction was intended to undo the advances wrought by the abolition of slavery, neoliberalism was designed to undercut the progress of civil rights, albeit in a very different way. Rather than function as a form of oppression, which is predicated on outright dominance (read: barring Blacks from participating in the game altogether), neoliberal governance prioritizes exploitation.[40] It is no longer the goal to keep Black people from participating in the mainstream of American society. This would go against the colonizing logic around which the United States was founded, which has always functioned to exploit Black labor without allowing Black people to own their labor. Given the illegality of certain forms of enslavement in contemporary society, overt oppression would cut off this essential economic valve. Neoliberalism represents a new strategy in which the extraction of Black vitality can continue under the guise of equal opportunity within a wider context where *everyone* is now being exploited to some degree.

Most insidious about this form of governance is that it extends perpetually from the (manufactured) "consent" of citizens. The existence of a neoliberal system relies on the public's performance of it as if it were the only real option. It operates as a kind of colonialism 2.0, back-ended by the politically derived plausible deniability that comes from the belief that the market itself is the only real arbiter of "civil" rights or capitalist achievements. Johnson refers to this swirl of strategic politics as a neoliberal "matrix of systems" that are designed to: "(1) *maintain* the full reign of the 'free' market, (2) *contain* left behind sectors of the population whose presence discloses the systems' inequities, (3) *control* those populations who pose a threat to the system's stability, and (4) secure the continued *contributions* of those who are indeed indispensable to the system's operations."[41] And since literal chains are no longer an option, Johnson rightly calls attention to hegemony as the primary way in which the interlocking forces that make up neoliberal governance can function without a culprit that can be called to account in any communal way. He writes:

> Hegemony operates at multiple levels in a society, exerting authority in the cultural, political, economic, intellectual, and material domains of life. Authority is not attained or sustained merely through the forcible imposition of power. Hegemony is attained and sustained by "coercion" and by securing a substantial degree of "popular consent." Neoliberal hegemony subtly and effectively encourages people to identify themselves with the habits, sensibilities, and world views supportive of the status quo and the class interests that dominate it. It is successful in persuading people to "consent" to their oppression and exploitation.[42]

The complex of contemporary sport lives within the political matrix of neoliberal governance. It spins from the feeling of freedom it creates based on its ability to normalize myths of individualism and meritocracy, while at the same time allowing those who already hold power to maintain it, to double down and increase it even, based on the culture of competition into which everyone has been recruited.

Inasmuch as Black bodies have been used to support this system, and Black athletic success to tell its story, Black athletes have exposed the racial inequalities of this cultural production on more than a few occasions. However, for every Colin Kaepernick who kneels to protest the bigger picture, there are a thousand more young Black athletes who need what neoliberalism provides more urgently than the felt need to be the martyr who makes a point that America has failed to listen to for centuries. It is by design that Black athletic success is propped up and promoted in such a way that materializes the myth of level playing fields in the minds of the public. Sport plays on and publicizes the vast minority of Black athletes who participate and "make it," presenting their bodies—adorned with the markings of the American Dream—as proof that anyone can achieve the same. But it does so with presentations of their bodies flattened into caricatures, which cloaks the real brilliance behind what they have been able to achieve in a persistently racist society that purports itself to be post-racial.

The political problem of *seeing* (race)

To bracket all this off as malicious might be convenient, but it misses the point. A deeper racial problem is revealed when granting that inhuman depictions cast as cultural celebrations of Black male inhumanity are *honest* mistakes—that those who make decisions ranging from editorial ads to which players they will draft are not *trying* to reproduce a racist caricature that has supported the dehumanization of Black men for centuries. Regardless of (ill) will or good intentions, however, every act of seeing these depictions performs the association between Black men and "beast" in the minds of viewers, whether they are consciously aware, consenting, or not. Such depth of racial conditioning points to the deeper complexities of race in contemporary culture. It is the kind of racism that exists outside of any moral way of making sense of it, where trying to locate the "racist" comes up short because white supremacy is written into the fabric of our daily lives. That someone can genuinely mean well and still reproduce deeply racist images and ideologies reflects the problematic way in which a trope like "beast" can become the stuff of celebration and criminalization, simultaneously.

Womanist ethicist and theologian Emilie Townes offers one of the most helpful analyses that highlight the subtle productivity of cultural productions such as "beast." In *Womanist Ethics and the Cultural Production of Evil*, Townes constructs a theoretical framework that highlights the way in which mythic ideological images of Black womanhood are proliferated into existence. She draws on Michel Foucault's use of "fantasy" and "imagination" together with Antonio Gramsci's understanding of "hegemony" to form what she calls the "fantastic hegemonic imagination."[43] Townes's primary purpose for constructing this framework is to expose the overlooked underside of structural evil in ways that reveal it as a cultural production. Rather than focus on the "rational mechanisms that hold forms of oppression and misery in place," Townes deals with the way "emotion, intuition, and yearning" are more deeply implicated in the constitution of reality.[44] Focusing particularly on the image of the Black matriarch, Townes argues that images and stereotypes employ a "politicized sense of history to create and shape its worldview."[45] Such images are presented as historical, then proliferated in myriad ways, which eventually cements them in the public imagination as something that just is.

Townes's assessment is crucial because it discloses how relational norms are shaped (subliminally) by fantastical images that proliferate without conscious awareness. She undresses the cultural process by which the Black matriarch was constructed as "real," highlighting the packaging, marketing, selling, and consuming of Aunt Jemima products as cultural performances that contribute to her "reality."[46] However, the deeper significance of Townes's project can be seen in the attention she pays to the relational play of race—how persons' attitudes, emotions, and even intuitions are recruited based on the productive function (and fiction) of mythic images. Couched within a celebration of Aunt Jemima is a deeper racial logic that literally creates a reality where the mythic Black matriarch exists. Despite being based in pure fantasy, the Black matriarch becomes "real" through a cultural performance of her presumed reality. In other words, though persons may not consciously relate fantastical representations of Black womanhood to Black women, their minds and relational patterns are still shaped by the taken-for-granted "truths" embedded within these images. The same goes for Black men, particularly when Black male athletes are propped up in public to propagate the racial logics of "beast." Certainly "racist" could be, and has been, located on persons like Amy Cooper or Derek Chauvin. But a deeper investigation into even these seemingly blatant displays reveals a depth of conditioning that exists underneath any conscious decision to dehumanize. And sport should be investigated as a unique stage where this cultural production plays out in front of millions who are kept unconscious to the effects of "beast" or their participation in it.

Raible's word choice was more than just a missed opportunity to disrupt a historically racist myth. This was an act of reproducing it. Caught by the excitement of the moment and the expediency of needing to give meaning to it, Raible drew on what he knew. He acted out of the ways he has been conditioned by society's incapacity to recognize the humanities of Black men, even when they happen to be elite athletes. And recognizing Raible's genuinely good intentions is critical. Steve Raible is beloved by the Seahawks' sports community, and for good reason. His deep love for the game, and for many of the athletes themselves, comes through clearly in his commentary, and his character has been vouched for publicly on numerous occasions. Steve Raible is known to be a good guy. And this is precisely the problem, revealing the level to which race is a matter of conditioning. Now to be fair, it would be asking a lot for any sports commentator to provide a more thorough analysis in real time. Time simply would not allow any commentator to capture Lynch's deployment of speed, strength, power, agility, and acuity in a series of split seconds, all while maneuvering through other elite athletes with similar skillsets who are hell-bent on stopping him. No. Moments like these call for something brief, like "brilliant." But for *brilliance* to break forth in the human mind when thinking of Black athletes, or Black people for that matter, we must learn to call the games (of life) differently.

CHAPTER TWO

Marshawn Lynch

"Beast" and the Historical Play on "Human"

> I know I'm gon' get got, but I'm gon' get mine more than I get got though.
>
> —Marshawn Lynch

"Beast quake" was not the first missed opportunity for the media to more fully capture the embodied brilliance of Marshawn Lynch. At various points throughout his career, sports reporters, analysts, even the 45th president took their turns fumbling his humanity with phrases like "jerk," "asshole," and "son of a bitch," not to mention the classic "thug," which was iterated on several occasions in response to Lynch's public resistance.[1] In many respects, the character assaults that Marshawn Lynch endured are a common occurrence when Black athletes protest. Whether having Olympic medals stripped for showing solidarity with the Black Power movement or being blackballed by the NFL for kneeling during the national anthem, Black athletes have been reprimanded when giving public voice to political realities that matter more than the sports they play. To the extent that these displays of resistance run the risk of raising public consciousness to the problems they are protesting, Black men have been muted in myriad ways. They are paid to play along and crucified when they do not. In Lynch's case, this ball was repeatedly dropped by the barrage of character assaults that criminalized him because he too had the nerve to say "no."

The most notable clash between Lynch and the media came during one of Super Bowl XLIX media days. These are typically days filled with excitement, where journalists, reporters, columnists, and the like are chomping at the bit because of the access they get to the athletes preparing to play in America's biggest football game. The Super Bowl is like a national holiday in the United States. This is a time when grossly overpriced tickets sell out early, some musical artist ascends to the next level of fame—or flop—as a result of performing the half-time show, and the public finally gets to enjoy the much anticipated Super Bowl commercials they have waited all year for; advertisements cost roughly $7 million for a thirty-second spot due to the predictable way in which this game galvanizes national, even global, attention.[2]

Super Bowl media day is just that, a day for sports media to feast on the forced availability of athletes they rarely get access to. It is an opportunity for them to capture whatever soundbites or storylines support the agenda of the organizations they represent. A chance for media players to make names for themselves. This is their Super Bowl, and because it is such a celebrated event they typically get to interact with happy-go-lucky athletes who give them lighthearted interviews, despite this day being such a nerve-racking distraction for most of the players. One can understand, then, why on this particular Super Bowl media day they would hope to get a different Marshawn Lynch than the one who had already committed to protesting the media because of how they had so routinely drug him through the mud since his time playing in Buffalo.[3] And a happy-go-lucky Lynch is exactly what they got, albeit not in the way they expected. Showing up with a lighthearted look on his face, and maintaining a playful air throughout the entire time allotted for his interview during the press conference, Lynch responded to every question the media asked him with the now famous line: ***"I'm just here so I won't get fined."***

Lynch repeated this phrase some thirty times in response to each of their varied, but increasingly frustrated, questions. They kept trying despite Lynch's announcement to them at the onset of the press conference how he was going to respond to their questions. After being overheard on the live broadcast asking the coordinators when his time starts, and being told it had already begun, Lynch started a timer on his phone and opened the interview with, "Hey, I'm just here so I don't get fined. So y'all can sit here and ask me all the questions y'all want to. I'm gon answer with the same answer, so... y'all can shoot if y'all please."[4]

There were only three brief breaks from Lynch's focused approach to his protest. The first was an encouragement to one writer to "make more with your time" because there were only three minutes left. The second was an acknowledgment of another reporter's presence with whom Lynch had a positive relationship. The last was a brief off-the-mic conversation with Hall of Fame cornerback Deion Sanders, who at the time was working for NFL Network and was the only one among the crowd who also had a microphone. Sanders asked Lynch a few questions—one about Lynch's distrust for the media due to the ways they construe him—to which Lynch gave him the same stock response that he had committed to, on air. Then Lynch and Sanders leaned off their mics and agreed that they would talk later. Lynch got back into character and proceeded to finish the interview with a silence that stymied their hopes of getting anything of substance from him.

This Super Bowl media day solidified Lynch's commitment to protesting the media, not to mention his creative approach to carrying it out. This was a commitment that cost him over $1.2 million in fines from the NFL for the times he previously refused to give interviews, much of which was collected retroactively once it was clear to the league that Lynch was trying to make a point.[5] Interestingly, he also incurred fines for wearing memorabilia that featured *his* Beast Mode brand during the interviews he did give, a brand that the NFL was happy to benefit from concurrent with their policing his promotion of it. Leveling six-figure fines is one of the primary ways in which the NFL coerces its athletes to play along with parts of the game that contribute to ratings and public buy-in. Many athletes historically have had to pay hundreds of thousands of dollars in fines when they have refused to endure the onslaught of often demeaning questions that come from sports reporters who get to narrate their stories to the public. Yet, once Lynch discovered that the NFL would use fines as a pretense for forcing him to talk, he found a loophole in the NFL Media Access policy:

> Beginning no later than the week prior to the opening of the regular season through the playoffs, each club will make players available during the normal practice week (based on a Sunday game) on Monday, Wednesday, Thursday and Friday to accredited media for player interviews. This includes mandatory open locker rooms sessions for a minimum of 45 minutes on Wednesday, Thursday, and Friday. On Monday, player availability may occur in an open locker room format, in an interview room or other location, or virtually, but players must be *available*.[6]

Lynch discovered that *availability* was the only requirement, and that there was nothing in the policy that said he needed to actually answer the questions they were asking. Hence, he made himself available to the media with a creative resistance that evolved from stock "yea" and "I'm grateful" answers—with the occasional "thanks for asking"—and eventually took on this Super Bowl form, followed only by "you know why I'm here," due to his realization of how well "I'm just here so I won't get fined" played. And it worked. Lynch played them at their own game, and much of the media's response reflected the criminalizing cadence that kicked off his protest in the first place: Marshawn Lynch is a "thug."

It is important to note that "thug" is not just contemporary code for "nigger" when used in the context of Black men. It is also a calibration to a criminalized history rooted in an (anthropological) assault on one's existence as a human being. Recognizing the rationale behind Lynch's protest is as important as appreciating the creativity of it. Lynch refused to allow the media to shit on him, and in so doing defended his humanity—a humanity that became more explicitly visible later that week during another Super Bowl media day press conference where he departed from his usual performance to level one final critique of the media before resigning himself to his usual disruption of their design:

> Hey look, I mean, all week I done I told y'all w'sup. And for some reason y'all continue to come back and do the same

> thing y'all did ... I don't know what story y'all trying to get out of me; I don't know what image y'all trying to portray of me; but it don't matter what y'all think ... what y'all say about me ... because when I go home at night, the same people that I look in the face, my family ... that's all that really matters to me. Y'all can go and make up whatever y'all wanna make up, because I don't say enough for y'all to go and put anything out on me. But I'll come to y'all's event, and y'all shove cameras and microphones down my throat, but when I'm at home in my environment, I don't see y'all.[7]

The grace Lynch extended in giving the media this glimpse of his humanity, given all that had transpired to this point, mattered little. They still did not listen as he disclosed the distrust and hurt that prompted his resistance. They continued to defecate on him by commentating his criminality in ways designed to discredit any of his endeavors outside of his (on the field) embodiment of "beast," narrowly understood.

If this was only about Marshawn Lynch, it would not be *as* problematic. The unfortunate reality, however, is that Lynch is but one example among many Black athletes who are recruited to embody "beast" on the field but expected to be Sambo in real life.[8] Lynch exposes a cultural tendency to appreciate the contributions of Black men only insofar as they comply with the status quo. When Black men assert their agency and voice—when they disrupt, even for worthy causes—society pulls the trump card of Black male criminality. This cultural tendency not only shades the *(r)evolutionary* contributions Black men have made to society—whether in sports or otherwise—but it completely ignores the humanity embedded in their rationales for resistance. But defecating reveals more about the poison within one's own body than it does the location of its smearing. And in this case, it reveals the extent to which players, the press, and presidents alike remain caught up together in the remnants of a relational shitstorm occasioned by the colonial occlusion of Black men from the category called "human."

Bracketing morality

It is safe to surmise that those who comprise the commentating community mean well, for the most part. It would be a stretch to assume that persons working under the banner "the media" show up to these interactions with malicious intent in their hearts, and even more misguided to assume that people who commentate Black men's existence more broadly have a handle on the deeper consequences of "beast" understood in relation to its racial history. Yet, even if there is a modicum of malice in their portrayals, it is unfair to assume there is an active awareness that calling Lynch a "thug" reproduces a centuries-old trope designed to disempower someone because of the meaning inscribed onto the appearance of their (Black) body. This level of sick genius is simply untenable, and certainly not in the forefront of people's minds when they question Marshawn Lynch, or when reporting based on answers he refuses to give.

A more accurate assessment would understand these cultural responses as regressions that revert back to the reptilian brain, which comes programmed with racialized beliefs that many do not know exist until they find themselves uttering the very things their neocortex told them they would never say, at least in public. It is a survival response that happens in moments of confrontation, where one's brain instinctually dives to the depths of what they know in service to surviving an encounter of uncertainty. And to the extent that neuroscience has demonstrated that the human brain cannot distinguish the difference between perception and reality[9]—between disruptions of privilege and actual threats to one's life—one can understand how someone like Marshawn Lynch could trigger such autonomic responses of racism even among people who are "post-racial." This is why Emilie Townes's concept of the *fantastic hegemonic imagination* is so important. By noting the ways stereotypes performed publicly can shape "private" sensibilities even down to intuition or desire,[10] Townes points to what I would call the *reptilian racism* that enlivens relational interactions, sometimes against the will of the ones interacting. And yet, such interactions remain productive.

Appeals to morality have proven faulty for fixing America's racial problem. White supremacy is embodied beneath the language one uses to dress it up. The lingo may have changed, but the logic remains largely the same. As a feature of human life that extends from the same imaginative space that myths such as "beast" originate, the constructs of morality do not provide a firm enough foundation from which to understand the nature of white supremacy or to transform society accordingly. Focusing on racism primarily as a moral problem not only fixates attention on faulty (read: incomplete) interpretations of racist (inter)actions—because of the need to make moral sense of things— but debates as such only contribute to further polarization. It is like comparing apples to oranges, especially in a world that is increasingly fragmented by algorithms that are only designed to provide more of what one already believes about one's social and political milieu.

Moral analyses of race fall short to the degree that they are contingent on the rationalities that support the status quo of whatever social and political realities predominate in a shared cultural space. Certainly, there are variations when it comes to the moral codes people across cultures live by. However, as white supremacy in the United States would have it, moral codes in relation to America's racial problem have always been skewed toward the preservation of national myths that support the idea of *Anglo-Saxon exceptionalism*[11]—the presumptuous priority of people who are "white." At any given point in US history, human beings have employed a sense of morality in order to distance themselves from the normalized dehumanization of times past. People are wired to reference real-time evidence of progress made. And while this ploy is available to everyone, white people in the United States are particularly susceptible to its slipperiness. In this sense, morality serves a psycho-emotional function that staves off despair, and guilt, but ultimately eclipses an understanding of the deeper embodiment and interlocking relational nature of racism, especially if the moral explanation seems sufficient for the situation.

With the benefit of hindsight in hand, (white) people—supported by the cultures they create—employ meaning-making strategies that help them stomach things about their past that they find sickening, even when self-deception becomes necessary to convince them that it is in fact not *their* past. One such strategy is to see the optimism of right now in relation to a moralistic, if not pessimistic view of history. After all, Black athletes can now make millions of dollars playing the sports they love. How can the United States still be racist when this would have been impossible four hundred years ago? And this rationalizing logic works in real time. Rather than sit with something like slavery and recognize how its underlying political dynamics still animate social life today—an invitation that Black scholars and activists have extended repeatedly—the tendency is to explain it away in relation to how things are currently different, thus ignoring the behest of Black voices in favor of the comfort that comes from the belief that "I am better." The logic is circular in that it creates the bias it needs in order to only see how things have changed, blinding itself to that which has not. Such is the misdirection of morality when analyzing the nature of racism.

Perhaps the biggest black eye to a trustworthy use of morality to make sense of white supremacy is the fact that Black people do not have the same luxury to forget. Black people in the United States continue to have to navigate a series of obstacles that have become increasingly sophisticated but are consistently oriented toward their demise. And this continues to take place *within* the moral rationalities of dominant American culture. One must remember that this play of morality has been operative from colonial conquests through to the current moment. According to the status quo at the time, there was nothing morally wrong with enslaving Africans. Once Black being broke through *that* configuration of the lie, however, a reality was created where whole families showed up to public lynchings, children included. And today, Black men continue to be incarcerated and killed at rates far exceeding that of anyone else with a normalcy that can be seen in how numb society has become to it, not to mention the cadence of criminalizing justifications that conclude, "he must have done something wrong."

Considering the cultural rhythm of rendering Black men inhuman *as a matter of legibility* begs a deeper explanation of cultural logics that invites us to investigate the relational science of racism as it plays out productively across the spectrum of moral sensibilities. Looking at the level of legibility gets underneath analyses of will or want to, but rather analyzes white supremacy as a cultural production that extends from deeply embodied beliefs and the performances of racism they enliven—performances carried out by actors, many of whom have no idea they are even part of the production and would never otherwise choose to be. White supremacy should be read for the ways it can seemingly possess people to (en)act against their will when it comes to being "not racist," which itself reveals a deeper misunderstanding as to the insidious ways in which supremacist sensibilities have been woven throughout parts of human existence that seem private and under one's own control. This approach brackets morality, shifting attention from questions as to *why ("this keeps happening")* and instead prioritizes the need to understand *how* (the racism of) "beast" can be reproduced despite articulated commitments to the contrary.

The commentary across this country belies a genuine hope in post-raciality, which itself is part of the problem. The aspiration to be post-racial is based on a misdiagnosis of racism. Scholars like Ibram X. Kendi have contributed significant work toward changing people's minds regarding their racial orientation toward life. Every aspect of it. He argues that there is no neutrality, but rather one needs to perpetually orient oneself against racism in all that one does. Hence, "anti-racism."[12] But there still exists a cultural pull toward "post-raciality" as a possibility, which testifies to a cultural failure to understand how racism operates at levels unseen and unintended. Analyzing race as a matter of legibility allows one to reread criminalization *as a cultural logic* that is meant to perpetually colonize Black men's bodies based on the need to exploit and extract vitality from them. It is to peer with curiosity at the consciousness behind the commentary, investigating the cultural play regardless of what commentators say. Bracketing morality invites us to question the origins of deeply held racist beliefs before getting analytically caught by their material consequences. This approach examines the criminalization of Black men in particular, understood as merely one feature (among many) of white supremacy's colonizing logic that is deployed as a defense mechanism that filters noncompliant Black men into cycles of containment and, if necessary, crucifixion. And like Emilie Townes, theologian Willie Jennings argues that this too is a product and problem of imagination.

Constructing the criminalized body of "beast"

The mythic body of Marshawn Lynch—the criminalized body of "beast"—was born from a tragic history of colonial conquest built epistemologically on a politically convenient creation narrative told by European imperialists in service to making the world over in its own image. It was an iterative relational process built on European idealisms that manifested power from its own imagination—more specifically, what theologian Willie James Jennings calls the "diseased social imagination" of Western Christianity.[13] In *The Christian Imagination*, Jennings unmasks the origins of race as understood today, representing it as a colonial creation with a uniquely European Christian heritage. He reads the relationality behind some of the earliest connections and disconnections that cleared the way for a color-coded caste system that still predominates the contemporary world. Jennings's work details how the fiction of race and its consequences through the last six centuries grew from the imaginative play of European Christians who made moral sense of their malice by dressing it up as divine sanctioning within an echo chamber of imperial power and Christian theology.

To understand, then, how the myth of "beast" has become such a second-nature cultural performance that shapes relational interactions at levels beneath moral commitments, one must learn to appreciate colonization as a process that was designed to *produce* and normalize social relations based on the politically convenient beliefs of people in power. This reading would allow us to more clearly recognize the ways contemporary normalcies ranging from incarceration to competitive sport are racially calibrated by commentary that criminalizes Black men as part of an *ongoing* colonial process. Three interrelated features of Jennings's theological analysis help to narrate the racial origins of this white supremacist *spirit* as it emerged to create the *sinews* of what would eventually become the mythic Black male body.

In the "beginning" was **spatial displacement**, which refers to the very stripping of people from their lands, their culture, and their communities. Displacement was a foundational theological operation that undergirded the creation of race as something eventually denoted by skin color. Before European conquests, identities were connected to geographic locale. Africans and Indigenous people, for example, were not thought of as "black" or "red" respectively, but were rather identified by their connection to geographic space, with the cultural customs and cosmologies that came with it. Spatial displacement disrupted the epistemological and embodied realities of African and Indigenous peoples. Jennings highlights this by reading the political underbelly of "expansion" as seen through the eyes of the Christian intellectual and royal chronicler Zurara. Jennings writes:

> The often-used term European expansion fails to capture the spatial displacement taking place at this moment, a moment beautifully captured by Zurara. This Portuguese chronicler is watching and participating in the reconfiguration of space and bodies, land and identity. This is the newness in Zurara's simple observation. Again, land and body are connected at the intersection of European imagination and expansion, but what must be understood is the point of connection—the Portuguese and the Spanish, that is, the European. He is the point of connection. He stands now between bodies and land, and he adjudicates, identifies, determines.... With those twin operations, four things are happening at the same time: first, people are being seized (stolen); second, land is being seized (stolen); third, people are being stripped from their space, their place; and fourth, Europeans are describing themselves and these Africans at the same time. There is a density of effects at work here far beyond a notion of expansion.[14]

Jennings denotes the ways European *commentators* used a variety of political means to render their own aesthetic judgments of non-European people as theological truth around which the "new" world could be built. The relational simplicity of the whole process should not be ignored. Stripped of their land, displacement left persons open to the absurdities of European aesthetics. Their identities were divorced from their geographic homes and reinscribed based on the epistemological limits of European understanding. Such judgments constituted the (not so) subtle creation of a *zero point*, an epistemological scale where whiteness became the organizing principle around which people globally would be organized.[15] Hence, while whiteness enjoyed the invisibility of functioning as the organizing conceptual frame, Blackness was simultaneously constructed as its ever-visible counterweight to be used in Europe's reconfiguration of the world. Colonizers used this constructed racial scale to report back to authorities about the people they were encountering. And the content of such aesthetic judgments was even more problematic. Since whiteness was the zero point, colonizers measured beauty and characteristics in terms of their proximity to the overblown and idealized qualities of Europeans. Hence, Blackness was not only construed as ugly, but also increasingly associated with savagery, debasement, and the like—in essence, the opposite of the idealized qualities Europe casted of itself.

If the original construction of Blackness relied on Europe's aesthetic judgments in relation to itself as the invisible norm, then it was the added layer of ***ecclesial authority*** that allowed such judgments to be grounded in explicitly theological terms. After acknowledging the audacity of both papal and monarchical authority to understand their reconfigurations as the sanctioned work of God, Jennings discloses the even more insidious ways in which ecclesial and political leadership adapted theological content to narrate their imperialist activity:

> In his *Chronicle of the Capture of Ceuta* Zurara masterfully ascribes to the prince the trappings of anointed sonship. His mother, Queen Philippa, is described in *theotokos*-like

ways. Her deathbed imperial oration to her sons, especially to Henry, prophesies and commands him to lead the elite of the nation to the glory that is their due. This holy beginning of his reign is further established by the appearance of the Virgin Mary next to Philippa as she lay dying. On her deathbed Philippa contemplates the divine, transfigured in the Holy Virgin's presence. The religious reality of Prince Henry approximates that of the chronicle. A very pious and theologically astute man, he was known to quote Scripture to strengthen his arguments and had even considered taking religious vows.[16]

Jennings illustrates here the entanglement of ecclesial authority with a deeper understanding of God's providence. This heinous association allowed Europeans to mask the brutality of their conquests, presenting them instead as acts of God saving the world through Christian missions. Such presumptions of divine sanctioning were connected to the aesthetic judgments previously highlighted, presenting this new construction of Blackness—with its presumed sub-humanity—as a "natural" (read: ordained) reality to be discovered—a mere fact of life.

Casting Blackness as the qualitative antithesis to whiteness, and eventually the face of evil, became cemented in the colonial consciousness with the addition of ***theological discourse***, the final feature of Jennings's analysis to be highlighted. It was ultimately the content of theological reflection—as colored by aesthetic judgments and justified by ecclesial claims of divine authority—that laid the scriptural foundations for the sub-humanity of Blackness. Doctrines of election and salvation were reinterpreted through Europe's racial scale, which resulted in a transference of Jewish election to Europeans, while the presumed reprobate nature of Africans left them incapable of achieving salvation on their own. Europeans believed Africans were "brute beasts" who existed without a culture. Hence, Christian missionaries thought it was their divine mission and political duty to bring salvation to Africans, which also meant "civilizing" them for a life of servitude unto God via the colonial empire.

The embodiment of this belief was supported by the writings of Jesuit missionary José de Acosta, specifically by Acosta's doctrine of creation which narrated the "New World" in a way that tracked scripturally in alignment with the aesthetic and political foundations laid prior. In essence, Acosta made theological sense of native people around the world by supplanting their local knowledge with his own creationist interpretations of how they fit into the larger scheme of Europe's perceived election.[17] Acosta spoke *for* non-Europeans, naming lands, animals, plants, and native people around the world in the list of objects he sought to understand on Europe's behalf. When considering his prominence in the Jesuit order, coupled with the theological content he produced, one realizes how relationally formative Acosta's theological reflections were for the colonial enterprise. His theology (among others) contributed to the foundations on which theologians and philosophers alike would increasingly theorize Blackness in opposition to whiteness. However, because of the extent to which European aesthetic judgments and ecclesial authority were already established toward this end, the equation of Blackness with sub-humanity was an established norm that shaped European thought prior to any formal theologizing. Hence, Black bodies were marked—presumably by God—from the beginning and were subsequently read back into the scriptures demonically throughout Europe's (re)construction of the Western world.

Whereas Jennings articulates the colonial Christian origins of race in service to showing how the early spirit of white supremacy emerged to form the sinews around which the mythic Black body would be formed, womanist theologian Kelly Brown Douglas's overlay demonstrates how that same spirit breathed criminality into Black *skin* and the *structures* that hold this association in place in the United States. And like the way Jennings grounds the origins of race as a problem of imagination expressed in the interstices of relational (dis)connection, Douglas too highlights the ways myth found material expression among cultures of people acting in concert with the moral order of the day. More specifically, she places the murder of Trayvon Martin and the acquittal of George Zimmerman within what she calls a *stand-your-ground culture*, a body of beliefs and practices designed to justify the mistreatment of Black bodies based on the need to preemptively protect the myth of Anglo-Saxon exceptionalism on which white American identities still rest.[18] She writes:

> A stand-your-ground culture is nothing other than the enactment of whiteness as cherished property. It is the culture that protects the supremacy of whiteness, hence an inexorable cultural expression of whiteness as cherished property— that is, of white supremacy. Stand-your-ground culture spawns its own means, legal and extralegal, to insure that nothing nonwhite intrudes on white space. In other words, stand-your-ground culture protects the rights that come with cherished white property. With this understanding, we can now answer the following question: "Could Trayvon have stood his ground on that sidewalk?"[19]

Clearly, the answer to her rhetorical question is "no, he could not." The reason can be read by the way in which Blackness was defined, by default, as the divinely ordained antithesis to whiteness as it was understood to be *cherished property*[20] to be protected at all costs. Hence, if whiteness was constructed as cherished property to be protected, Blackness was to be understood as the threat from which it needed protection, regardless of situation or circumstance. The problem with this logic is that such protection followed whiteness wherever it invaded. With the swirl of divine sanctioning and the doctrine of discovery[21] in Europe's back pocket, "free" space was rendered the property of whiteness by nature of being within its reach. White settlers were given license to simultaneously protect and *seize*, which applied to space they had not yet taken over. In other words, white people could move with the audacity of believing they owned everything, even when it required them to steal in order to bring such ownership to fruition.

The cultural logic of this configuration was more deeply rooted in the notion that the nature of the Black body was to be, perpetually, chattel. Hence, enslavement was the logical (and moral) conclusion, and the prevailing structure that extended from Europe's epistemological imposition. But Black being broke through the absurdity of white control, finding relational resonance among collaborators with whom they pushed the envelope toward abolition. However, the "freedom" that followed abolition created a cascading effect. Once Black people could no longer be enslaved legally, there became the need for new forms of control. In a sense, the transition to Jim Crow could be considered akin to one of the earliest collective bargaining agreements, wherein "owners" were forced to renegotiate with players who did not have enough political power to challenge the fact of ownership itself. But they did challenge the degree and terms of ownership. Hence, players resisted and consented to *more* freedom than they had, while still being coerced to concede components of their createdness from which they would have been able to otherwise demand a more complete liberation.

Intersectionally marked, "beasts"

The period of Jim Crow is where the intersectionality of "beast" took center stage. It entailed a cultural shift where brokers of colonial power used sexuality to shape the psychology of a public that was beginning to see beneath the skinfolds of structures built upon the myth of Black inhumanity. Black men were reconceptualized and recast sexually against the idealized fictions of European men—and across the newfound "freedom" of this era—marking them as "beasts" from which society would perpetually need to be saved. "Beast" was born from the confluence of theologically rooted stereotypes articulated at the intersections of race, gender, and sexuality in particular.

The prevailing image written onto Black men during Jim Crow was that of the oversexualized "buck," or "beast." This image was constructed based on interlocking assumptions that Black men and women were sexually out of control, cast contrary—of course—to the idealized fiction of white chastity and the purity culture it created. These caricatures cut across white men's infatuation with the physicality of Black men, not to mention their need to justify their sexual abuse of Black women. Douglas notes, "Black male sexual prowess has become almost legend in the stereotypic logic of White culture. The idea that Black men possess an unusually large penis has only reinforced notions of their sexual aggressiveness and mastery."[22] Theologian Dwight Hopkins notes the theo-biblical origins and evolution of this sexualized trope. His analysis also reflects Jennings's deeper awareness of the colonial legacy behind these cultural and theological attacks, but does so with the specificity of Black men and the role of sexuality in mind:

> The religious concept of sexualized black beast body (cemented in a theology of antagonistic dualism and a theology of prudishism) did not fall from the sky. A historical legacy has birthed it with white, European Christianity as a main architect. "The church officially reinforced this entanglement of aesthetics, carnality, and negativity of blackness at the fifth-century Council of Toledo." White religious men decided that Satan was a monster with huge genitalia. Three centuries later, one finds a naked black devil painted in Europe.[23]

Subsequent historical developments contributed to the growing association of Black men with a unique kind of carnality—via presumptions of sexual character(istics) and abilities—that required the control of white Christianity. Ultimately, Hopkins's assessment reveals the extent to which Black men were rendered synonymous with Satan. It illustrates how the "mark of the beast" was the Black penis, concocted from the confluence of race, gender, and sexuality and canonized in the form of the ultimate criminal—a "super predator," if you will.[24]

Commentating criminality

It was also during Jim Crow that commentary was put on the clock as a last line of defense in service to colonization, a strategy that has been forced to incrementally move its goal posts back because of the inherent blossoming of Black being based on a divine essence that can never truly be controlled. This did not stop colonizers from trying, though. To support new legal structures like "separate but equal," and extralegal forms of control such as lynching, white power-brokers turned their attention toward the minds of Americans more broadly. For the political dynamics of white supremacy to be maintained, the public needed to be convinced of the myths being told about Black men. In a real sense, the public has always been the target audience for the criminalization of Black people. They were the ones recruited to manage the morality of mistreatment then—during Jim Crow—and the public remains largely responsible for materializing the normalcy of policing Black bodies today. From films like *Birth of a Nation*—which reinvigorated the Ku Klux Klan—to contemporary celebrations like "he's a beast," commercializing Black men as criminals has always been designed to advertise a certain animalistic nature believed to be lurking just beneath even the most "civilized" surfaces, regardless of how well Black men can dress up and perform their (Black) masculinity.

Though "beast" as a formalized representation of Black masculinity took center stage during segregation, the tendency to associate human beings with animals for the sake of mistreating them goes back much further. This point may seem redundant, but it is important to the degree that it illustrates the anthropological depth of criminalization. To be sure, cultural misinterpretations of Black male athletes do extend from a historical failure to recognize the humanities of Black men. However, they also draw on and develop the history of animalisms that fund this failure. There is an important difference between merely noting assumptions of inhumanity—whether feared as subhuman or fetishized as superhuman—and exposing tendencies to render one an animal. Stating what one is *not* usually eventuates in apathy, or invisibility altogether. On the other hand, is-ness implies presence, and acknowledging one's presence invites attention—in this case, a culture of death-dealing attention paid with the currency of "beast" by common people.

The deployment of denigrating distinctions between humans and animals throughout history can be seen in early philosophies, the sciences, and in contemporary culture. One early conception that dates back to (at least) Aristotle understood animals to be "failed humans" in that they did not possess the capacity for moral reflection, which further implied a lack of ability for intentional action (read: rational control of oneself). The assumption was that animals and children (narrowly understood) were similar, except animals did not have the capacity to develop in the way children did.[25] This relatively benign view of the distinction took on more malignant form in the world of René Descartes, which reveals a latent racism that was present in his philosophies even if not articulated as explicitly as later thinkers, like Immanuel Kant, did.[26] Descartes' perspective was shaped by a view of animals as purely mechanical, lacking a rational soul, and thereby "dumb" beasts. However, Descartes also assumed animals were physically superior by nature of their closeness with the materiality of the earth. His view was coupled with the presumption that animals lacked rationality, which was based on a deeper logic that assumed an inverse relationship between rationality and physicality. Cartesian dualism—the notion that the mind is fundamentally separate from, and of a higher order than, the body—was conflated with the conclusion that human beings were of a higher (moral) nature than animals and should therefore "master" (read: exploit) them and the earth for human purposes.[27] Hence, associating Africans with animals also functioned as a strategy to bind Black people to the body, thereby rendering the mind (read: humanity) as something uniquely monopolized by Europeans.

These philosophical conclusions eventually made their way into the sciences, supporting centuries of sense-making that shaped public sensibilities without requiring malicious intent or conscious awareness to be carried out. Animalizing Africans was a tactic that was central to colonial imperialism and a primary justification for funding the transatlantic slave trade. This strategy then provided a philosophical basis for the caricature's legendary spread during the period of Jim Crow. Today, "beast" continues to function as a bridge that brings assumptions of inhumanity and physical superiority together to sustain a culture of criminalization for which the only logical conclusion is to commodify, contain, or crucify Black men.

Marshawn, Lynched

The crucifixion of Marshawn Lynch in particular can be seen not only in the ways his silence was recapitulated with refrains of "thug" during his media protest, but also in the ways his message gets misread on the rare occasions that he does open up to share his humanity. In a 2016 interview with John Wertheim on *60 Minutes Sports*, in which he announced his retirement, Lynch provided a literal and figurative picture of his approach to life and football, which is suggestive of his particular brand of brilliance. Upon being asked what he learned from his Uncle Lorenzo, who played linebacker in the NFL and was shaped by similar experiences growing up in Oakland, Lynch shared this story:

> We went to his house one time, and uh. . . . And he told me something like this. He say, "It's 4th and 1, the running back is coming through the hole. I'm going to kiss that motherfucker in the mouth." That's what he told me, "Smell his breath." And this was a young age too. I think that's when it just clicked in my mind that if you just run through somebody's face, a lot of people aint gonna be able to take that, over and over and over and over and over and over and over and over and over . . . (pauses) and over and over and over and over and over again. They just not gon' want that.[28]

In an attempt to get Lynch to translate his philosophy to a vernacular more palatable to the typical American viewer, Wertheim asked, "Do you think there is a deeper metaphor there?" To which Lynch bluntly replied, "Run through a motherfucker's face, then you don't have to worry about 'em no more." With this response, Lynch captured the kind of cultural grit that would have been necessary to navigate the sociopolitical conditions that impacted his upbringing in Oakland, California. He notes being regularly exposed to violence, drug paraphernalia, and an overall lack of resources. Hence, his grit was appropriate not only for the gridiron, but because it helped him deal with these difficulties without succumbing to them. In a pragmatic sense, Lynch authorizes an approach to life (and football) that proves advantageous for other Black men seeking to survive, or find success amid similar circumstances. To "run through a motherfucker's face," repeatedly, speaks to Lynch's use of *force* in the face of a cultural onslaught that many Black male athletes must navigate, both on and off the field. But the brilliance of force can only be seen when looking more deeply at the body, rather than away from it. Unfortunately, Lynch's developed forcefulness is misread as a revelation into a deeper racial nature rather than the neurophysiological phenomenon it is.[29]

(e)Strange(d) Fruit(fulness)

If "beast" is currency, Marshawn Lynch exposes both sides of the coin. On one side, "beast mode" represents the celebratory flattening that tends to only appreciate Black athletes as commodities fit for the consumption of crowds hungry for entertainment. On the other side lives a culture of criminalization based in racially coded commentary that extends from Jim Crow into contemporary society. Together, both sides converge on the bodies of Black athletes in ways that signify an inscribed inhumanity that can be cashed in whether one's motivation is fear or fetish. Reading the receptivity of Marshawn Lynch reveals the way in which Black men's bodies appear in the American consciousness *without humanity* based on an underlying suspicion of wrongdoing—how the mere presence of the Black male body performs beyond the intentions or actual practices of Black men, and how this puts them in proximity to the possibility of being crucified when they refuse to consent to their own commodification. In this sense, Marshawn Lynch epitomizes the *(e)Strange(d) Fruit(fulness)* of Black men's bodies, which reveals the deeper anthropological consequences of criminalizing misinterpretations of Black embodied brilliance.

On a cultural level, *(e)Strange(d) Fruit(fulness)* is a concept that captures the regularity, moral permissibility, and continued legacy of lynching Black men who do not comply with the caricatures meant to contain them. It understands the cultural assault of misinterpretation against a historical backdrop of Billie Holiday's iconic cry, "Strange Fruit," which still testifies (read: detests) to what had historically become the nutritional value for white America to witness Black bodies hanging from trees, crucified for all to see:

> *Southern trees bear strange fruit,*
> *Blood on the leaves and blood at the root,*
> *Black bodies swinging in the Southern breeze,*
> *Strange fruit hanging from the poplar trees.*
>
> *Pastoral scene of the gallant South,*
> *The bulging eyes and twisted mouth,*
> *The scent of magnolias, sweet and fresh,*
> *Then the sudden smell of burning flesh.*
>
> *Here is a fruit for the crows to pluck,*
> *For the rain to gather, for the wind to suck,*
> *For the sun to rot, for the trees to drop,*
> *Here is a strange and bitter crop.*[30]

The interchangeability of lynching and crucifixion is intentional. It is also instructive in that it illustrates both the brutality and political function shared by these mechanisms of control. James Cone, the father of Black theology, makes this connection in a way that illustrates the public spectacle of the untimely, and far too often wrongful, deaths of Black men. In *The Cross and the Lynching Tree*, Cone links crucifixion with lynching because they both represent the ways state violence also serves a terroristic function meant to deter acts of resistance against empire. Crucifixion was a public execution used by the Roman empire to punish rebels and to squelch any insurrections that might arise accordingly. Cone argues convincingly that lynching functions in much the same way. In addition to exacting torture and death on the person in question, the visibility of Black bodies hanging from trees was designed to induce terror in other Black people, compelling them to comply with whatever demands those executed resisted.[31]

Kelly Brown Douglas develops Cone's connection further. Whereas Cone notes the sexualized tropes related to "beast" as the primary rationale for lynching during segregation—the myth that Black men were in sexual pursuit of white women—Douglas links their crucifixion to the mere fact of Black bodies existing in (read: encroaching upon) the "free" space presumably owned by "cherished white property." The creation of a stand-your-ground culture, according to Douglas, is a mechanism that uses various forms of crucifixion to control Black men based on the assumption that they are inherently dangerous.[32] Hence, any time they step out of line—sexually or otherwise—they are justifiably, and publicly, hung out to dry as retribution and a warning. The undertones of salvation are telling. Both Cone and Douglas reveal how crucifying Black men takes on a salvific quality for a larger purpose. In Cone's analysis, lynching was thought to save white women from the sexual threats of Black men. Salvation in this sense was directly connected to preserving the presumed purity of white bloodlines by not allowing miscegenation—in effect, to *save* the white race. Douglas links the historical and contemporary murders of Black men to a broader goal of saving America from a perceived threat to its very (ideological) existence. In both instances, the crucifixion of Black men is simultaneously connected to a larger salvific goal, which is to eradicate Black bodies once they can no longer be used to support (white) America's profit margins.

On a deeper level, however, *(e)Strange(d) Fruit(fulness)* reveals the extent to which the (r)evolutionary brilliance of Black embodiment is lost on the species due to the historical ways in which whiteness has gotten hung up on "human." Like morality, "human" plays culturally as a concept that can be used to include or exclude based on the conceptions and configurations of power around the subject at the center of its usage. It is a *construct* that is meant to capture the essence of an evolving species in real time, conceived in relation to incremental changes believed to set said species apart from, say, animals—or Black people, historically. Politically, "human" has functioned as a social safety net within which one can secure certain "rights" not afforded to the other species that it is defined in opposition to. This is why Black posthumanist scholar Philip Butler argues that (Black) people should stop trying to be human, technically.

Bracketing "human" with Butler

In *Black Transhuman Liberation Theology*, Butler invites (Black) people to unsubscribe from the use of "human" because of the extent to which it is politically fraught and continually caught by European epistemologies that preclude Black existence from the safety it provides. And this happens whether one is adopting predominant worldviews or resisting them.[33] In this sense, Butler's critique of the category "human" connects with the zero point previously noted. If whiteness has been constructed as the organizing center of all (colonized) existence, then its linguistic codes have also been imposed and normalized. Such codes have Eurocentric cosmologies embedded within them, which means any relation to them—whether collusion or resistance—reifies them as normal, as "real." This suggests that even revolutionary movements that employ "human" as a foundation from which to resist or pursue more rights is, in a deeper way, reinscribing the worldviews of white supremacy.

In other words, Butler's analysis points to the impossibility of someone like Marshawn Lynch ever being able to dress up his Blackness enough to achieve some unanimous affirmation that he is (fully) "human"—that no matter what Lynch does or says (read: his performance), his very appearance bears a historical marking that will always disqualify him from a category that was constructed to preserve the priority of whiteness. It is like existing with a clause within a culture's consciousness that holds out the possibility of proof that one is not human. And criminalization is like the "aha" moment that says, "I told you so." By nature of the conceptual cosmos that has been created to encompass "Black," people who wear this honor appear in European consciousness as Other. And in many respects, Black people too are recruited to appear in their own imaginations with this caveat. This is by design.

The gravity of this claim can only be grasped when "human" is understood as a linguistic *technology*[34] that extends from the same European imagination that manufactured race as a politically operative measuring scale that literally colors every aspect of human existence, and one that has normalized "beast" as a particular expression within its world of meaning. In much the same way that morality cannot be trusted to understand the relational science of racism, "human" will always function politically in concert with the presumed preeminence of whiteness. In this sense, "human" is never apolitical, though it presents as such. Nor is there anything inherently true about its ability to fully capture the embodied realities of the species it purports to understand, regardless of their hue. As Butler writes:

> Essentially, the human classification functions to protect the proto normativity of white supremacy by upholding epistemological systems of anti-blackness, which are dependent on the meaning disproportionately imbued upon those who bear its moniker. When we consider the role that the technological apparatus of language plays in undergirding anti-blackness, it could also be inferred that white people are not human either. White people are simply the benefactors of this technology, given their status within the cultural milieu in which it is employed. So, when Black people insist upon participating within the supposedly protective schema of this term, Black folks are actively reifying anti-Black hierarchies inherently imbedded within its cybernetic reach.[35]

The depth of Butler's argument is perhaps best illustrated by the ease with which the negativity associated with "black" lands as commonsensical when used as a descriptor in the English language. To be blackballed, blackmailed, or blacklisted all bear negative associations akin to the ways "dark" drums up the same sentiments. It is no coincidence that cultural connotations of darkness, or Blackness, land in consciousness as something bad. Because in large part, the contents of contemporary human consciousness have been curated by Eurocentric understandings of the world and its people, grounded by and oriented toward colonizing ends.

In a real sense, the human race has been held back by "human" and race. By nature of its need for control, white supremacy inhibits the flourishing of the species. And as a result of its racism, the contributions of Black people within sport and society can only be received and related to capitalistically as far as caricatures like "beast" allow. Rendering the body uniquely "black," and thereby evil, has closed everyone off from the possibilities that come from a full-bodied appreciation of Black being. As it stands, the bodies of Black people must field cultural assaults rooted in a collective consciousness that has been curated by a colonizing history. Catholic theologian M. Shawn Copeland speaks to this convergence of racial politics on Black bodies. She positions the body as a mediating field between the "essential freedom" of the soul and the political realities in relation to which such freedom must be actualized.[36] For Copeland, every "human" body discloses a "more" to its own existence, which can be understood only when prioritizing embodiment accordingly. She writes:

> For the body is no mere object—already-out-there-now—with which we are confronted: always the body is with us, inseparable from us, *is* us. But, always, there is a "more" to you, a "more" to me: the body mediates that "more" and makes visible what cannot be seen. "The body," Yves Cattin writes, "is that ontological impotence which prevents the human spirit from presenting itself as pure absolute spirit. And in being human, the body is an essential quality of the soul." Spirit or soul and body, he continues, "are not two realities of which we are composed, [but] the originary totality

that we are." The body constitutes a site of divine revelation and, thus, a "basic human sacrament." In and through embodiment, we human persons grasp and realize our essential freedom through engagement and communion with other embodied selves.[37]

Copeland's understanding of the "more" with which every person exists posits a spiritual dimension that is glimpsed by deep engagement with the body rather than a denial of it. She discloses the anthropological depth to the racial struggles that play out uniquely on the terrain of Black bodies, and Black athletes—when read correctly—offer insight into the impossibility of controlling Black being, despite colonial attempts. Trying to control that which cannot be controlled, in theory or practice, has always been the goal of white supremacy. And as long as "human" operates within the linguistic heritage of European epistemologies—with its conception of, and commitment to anti-blackness—then it will forever be bankrupt when seeking to understand the depth and dynamics of Black embodiment.

While the treatment needed to justify a permanent move beyond "human" is outside the scope of this book, the fact that it has been racialized and deployed as a technology of empire is sufficient reason to set it aside for the sake of deeper analysis. Bracketing "human" allows the intellect to be placed back in its rightful context: the body. Inasmuch as the intellect—narrowly understood—has played politically as a historical reference point in determining who can be "human," considering it outside the context of Eurocentric understanding reveals significant insights into the nature and nurture of (Black) athleticism. This approach reimagines human intelligence as a *biotechnology*[38] *of becoming*, which enlists and extends from the totality of one's embodiment, including a "soul" that animates every movement. It brings brain and body back together to speak about being in a way that connects athleticism to anthropology and anti-racism.

Bracketing "human" holds space for the embodied brilliance of Black athletes to become legible—to shine through—which sheds light on the (r)evolutionary significance of Black athletic achievements in relation to America's legacy of white supremacy. Without the cultural baggage of "human" casting a disembodied (white) shadow over consciousness, Black athleticism can be reconceived as an expression of the intellect that demonstrates the struggle between incarnated spirit and cultural assault. It provides the opening needed for (Black) athleticism to be understood as both a form and blend of intelligence(s) that have been *developed and deployed* in service to skillfully navigating fields of players within cultural domains that still reek of racism. This perspectival shift opens into an analysis of (Black) athleticism that can truly take place on a more level playing field: the body and its interworking. And the consequences are far more significant than typical connotations of "sport" allow for. As a result of this shift, the contributions of Black people within sport and society can be appreciated for their (r)evolutionary significance, despite the ways they have been trivialized—or criminalized.

A (kind of) crucified Christ

Marshawn Lynch already accepted Butler's invitation to stop trying to be "human" on the terms set by a supremacist society. And like Jesus, he is crucified by the realization that the category was never meant for him, buried with his own refusal of its enforcement. Not giving a fuck is what makes Marshawn Lynch messianic. To the degree that he has bracketed the opinion pieces of society, he has also transcended their ability to keep him housed within the racialized reach of "human." He no longer lives in relation to the category, but rather has reoriented his life to a purpose of his own choosing. In this sense, Lynch embodies what theologian Dwight N. Hopkins calls the "outlaw," an African folk hero whose resistance of dominant cultural norms is read anthropologically as an embodiment of freedom on behalf of a community that has been targeted by empire. Hopkins describes the outlaw as one who is willing to shatter "conventional seductions of success" as part of an unlikely exercise of a "healthy human self"—perhaps a *healthier* "human" self. The outlaw's willingness to resist is salvific in that it wakes up the same capacity within others from similarly subjugated communities. It makes legible another way. Rather than succumb to the *policy-ing*[39] designed for their subjugation, the outlaw accepts criminalization and in so doing transcends the category by which they have been criminalized. In other words, they do not reinscribe the lie by resisting the label on its terms. Instead, the outlaw is willing to be whatever empire says they are because they recognize the absurdity of the terms in the first place.

Marshawn Lynch has resisted criminalization by disregarding its cultural logic and disentangling himself from its world of meaning. His assertion of the *Homo sapiens*[40] he knows himself to be is an embodiment of freedom despite even the possibility of death that he knows is lurking no matter what he says. And it is clear that the few things Marshawn Lynch *has said* resonate with people in ways that reveal the failure of criminalizing narratives to persuade their target audience. Lynch is all over the media now, featured on podcasts, late-night talk shows, movies, and the like. But what makes his story so salvific—so instructive—is the fact that he plays "himself" in the majority of his features. He is more popular now with his helmet off than "beast mode" ever could be on the field, despite the criminalizing messages that threatened his legacy. In a deeper way, however, Lynch's popularity reveals a growing reciprocity between the uniqueness of his voice and the cultural demand *for* the uniqueness of his voice. In other words, he has created a legibility for his humanity, on his own terms. His embodied brilliance is an exercise of essential freedom that has disrupted the logic of criminalization in ways that allow his spirit to withstand the social death that comes with his refusal to play along, rendering unsuccessful the barrage of attempts to silence him, or to make him speak against his will. And yet, by nature of his Blackness in relation to the category of "human" itself, there will remain those who cannot escape the racialized cadence of "crucify him."

CHAPTER THREE

Steph Curry
Range Beyond the Ploy of Neoliberal Rationality

> I am what time, circumstance, history, have made of me, certainly, but I am, also, much more than that. So are we all.
> —James Baldwin

ROOM IS NOT often made for Black men to have range. Because range signals capacity, a spaciousness within which one can wield oneself with a level of expertise that is undeniable. If an actor is said to have range, it means they have mastered the art of channeling dimensions of themselves—psychologically, emotionally, even spiritually—in order to *play* a variety of roles and make them all believable. To portray a character as if they were real. To make them, real. It means they have successfully become that which the script called for, having learned the relational technology written into the role but (em)*bodied*[1] it in their own way. It is when one's performance testifies to the expansiveness of their being, because to *per-form* literally means "to bring to fruition, completely."[2] Range signals the capacity to become, which registers *being* at a level of depth that can never be colonized. It signals the kind of adaptive intelligence a species needs to survive, and eventually find flow amid new circumstances. But range has to be developed, and its development is limited by the level of freedom it has to be—the room within which it can practice. To develop range, one must have the space to shoot, and to miss. To shoot again, and to miss many more times. To shoot, over and over again, until shooting becomes second nature, and "swish" white noise.

On December 14, 2021, Wardell Stephen Curry—affectionately known as "Steph"—launched and sank a three-point shot against the New York Knicks in the legendary Madison Square Garden to become the NBA's all-time leader for three-point shots made during the regular season. In addition to his prowess as a shooter, the one nicknamed "Chef" is known for *cooking* even the best defenders and double teams with his blend of agility, speed, and stamina. To say that Steph Curry has had an influence on the way basketball is played in the NBA would be an understatement. But it is a part of Curry's story that should not be overlooked, especially considering how grim his NBA pre-draft scouting report looked in 2009 despite his displays of athletic brilliance while playing at Davidson College. In a 2015 ad with Coach Up, shortly after winning his first championship, and with musical artist Drake's "0 to 100" playing in the background—a song in which "Chef" Curry's top-tier shooting ability is referenced—Steph read his own draft report in a voiceover while performing some of the very skills experts said would be his demise:

> Stephen Curry, 6'3" 185lbs.[3] Position: point guard. Stephen's explosiveness and athleticism are below standard. He's not a great finisher around the basket. He needs to considerably improve as a ball handler. Often struggles against physical defenders. Stephen must develop as a point guard in order to make it in the League. *He will have limited success at the next level.* Do not rely on him to run your team.[4]

All sensationalism aside, since this ad was released, Curry has won three more championships, two league MVPs, one NBA finals MVP, a gold medal at the 2024 Paris Olympics, and is a ten-time NBA All-Star, and counting. Beyond his personal accolades, however, Steph Curry's impact on the NBA can be seen most clearly in how the niche he has created for himself has become the standard across basketball teams at all levels.

It used to be that three-point shots were a rarity. In 1979, when the three-point line was introduced in the NBA, there were only an average of 2.8 three-point attempts per game. In 2008, the year before Curry was drafted, that number had risen to eighteen, with the Golden State Warriors—the team that drafted Curry after that season—boasting the leading average with 26.6 three-point attempts per game. As of 2024, after Curry's record has been set and extended, and his Warriors now have seven NBA championships on their record—four since he arrived—no team in the NBA is attempting fewer than thirty-one three-pointers per game. Hall of Fame center Shaquille O'Neal says Steph Curry has "messed up" the game of basketball, and that Curry is his favorite player because of it. By messing the game up, he means Curry has radically reshaped the NBA, shifting the very logic by which players and coaches must approach their strategies and execution of game plans.

Before Curry, any given sequence of play did not truly begin until after the ball handler—usually a guard—crossed half court and approached the three-point line.[5] This is when defenses knew they had to engage, especially if the offense had players that could shoot with accuracy from beyond the arc (or three-point line), which sits at a distance of 23.9 feet at its furthest point from the rim. In this era, "big men"—players like Shaq and others whose dominance was based primarily on their height and physicality—were more often the focus of offensive schemes, which meant more defensive attention had to be paid in the "paint."[6] Since Curry, attention has shifted to the perimeter. Now defensives must engage as soon as he touches the ball, and certainly once he crosses half court, because they know his range reaches well beyond the arc. This creates a chaotic scenario where the floor is "stretched" and defenders are forced to engage further away from the basket, leaving more space for movement and for more points to be scored.[7] In a press conference after winning the 2017 NBA Championship, Steve Kerr—Curry's coach and confidant—explained the implications of his impact in more detail:

> It's just stunning, really, the impact he makes. Um, I've never seen anything like it. I mean there's, uh, obviously been so many great players in this league who have dominated, and . . . you

know, you think about Michael Jordan immediately, or Larry Bird, or Magic, and ... uh, you know, Shaq, you know, what he did to the defense. You had to pay so much attention to him. And Steph is similar but in a different way from everybody else. You know, I've never seen anybody put that much pressure on the defense 35 feet from the hoop and generate the spacing and the pace, *and the chaos* that ensues defensively once he gets going towards the rim. So, everything we do, you know, starts with Steph. And um, he's uh ... he's brilliant ...[8]

Curry's contribution goes much further than the NBA, however. Curry has *(r)evolutionized* the game of basketball, period. In the same way that Usain Bolt has stretched our imaginations when it comes to how fast a person can cover a distance of one hundred or two hundred meters,[9] Steph Curry has opened up a new dimension to the game of basketball, and with it an embodied capacity previously unknown to humankind. His novelty has become a norm around which the game itself is played, making him a messianic figure in the minds of young hoopers who hope for similar success. By setting the NBA's equivalent of a "world record," Curry has accomplished something that no other person has done.[10] On its face, this is what is meant by *(r)evolutionary* when speaking of Curry's contribution. The fact that his protest of previous basketball logics has resulted in the game's evolution speaks to the revolutionary significance of his athleticism in relation to the sport. It is no small thing that Curry's brand of basketball play (read: blend of intelligence) has disrupted the logic of the sport itself. On a deeper level, however, this concept reads revolution as a corollary to legibility. To call Curry (r)evolutionary references the constitutive consequences of his range based on an understanding of how any radical reshaping of something suggests its own evolutionary significance. It signals the connection and constant tension between *being* and *becoming* wrought by performances that push us forward. Moreover, it posits the evolutionary significance of *seeing*, which suggests that legibility is simultaneously a product of, and precursor to, sustained social change. In other words, it is the act of seeing the way Steph Curry plays basketball that makes legible the possibilities that have now become preconceived notions of how basketball should be played. He has literally reshaped the logic by which success happens in the sport, not to mention expectations for how success *should* happen.

This is the other reason Shaq says Curry messed the game up. He tells a story about how his son Shareef, who is 6'10" and 220lbs, now prefers to shoot a three-pointer instead of driving to the basket, which would have always been the custom for a player his size ... until the "Steph Curry effect." More than his influence on "big men" shooting three-pointers, Curry has created space for undersized players to pursue their dreams of playing basketball and has made legible the very real possibility that they can be successful despite their size. Because of Curry, it has become commonplace to see youth basketball players shooting (and making) 30-foot three-pointers, not to mention dribbling with fluidity through defenders, dropping dimes to their teammates, and doing it all with style. Certainly, legends like Allen Iverson—aka "The Answer"— have influenced the game of basketball in similarly inspiring ways when it comes to the blend of skills Curry embodies, but his range raises new questions, which sets him apart and signals the resilient capaciousness of Black being more broadly. However, the deeper cultural significance of Curry's range only becomes clear when it is read as a feature of his athleticism that was developed in direct response to the disharmony between his body and the economic logic by which Black athletes are typically recruited and commodified in the context of sports.

The neoliberal rationality of recruitment

Despite political attempts to erase the racial history of this country, it is well known that the Black body has always been big business in the colonial United States. From tobacco, cotton, and sugar cane to sponsorships, sports betting, and merchandise—not to mention revenue based on ticket sales and television ratings—Black (athletic) bodies have lived behind the billions of dollars enjoyed by primarily white, wealthy owners, whether of plantations or sports teams. But the normalcy of the latter did not emerge until the advancements of civil rights indirectly kicked off a resurgence in the economy of Black bodies (for sport). Prior to integration, Black athletes were relegated to competing against each other in leagues set aside by segregation. This means, at least in part, that the carceral system—with its policing practices—would have been the primary way in which to "recruit" Black male bodies for the exploitation of their labor. Certainly, Black men were a growing part of the American labor force after integration, but the carceral system was unique in that its business model was predicated on the presence of Black bodies for the purpose of exploiting them—still for sport, but in a much different game. The asymmetries of power in this relationship were permissible because criminalization justified the imbalance. In this sense, (mass) incarceration has always functioned as an extension of the political dynamics of antebellum slavery. It is a system that was formalized as a political structure during Jim Crow, and increasingly privatized as part of the neoliberal turn in contemporary society.[11]

However, as sports organizations slowly began to pepper their teams with Black players—enjoying much success as a result—the trend of trafficking in Black athletes took hold. Eventually, a system of recruiting was born whereby the wealthiest (white) organizations and educational institutions poured over each other to scout (read: salivate over and stalk)[12] and hopefully sign the most talented Black athletes from around the United States. Given the growth of the sports industry since integration, some institutions now enjoy global access to players who show promise. Bill Rhoden calls this phenomenon the *Conveyor Belt*,[13] an industrious system of recruitment by which the most (physically) talented young Black men are plucked from their locales and put to work in the fields of athletic competition. And it promises them scholarships and sponsorships as penance for the ways it will pimp them out throughout their tenure. Rhoden critiques this recruiting apparatus based on its extractive economic logic, arguing that it effectively functions as an arms race wherein white institutions race to recruit and put on display a labor force featuring the biggest, fastest, and strongest specimens respective to their sport. He writes:

> The sports industry is not just a signature aspect of the American way of life, but has also become a major component of the American economy. What distinguishes sports from other industries is the nature of its raw material: For the past fifty years, the prime raw resource in the sports industry has been black muscle. The work of the industry is to extract those bodies from where they primarily reside—in the black neighborhoods of rural and urban America—and put them to work. Now a sophisticated recruiting apparatus has been created for just that purpose.[14]

Prior to the integration of Black athletes into mainstream sports, the ideal athlete was defined in terms of philosophical, artistic, and other racially driven conceptions of the ideal (white) *man*. Even down to the proportions of one's body, sports were generally calibrated based on the "average" body type as defined by European philosophies and artistic renderings. This meant that elite athletes would have been the same size, whether they were playing basketball or throwing shotput.[15] This paradigm did not begin to shift toward the sport specialization that is the standard today until the neoliberalization of society curated a "winner takes all mentality," concomitant with technological advances (i.e., television) that contributed to the growth and popularity of sports as an industry that could simultaneously stimulate and satisfy the public's desire to be entertained, if not utterly mesmerized. This gave rise to a cultural phenomenon that has come to be called the "big bang of body types," because it marks a time when sports became highly specialized based on the particularity of the bodies within them.[16]

In contemporary society, it is commonplace to assume that volleyball players and shotput throwers would be built differently. And pretty drastically. The same goes for basketball players, whose specialty has become so phenotypically focused that everything from a player's draft status to the size of their contracts, and their hands, are scaled based not only on height, but even more specifically on wingspan—because (dis)proportionally basketball players are prized for how well the length of their bodies fit the logic of the game, and the positions they play within it. To be sure, skill has its place. But as can be seen in Curry's draft report, skill can be easily overshadowed if one's body is deemed insufficient for the tasks tailored to the sport.

It is important to note that the economic logic of this recruitment system functions similarly to the carceral system in that the exploitation of bodies and labor is bookended by asymmetries of power that are the name of the game—mere facts of the way the economy of sport is structured. Furthermore, the attending economy of bodies in sport leaves little room for (even the idea of) Black range. By nature of its extractive logic and entertainment value—both of which are directly tied to the fetishizing indispensability of (Black) bodies as its "raw material"—the economy of sport exercises a rationality of control that is designed to maximize profits while protecting the bottom line at all costs. This is why premiums are not only put on the most physically gifted specimens, but also on athletes who prove compliant. Outspoken players like Colin Kaepernick make it hard to control a narrative that needs investors. Yet, even while the attitudes of Black athletes matter, it is the presence and productivity of their bodies that form the basis of the business. Such was the deeper reason for the pause many teams expressed when it came to drafting Steph Curry. Truth be told, they really only found his skills wanting *because* of his size.

Everything about Steph Curry confounds the economic logic by which (Black) athletes are typically recruited and commodified in the context of sport. He is not from "the hood," he grew up with both parents present in the home—with a father who also played in the NBA—and basketball was not his only option. In other words, Steph Curry did not *need* basketball, even while it was always his passion. Furthermore, his fair skin, small frame, and cool demeanor all fall outside the contemporary fascination with "bigger, faster, stronger," and blacker, which is a phenotypical blend that has always functioned as a colonial impetus to invest and exploit. If Marshawn Lynch epitomizes the historical fear of Black men found in the physicality of "beast," Steph Curry eludes its fetishization altogether. Where Lynch embodies the brilliance of force expressed through resistance, which is only strategically brutish, Curry epitomizes the finesse of being elusive—brilliance, but in a different neurophysiological key. Steph Curry is not the "power generator" Mike Mayock would be looking for if his exploitative analytical expertise was translated to basketball. In a real sense, Curry would be left on the same auction block from which Lynch would be a first-round pick. He does not fit the idealized frame for the role Black bodies play in the economy of sport, whether physical or ideological. Hence, his dominance creates a conundrum because it forces a recognition of range for which space is not typically held.

Painting a picture of Black pathology

Even though Curry's embodiment eludes the stuff that typically gets spun into the kinds of "rags to riches" stories that sports media uses to pat itself on the back as uniquely "post-racial,"[17] the particularity of his success still provides the plotlines needed to pathologize Black youth and families while pedaling a neoliberal narrative that fails to tell the whole story. After winning his NBA MVP honor for the 2015 season, Curry closed out his acceptance speech with the following words:

> You don't have to live anybody else's story. Sometimes people make it seem like you have to have certain prerequisites or a crazy life story in order to be successful in this world. But the truth is you really don't. It doesn't matter where you come from, what you have or don't have, what you lack or what you have too much of, but all you need to have is faith in God, an undying passion for what you do and what you choose to do in this life, and a relentless drive and the will to do whatever it takes to be successful in *whatever you put your mind to*.[18]

In an attempt to inspire the *range* of embodiments and expressions among those who might have been listening—especially Black children[19]—Curry uttered words that would make any proponent of neoliberalism salivate. To suggest that anyone, anywhere, can make it, no matter what they have or do not have, and moreover if they merely "put their minds to" it, plays perfectly into the ploy of neoliberal rationality, which is hopelessly romantic about convincing the public that anything is possible in the land of the free. This belief rests on the constant interplay of *individualism* and *meritocracy*, ideological soulmates whose coital relation gives birth to an economy where competition and inequality—and the asymmetries of power that follow—are as normal as the relationship between owners and "their" players. In a more insidious way, however, this rationality is also designed to explain away suffering as ultimately the fault of people who suffer.

One of the most insidious ways in which neoliberal rationality makes Black pathology legible is by emphasizing storylines that flatten the range of Black youth. Black kids are often filtered through the same exploitative recruiting apparatus that more mature athletes navigate, and the "success stories" that follow become the fodder from which anti-intellectual notions of Black athleticism are normalized. Stated plainly, there are consequences to *casting* Black boys as the up-and-coming "beasts" that fans can look forward to fetishizing. And since the recent NIL changes, this recruiting apparatus is now able to reach into the lives of Black youth more easily, initiating its seductive pull earlier into childhood.[20] The psychological effects of seeing Black athletes boast multimillion-dollar contracts should not be ignored, particularly for kids whose everyday life is lived hand to mouth—never mind the fact that these contracts pale in comparison to team owners and corporate executives, both in terms of wealth and the power that comes from it in a capitalist political economy. Despite these discrepancies, sport is by far one of the most lucrative professions where Black men are used to seeing themselves successful and are made to believe they have a chance at making it to the pros. And if the problem of legibility is taken seriously, one understands that *seeing* this play out is largely the reason Black youth continue to aspire to professional sports despite the probability that most will never make it past high school.[21]

The NBA and the NFL are the only professions where Black males are overrepresented, making up roughly 70%[22] and 53%[23] respectively. In fact, the percentage of Black males in the NFL alone exceeds their representation across the top three occupations combined that represent employment statistics for Black men in the United States.[24] Even across the entertainment industry—a domain that is typically held alongside sport as a unique aspiration among Black youth—Black males are a minority. And these statistics hold when singling out the music industry in particular. In hip-hop specifically—a genre built around the free expression of young Black men and women—one must acknowledge that artists have little control over the stories they tell, especially if they hope to make it in the mainstream. White male CEOs make up the overwhelming majority of record executives, which means they are the ones signing off as to what plays publicly. Michael Eric Dyson has rightly noted how doubtful it is to assume a white male CEO would sign and support the promotion of a hip-hop artist who challenges the establishment, especially if their critique targets the embodiment of the one who is paying them (even if indirectly).[25] Stated plainly, hip-hop artists are often coerced into careers of performing Black pathology as a means of escaping Black poverty. And this is productive.

Outside of sports, the only other measured data where Black males are overrepresented is in statistics that coincidently "prove" the criminalizing narratives told as justifications for incarceration, police brutality, or premature death.[26] In one sense, then, the aspiration to become a professional athlete could be understood as an attempt to escape the political circumstances for which so many young Black men are targeted. It is understandable how sports would be seen as a way out. Beyond an escape from alternatives, however, there is also a neoliberal pull toward the financial security (and fame) that professional sport seems to offer. bell hooks speaks to this cultural allure in *Where We Stand: Class Matters*, citing mass media as a primary mechanism through which class divisions between wealthy and working-class people are mediated based on positive television portrayals of the rich. For hooks, consumerism has been cast as the vehicle through which class differences can be mitigated.

She illustrates how the ability to acquire the same accoutrements one sees depicted among rich people on television became a signal that one had transcended one's circumstances and achieved at least a slice of the American dream, at least according to what cultural definitions of "success" look like.[27]

To the growing degree that success in sport looks like Black men such as LeBron James or Marshawn Lynch—or Steph Curry, for undersized kids who previously did not think they had a shot—then one understands why Black boys continue to aspire to careers in sports over and against other professions that are not already legible to them as "real" possibilities. This explains why some studies have found athletic aspirations to be the highest among Black male youth in comparison to their peers.[28] Studies also show that rates of educational attainment are the lowest among Black boys across the same age groups. But the stories we tell ourselves about this data matters—it materializes—because for any statistical connections that have been found between athletic aspirations and educational failures among Black boys, there are even stronger correlations between lower educational achievement and racial socioeconomic disparities. In other words, by including structural factors such as racial gaps in income, poverty rates, unemployment, and educational attainment, researchers have essentially been able to predict rates of educational achievement based on the demographics of race as they intersect with economic disparity.[29] To be sure, there is a structural critique that must always be considered when trying to make sense of why Black boys continue to fall behind in school even while they excel in sports. And this is not even to mention the school-to-prison pipeline, which adds an element of hypervigilant policing to Black adolescents in ways that constrain the space within which they *should* be able to develop their range.

What is even more disheartening are the ways Black families are blamed for it all. In ways specific to the struggles Black men and women face respectively, Black fathers and mothers are routinely cast as the problem. Portraits of single Black mothers in particular are routinely cited as evidence that Black homes are "broken," when in reality, there remain structural impediments that cannot be detracted because neoliberal rationality denies they exist. And since its logic is predicated on unfettered competition grounded in ideologies of individualism and meritocracy, any measurable failures among cultural groups can be easily (mis)read as evidence that they do not possess the stuff needed to succeed in the ways their white counterparts do. Educational psychologist Jennifer D. Turner decries the way in which data relating to the education of Black youth has been spun into what she calls the "myth of low aspirations." This myth invites interpretations of athletic aspirations as a misplaced priority, which is an underhanded way to reference a pathology because it puts the onus on the youth and their families, without any acknowledgment of the interrelated factors that occasion, if not streamline, such dreams. To challenge this myth, Turner conducted a study wherein children were asked open-ended questions like "who they are, what they think, and what they desire in their lives," and then invited them to draw themselves accordingly. She found that the range of aspirations among Black youth changed drastically when space was intentionally created for them to dream outside of the categories that questionnaires seeking the same data typically used. In other words, when given a truly blank canvas, Black children paint pictures of their lives that reveal a belief that, in the words of one participant named Paris, they really can achieve "whatever they put their minds to."[30]

Re-membering our (common) African heritage

The ploy of white supremacy is revealed when one recognizes that neoliberal rationality shares an epistemological heritage with "human" as discussed in the previous chapter. At its core, it is designed to orient the public toward the superiority of whiteness, which is part of a broader cultural need to protect the myth of Anglo-Saxon exceptionalism. But it seduces this way of seeing with subtle messages that recruit the public into its play. Such cultural performances span the spectrum of relational interactions, imbuing our imaginations with racial subtexts that cultivate a consciousness fit for capitalism. And Black pathology is so woven into the script that most of the actors have no idea they are performing it, which makes their roles that much more believable. This method (of) acting is *muscle memory* in the United States, a series of meaningful, yet mindless, movements that reinforce the rule of white supremacy. And its rules are grounded in a cultural belief that Black people are intellectually inferior—that, without white control, Black talent will flounder. And this conclusion is drawn despite a DNA paper trail that testifies to the expansiveness of a genetic heritage from which *all* "humans" come.

Genetically speaking, no embodiment of *Homo sapiens* has more range than persons who possess African DNA. The genetic variations that exist on a single strand of an African-descended double helix exceed that of any other ethnic group, which means more possibilities for embodiment in *every* direction.[31] In other words, the mere fact of being Black typifies *range* down to molecular levels. Culturally, however, the phenotypical evidence of African DNA has been cast in ways that support a colonizing agenda. And even benign cultural messages seem to support the conclusion that Black men are uniquely cut from a cloth of carnality, useful only insofar as they can be contained. Such is the reason "beast" plays so well, whether celebrated in the context of sport or cited as a rationale for imprisonment. Its delimitation of Black men's range lands (as true) no matter how we spin it, simply because it is already legible. And to the degree that it foregrounds the physicality of Black bodies in relation, sport is the perfect play space for this caricature to continue to shape the consciousness of Americans within a world (of meaning) that is none the wiser.

Taking Curry's range seriously exposes the ways Black athletes are expected to exist within a racist rationality which was built on an extractive logic that is wired to control Black bodies based primarily on economic (e)valuations of their machinery, which plays into the "anti-intellectual" assault on Black athletes. Yet its conclusions have been drawn without truly understanding this (Black) machinery, or the nature of the intellect for that matter. One of the most helpful aspects of Philip Butler's declension of "human" is that it invites a fresh look at the technology of Black bodies. By reading the Black body as *technology*,

Butler begins a necessarily open-ended exploration into the range of Black being without "human" as *the* reference point. Certainly, other Black thinkers have explored similar dimensions of decoloniality—and Afro-futurism—while holding "human" in check. And we need all of them. But Butler is unique among theologians who are engaging the deep biological complexity of Black bodies with such theological questions in mind.

The very premise of Butler's project is based on the claim that "Black people are not human."[32] On one hand, he means this as a statement of fact. To the degree that "human" is a technological apparatus that has been used to support the supremacy of whiteness, no person, technically, fits the category. Butler is right. No amount of categorization, racial or otherwise, can capture the evolving nature (or nurture) of *any* embodied iteration (read: person) within the existence of *Homo sapiens*. "Human" is a name, much like the names of people or places or things. And to the demise of millions of Black people over centuries, our capacity to name things and places and people has proven faulty. This recognition is built within Butler's claim. From a critical perspective, Black people have never had the luxury of feeling safe within this category, or its imperatives, because it was never meant for us. Kant admitted as much in both his blatant racism and the individualism that grounded his notion of *Reason*.[33] On the other hand, however, Butler's claim leaves room for *us* to (be)come something outside the category altogether. To simply say "not human" does not provide another moniker. Rather, it is an invitation to look more closely, to explore the tangible depths of embodiment outside even the most widely held claims of a colonial history.

What is particularly welcoming about Butler's invitation is that it is undefined but specific at the same time. It is undefined in that it leaves space for discovery—we might find out that we are *all* either something akin to animals or something closer to gods, and perhaps some blend of both. Yet, it is specific in that the answer lies in the materiality of the body. In other words, *being* is more clearly glimpsed when understanding the interworking of embodiment. Butler levels the theological playing field by centering the (Black) body as *the* mediating center for (Black) being *and* the primary text for theological understanding. For Butler, *Black being* is expressed through the technology of the body, disclosed in the complexity of biological systems that work collaboratively to sustain (its own) and create (new) life. It is through the enactment of such systems that Black being expresses and develops itself in the world. Said differently, (Black) being emerges from, and is bound by, the machinery of the (Black) body-in-relation.

The genetic heritage of *Homo sapiens* suggests that reading the embodiments of Black people is the best way to understand the nature of "human" existence as a whole. Because embodied being is always forming itself in relation to its cultural surround, every part of its adaptation reflects that which it must navigate in real time, for better or worse. In other words, the process of becoming emerges from the material tussle of one's being-in-relation. M. Shawn Copeland rightly notes the extent to which we are *caught* in our embodied becoming. She argues that the *physical body* is constantly constrained by the consequences of the *social body*.[34] In other words, even discursive conclusions about one's being circumscribe their becoming in deeply consequential ways that either limit or accentuate one's range. She writes:

> In other words, while interaction and engagement with others is crucial to realizing essential freedom, that realization in large measure hinges upon cultural perceptions and social (i.e., political, economic, technological) responses (affirmation or rejection or indifference) to the physical body. So the social body's assignment of meaning and significance to race and/or gender, sex and/or sexuality of physical bodies influences, perhaps even determines, the trajectories of concrete human lives. Thus, a social body determined by the arbitrary privileged position and, therefore, power of one group may enact subtle and grotesque brutality upon different "others."[35]

Copeland's analysis highlights the extent to which people must navigate a variety of power relations that either occasion or occlude their becoming. Connecting discourse and embodiment invites a recognition of the way political narratives function to delimit the embodied possibilities of persons based on what is believed about them, and then structured into existence. And when it comes to Black people in the United States, it posits the real problem of white supremacy. Considered together, Butler and Copeland help to disclose the materiality of racism, as well as its consequences for Black being and becoming—consequences that work on and in the body. Whereas neoliberal rationality would have us believe that power and privilege are of little consequence to those who have the wherewithal to "pull themselves up by their bootstraps," acknowledging the (Black) body as a technology that must navigate often oppositional forces for its own fruition illustrates how the materialization of myths such as "beast" forecloses the full flowering of Black men based on the fiction of race.

The tragic (racial) dimensions of "I am because we are"

A tragic dimension emerges when considering how any "being" could be "Black." To the degree that race is a social construct, and "beast" a myth that is inscribed *onto* persons based on the slipperiness of phenotype, how can the core of one's existence be considered in such terms? Would not this make the same essentializing mistake that Victor Anderson corrected in his critique of "ontological blackness,"[36] or mistakes made by philosophical and scientific histories that are largely responsible for persistent views of Black athletes as particularly wanting when it comes to intellectual range? Butler's is not an essentialist argument, however. It is not meant to determine who can or cannot be considered "Black." Rather, it is recognition as to the genetic depth with which one must deal with political life. The fact that such racial inscriptions factor not just in the ways Black people are (mis)treated, but also in their formation, points to a depth of relationality that, if taken seriously, obliterates even the idea of *individual* existence.

Pastoral theologian Archie Smith Jr. is helpful here. Writing during the unfortunate upswing of neoliberal rationality—and largely because of it—Smith argues that the "human" self is to be more accurately understood as a *relational* being, social in origin and reflexive in nature.[37] As a pastoral theologian writing in the late 1980s, Smith's primary concern in his groundbreaking work, *The Relational Self*, was the care of Black folks who sought support in a therapeutic world that was designed to help people *adjust* to society as is, *as if* society already knew how to properly hold all its people. Beyond the ways it clearly did not, in practice—which is why healing is necessary—Smith's primary critique was that it *could not*, in theory or practice. The problem was prior to revisionist attempts to make therapeutic practices more attentive, which can only be accomplished by asking therapists who were trained one way to practice another way. Certainly, educating practitioners regarding the politics of race, class, gender, sexuality, and the like has helped. There are now many more therapeutic options for melanated people across gender expressions, sexualities, and class status. But to the degree that therapies continue to operate toward adjustment, they will never be able to address the political realities that occasion the need for therapy in the first place, especially for marginalized people. The cycles will continue, and the market will not complain. Hence, for Smith, revising therapeutic practices is not the answer, because the error is located in the predominant conception of the *self* around which therapeutic theories themselves are built. Of this *self*, he writes, "In this perspective society is an organization of essentially interdependent, self-reliant individuals who actualize their inborn potentials within their social context. Relationality is seen as a by-product of human association, rather than the fundamental datum constitutive of human existence."[38] He offers this corrective:

> My position, by contrast, seeks to establish the social, historical, contextual, and, hence, the relational character of the self. The notion of sociality or the underlying relatedness of reality is the web which is the primary constitutive condition out of

which social and personal reality emerges, and it thus becomes the basis for critical reflection. The idea is that reality is fundamentally interrelated and social and perspectival or plural in character, and it is ever differentiating and evolving.[39]

Smith's replacement of the individual self with a relational self better recognizes the *depths* of interdependence that individualist theories have merely learned to accent therapeutic practices with. It sounds good to acknowledge how "interdependent" we are, especially when marketing to millions for the purpose of building a customer base. After all, using rhetoric that resonates is marketing 101 when you need to sell something. And to complicate things even more, the people behind such advertising likely also believe (in) the messages they are crafting. And this applies to more than just therapists, but to any organizations who seek to *serve* the public based on structures that are built to support the market. No amount of goodwill or heightened attention will enable a system to reach beyond its own design. The structure of neoliberal rationality itself idealizes individual "human"[40] existence, which coerces us all to act as separate entities who will p(l)ay the game.

Pastoral theologian Barbara McClure builds on Smith's epistemological shift but goes further in illustrating the mutuality of selves *and* society. Her "synergistic" model of theological anthropology offers a corrective for pastoral theologians who continue to fall into the trap of revision based on not taking Smith's relational shift seriously enough. Despite efforts at paying closer attention, she argues, pastoral theologians have been hamstrung by a lingering self-versus-society assumption, which reveals how deeply held the assumptions of individual existence continue to be. For McClure, "synergism" best captures the mutual nature of the relationship between persons and the political world.[41] In other words, every person exists and emerges from a constant creative exchange with their social surround, at every level of existence. This includes those immaterial parts of our being that we are made to think are untouchable, or that we experience as automatic, and therefore would never assume are manufactured.

Manufacturing "humans" is precisely what the market is up to, however, and no part of the self is off limits. In *Emotions: Problems and Possibilities for Human Flourishing*, McClure demonstrates the psycho-emotional depths of relational formation, emphasizing even the *emotional* synergy of selves *with* society. She argues that emotions are social constructs that simultaneously work on behalf of human survival—both socially and physically—and in service to the maintenance of the social order.[42] In this sense, emotions, like every other part of the self, have social origins that function to help persons perpetually fit themselves into the social systems they depend on for survival. Which is to say we know how to act, emotionally. And when someone does not "know how to act," the naming of emotional "disorders" is only understood as such because of norms that are designed to shape our emotions to fit the logics of a social identity—even when that identity is a national one that exists in service to, and as an extension of, empire wrought through the epistemological worldview of "human."

McClure is right in her assessment of the emotional synergism that grounds our existence. We regularly create and maintain what I call *emotional equilibriums*, by necessity, which ground every aspect of our becoming. Such emotional states of balance are born in real time from the constant creative exchange between selves and their surround, inscribed with meaning that emerges from, and wires us toward, the logic of the relational milieu that makes us. Sometimes we notice the discrepancies, such as when a young Black boy must weep despite being constantly reminded that "boys don't cry." The very fact of his tears should compel a reconsideration. But to the degree that everyone around him is shaped by the same emotional logics—which extend from the same rationality—their empathic efforts are overridden by the urge to encourage him to put his helmet back on and get back in the game. No wonder rates of unreported concussions are higher in Black youth,[43] which may be connected to the racial disparities found among former NFL players experiencing neurological problems resulting from repeated brain trauma.[44] To be sure, these discrepancies can also be linked to the "race-norming" embedded within the NFL's process for assessing and potentially paying out Black retirees who had debilitating brain injuries—a practice that was only recently challenged, and resulted in a $1 billion settlement with Black former players.[45] Regardless, the felt need to not show weakness imprisons Black men, both because it is an imposed trait that reflects the toxic history of masculinity *and* because it unfortunately acts as a protective measure that might factor into his survival if he has the wrong encounter. Stated plainly, it is virtually impossible for a young Black man to nurture healthy vulnerability when everyone around him encourages him to be "hard," even if by political necessity. This is what McClure is trying to get at, albeit not with this level of specificity with regard to race as it intersects with (toxic) masculinity. But the thrust of her work is important in that it moves in this direction.

Emotions are tricky because we experience them as automatic. But they are not. Emotions are contextual in their development, constructed in their meaning, and consequential in the ways they simultaneously protect and propel us in our daily development. They are manufactured, and the inevitability of our participation in the manufacturing process is another reason why neoliberal rationality is so seductive. We are taken in ways that feel self-directed simply because we are the actors, which blinds us to the tragic reality of how deeply relational we are. Emotions simultaneously serve us in our survival, and function as a last line of defense to protect whatever rationality they have been synchronized in service to, for said survival, for better or worse. And this too is productive.

Racialization runs even deeper than emotions, however. White supremacy seeks to reconstruct the very *crux* of one's creativity. This concept is preferred to "soul" because of its disembodied historical baggage. "Soul" too often brings with it the assumption that one's body is some sort of vessel, and that the *person* they really are—their "self"—has a destiny that can only be reached apart from the body. This notion of "soul" reflects the individualist assumptions that Archie Smith challenges. It assumes uniqueness is innate and prevails in its triumph. It pictures "soul" as the driver behind the wheel in a race against finitude, seeking to find freedom *from* this life. ***Crux***, on the other hand, sees *this life* as the whole point. It takes seriously our capacity (and responsibility) to create, but sees such capaciousness as thoroughly caught and constituted in conversation with the political world. Like "soul," it similarly references that immaterial part of embodied existence, but argues that it *emerges* with increasing particularity the longer we live and experience life. In this sense, ***crux*** is an accumulation of experiences made sense of, brought to fruition by acting out its own emergence *as real*. And thus, it is real. ***Crux*** also acknowledges our connection to a consciousness that is greater than our own. It is that highly subjective spiritual dimension of life that each of us—in our own way—experiences as *being* connected to something beyond ourselves. It is our intuitive sense of what Copeland calls the "more" of embodied existence, where the deep materiality of embodiment and Mystery meet in the murky circumstances of life. Hence, ***crux*** challenges the historical notion that the "soul" is unaffected by political realities like racism, writing it off as a theological vestige of the triumphalist bullshit that is built within individualist notions of the self, which extend from the colonial attempt to remap the world with Eurocentric sensibilities. The fantasy might feel good, but it is not real.

The fact of the matter is, we suffer. We bear the scars of all the death and detainment that have happened in the name of race throughout the history of this country, collectively. George Floyd's murder is a wound that we all wear, regardless of political identity. But Black people cannot distance ourselves from the pain in the same ways others might be able to. We wear it subjectively, incorporated deeply in the ***crux*** of our creative being, whether we want to or not. *We* suffer. It is part and parcel of the human condition wrought by the tragedy of relational existence. And such suffering reaches the innermost parts of ourselves in ways that create traumas that live in the materiality of our bodies, even down to the level of DNA. Racism does not just harm the body, or the psyche. Its fangs do not just sink into one's emotions. Racism targets the very ***crux*** of one's being in the world, coercing spiritualities of subservience that compel us to forfeit and just *play* along. Wendy Farley calls this "radical suffering" because it "pinches the spirit of the sufferer, numbing it and diminishing its range,"[46] which references the possibility that the *crux* of a person can be snuffed out while they are still (technically) living. And that is tragic... and productive.

The "mind" of muscle memory

To call the scourge of racism *muscle memory* is more than metaphorical. Neuroscience demonstrates how what is commonly known as "muscle memory" is more deeply understood as a process of "motor learning," wherein the brain and body communicate back and forth in real time to create and sustain equilibriums out of which all embodied movement takes place. It is the underlying process that allows an adult to tie their shoes without having to think about it. While the technology of the movement remains the same across time—cross the laces, loop one side, tie the loop, secure—the ease with which one can carry it out develops the more one practices it in a ritualized way. A child tying shoes for the first time is completely absorbed in the process, flexing their neocortex as they concentrate to accomplish the task. Yet, for an adult who has probably tied their shoes a million times, the movements are as mundane as the task itself—because it has already been downloaded. This means that attention has moved from the neocortex, where executive functioning takes place, to the "back" of the brain, where previously downloaded programs live—in the basal ganglia and cerebellum, more specifically.[47]

Once movement patterns are downloaded, we experience them as largely automatic. At least until one breaks a thumb or experiences some other disruption to one's particular way of carrying out the task, which compels one to relearn the same task but in a different way. This is when executive functioning turns back on—in conversation with the motor cortex and company—and locates another neural pathway that allows one to perform the task to completion. But it takes a lot longer this time, like in the beginning of any new effort. This is because new neural pathways must be explored and created to establish new movement patterns. They do not exist prior to this exploration. However, once a task is successfully completed—meaning that movement pattern has proven trustworthy—one's brain will continue to send signals down that same pathway with each successive completion of the task. And the increasing effortlessness with which these signals flow is a direct result of dendritic spines being thickened with each successive, successful performance.[48] This is why the phenomenon is called muscle *memory*—because the coordinated movement among interdependent pieces that allows one to successfully tie shoes, prior to breaking a thumb and having to relearn, is downloaded and readymade to be pulled from in the performance thereafter. And this applies to all embodied movement-in-relation, whether made sense of or completely "mindless." Muscle memory demonstrates that there is really no distinction. The memories live in the neurophysiology of the body, regardless. In other words, once the cast is off, the shoe tier is now equipped with two ways of tying their shoes, both of which are neurophysiologically structured, or *programmed*, into their being.

The fully embodied nature of muscle memory should not be glossed over, however. Every part of one's being is fair game in the formation process of memorizing movements-in-relation. This is another reason Butler's focus on the technology of (Black) bodies is so inviting. On one hand, it illustrates an even deeper dimension to the tragedy of relationality. Take the trauma of racism for example. Like the memory of movement patterns, trauma is also downloaded and held in the body—in the brain, specifically. When someone experiences a traumatic event, it shocks the system, sending messages to the hippocampus and amygdala to be stored. These regions hold the details of the event—according to whatever rationality made them land as traumatic—to be drawn on for protection in the case that one confronts a similar set of stimuli that remind one of the previous incident. And to the extent that traumas are also tied to the release of stress hormones such as cortisol—which accompany adrenal efforts to fight, flight, or freeze—such stimuli can stymie one from engaging in, or fully experiencing, a host of tasks associated with everyday life.

However, traumas—real or imagined—are but one inhibitor of movement. Many other stimuli exist that similarly serve a restricting function, and most, if not all, of them are socially induced. Their ability to invoke fear is based more on the possibility that something traumatic *could* happen than the fact that something already has. And this too is marked in the body. Consider the embodied responses of two different people being pulled over by the police. In one scenario, a Black man who is conscious of race and the history of policing gets pulled over. He may be doing nothing wrong, but he notices an immediate tightness in his body, an elevated heart rate, and feels himself essentially preparing to go into survival mode. No matter how much he may remind himself that he has nothing to be afraid of, the stimulus of seeing those lights in his rearview mirror invokes an immediate embodied response that bears on the interaction itself. And potentially tragically. In another scenario, a white woman who has never been racially profiled, and who perceives being pulled over as minor inconvenience, does not feel the same tightness in her body. If anything, she might be annoyed and perhaps even volatile. The *range* from which they can each pull is drastically different, yet productive in both directions. Both of their embodied responses are automatic and directly connected to the meaning associated with their particularity in relation to the stimulus—being Black versus white while engaging the police. And such meaning is *downloaded* into their being in ways that either occasion or occlude movement, which is tied to the development of their range.

The neurophysiology of muscle memory sheds light on the chokehold that rationalities of race have on relational interactions and the deeper consequences of white supremacy. This can be seen even more clearly when considering the Central Park confrontation between Christian Cooper and Amy Cooper. When watching the footage recorded on Christian Cooper's phone, it is apparent that both were experiencing the physiological symptoms associated with feeling threatened. Their trembling voices suggest that their bodies were similarly stressed—shortened breath, tightened muscles, narrowed perception. They were both triggered, but for very different reasons. For Amy, the mere appearance of a Black man recording her in public was enough to send her into a panic. For Christian, it was the potential threat of having triggered a white woman in public, who weaponized her intention to get the police involved. Regardless of how one might interpret this encounter morally, the predominant rationality of race shaped how each of them could or could not show up.

Muscle memory gives neurophysiological legs to Pierre Bourdieu's *habitus* in that it demonstrates the way cultural narratives are internalized and then acted out as real.[49] Religious scholar Onaje X. O. Woodbine offers an apt sports metaphor to capture this, which he finds in Bourdieu's work. Building on the thrust of Bourdieu's *reflexive sociology* found in his concept of *habitus*, Woodbine writes:

> Born into a field of social forces, people habituate to the norms of the field, even if they are harmful to one's self. Over time these cultural narratives shape the thoughts and feelings of groups and individuals, such that their bodies become the historical "repositories" of a culture. *Employing sports metaphors, Bourdieu draws an analogy between this social process of internalization and an athlete's development of a "feel for the game." When an athlete possesses a feel for the game, the rules become second nature.*[50]

That second-nature "feel" that Woodbine highlights captures the subtle power of this phenomenon in that the neurophysiology of muscle memory reveals just how deeply trainable we are. And when it comes to the problem of race, how unfortunately trained we are. It discloses the extent to which privilege *and* oppression operate inside bodies and not just on them—how the relational privilege white supremacy creates is downloaded into white bodies, and how white people often only learn of their programming after they have been triggered. Similarly, muscle memory discloses the depth of conditioning Black people must negotiate, both internally and in the political world. It speaks to the function of *stereotyping*, which is a term in neuroscience that references the material ways we are designed to default to those well-established neural pathways that allow us to move more efficiently with little attention needing to be paid.[51] It is important to note that being wired this way is a feature of the adaptable intelligence that aids in *Homo sapiens*' survival. The problem, however, is that this wiring is subject to movement in any direction. There is no internal mechanism (of justice) that signals when a stereotype has been created around bad form ... except perhaps in cases of (cultural) injury, of which there have been an abundance. But stereotypes are only efficient *because* they represent the neural pathways that have already been taken, over and over again. Thus, muscle memory teaches us that we will literally become whatever we "put our minds to."

Flipping the script

Steph Curry tells a different story. He embodies Dwight Hopkins's trickster figure in that he "acts out the notion of human reversal in which usually the weak character (that is, poor and working-class black folk) deploys the weapon of wit to outsmart the physically strong owner of material resources (that is, elite whites with power)." Of the trickster, Hopkins further suggests:

> This dynamic produces a spirituality of human flourishing. Restated, the trickster character suggests a spiritual environment in which the disadvantaged majority can flourish and have abundant life by tricking the arrogant powerful few. Such tricking yields a human flourishing spirituality characterized by creativity, cunning, and balance.[52]

Curry has flipped the script, and in doing so made legible a different way to think about the intellect. He illustrates how "mind" is a fully embodied process of cognition that can be conditioned in ways that help one navigate the political world. This is what Curry means when *he* talks about putting *his* "mind to" something, or "obsessing over the details," as he cites "muscle memory" when asked how he is able to move in and out of *flow states* so easily.[53] The handle Curry has on himself, and anyone who tries to guard him, is a direct result of the conditioning he puts himself through each day in practice, at every level of his being. From training the "triple extension" of his hips, knees, and plantar flexion of the ankles, through to his fingertips—including the acuity needed to control the arc of the ball into the hoop—Steph has the magic of muscle memory down to a science.[54] He is a mastermind when it comes to playing (read: embodying) the game of basketball, and it is a result of the wherewithal he has developed *in direct relation* to the ways he was doubted from the beginning. The ability to contort one's being against oppositional cultural trends in such a way that has made legible new pathways for others to follow—and to do it with such ease while being undersized—is nothing short of a miracle. But the magic is in the mundane. Curry has literally conjured within himself the capacity to transcend the sport, and with it the relational rules that encouraged him to quit before he got started.

Freeing the "mind" by re-membering the body

It is critical to understand that sport is not dissimilar from other **cultural domains** for which extraordinary performances are held up as brilliant, and necessary. It would be hard to imagine cell phones today without Steve Jobs, or classical music without Beethoven, or physics without Albert Einstein . . . or space travel without Katherine Johnson, or literature without Alice Walker, or music without Beyoncé. It would be equally impossible to imagine the game of basketball today without Steph Curry. Each of these brilliant minds transformed the cultural domains in which they operated, and some of them had to do so from within constrained spaces that were complicated by the consequences of race. And yet, they still became so good at their respective crafts that they excelled in relation to a *field* of contemporaries and competitors, all of whom had to navigate the relational world of rules by which their "sport" was governed. The only difference is that Black athletes operate within a cultural domain that is easily trivialized because of sport's association with play (and entertainment), which is cast as a frivolous pastime that means little to the "real" lives of Americans. Developmental psychology notwithstanding, however, an awful lot of time is passed on the (political) *play* of sports, and there are few industries that contribute more to the everyday lives of Americans, not to mention the economy. If science was (seen as) a sport, scientists would be called "athletes" too. Similarly, *Breaking*—a form of dance that originated among Black and Latine youth in New York during the civil rights era—made its debut as a sport at the 2024 Paris Olympics, officially ushering break dancers into the realm of "athlete" as well.[55]

This brings us back to the problem of naming mentioned previously. Not only are the intelligences of (Black) athletes cloaked by the rationalities of race, but they are further buried because of the connotation "sport" has in the United States. This is because terminologies delimit by nature, which is a part of their function to *stereotype* for the sake of efficient understanding. Racialized notions of the "dumb jock" also have a genealogy that is linked with the mind–body dualism associated with Cartesian thinking, where the mind was assumed to be of a higher, more "pure," order than the body. But "I think, therefore I am," is yet another vestige of "human" and its political history, which was defined in opposition to Black embodiments as part of a (blindly?) racist exploration into the essence of the species. In other words, bracketing off what were thought to be the defining qualities of Black people grounded the pursuit to answer the question, "What does it mean to *be* 'human'?" And because Black people were uniquely associated with the body, European thinkers cut off a (neural) pathway into understanding the fullness of their own embodied existence as well. As a result, "mind" has been defined around individualist assumptions of singularity as separate from the body, and conflated with concepts like *rationality* and *cognition*. Definitions of intelligence followed this logic and found normalizing expression in the IQ test, which became the standard way in which to measure whether someone had *it* or not.[56]

The truth is, scholars have debated the nature of intelligence for centuries and, depending on their field, their focus has overemphasized some parts while neglecting others. But by and large, "mind" has continually been conceived as singular, separate, and largely synonymous with "soul." A more accurate—and helpful—way to speak about the nature of intelligence(s) is to acknowledge *them* as multiple, fully embodied, and relationally linked to the need to navigate a social and political world for survival. One thing scholars have agreed on is that the intellect references that adaptable aspect of being "human" that helps us survive by evolving to fit whatever circumstances are necessary. In other words, intelligence is adaptable and creatively oriented toward survival. Furthermore, it is distinguishable by the ways it allows one to both *answer* questions and *raise new ones* in relation to the rules of a cultural domain.[57] Intelligences are also translatable from the standpoint of applicability across situations. In more recent neurobiological views, which have worked to hold space for the mysteriousness of intelligence, scholars argue that intelligences should be seen as "relatively autonomous" intellectual proclivities that extend from one's DNA and find expression in myriad ways as people navigate life. And they are able to isolate regions of the brain–body connection that suggest the neurobiological basis of such proclivities. In this sense, *intelligences* can be spoken of in at least three ways. They are: (1) **multiple**, in that they reference the multiplicity of adaptive cocktails persons employ in order to meet and master their respective social worlds; (2) **fully embodied**, in that those cocktails represent unique embodiments that are similar in wiring but as varied as the DNA compositions that form the ingredients (read: biological bases) from which such cocktails are crafted; and (3) **relational**, in that they can only be known by the extent to which one successfully navigates the rules of a cultural domain, in relation to a field (of players) who collectively judge the competence of the actor in question.[58]

Acknowledging the technology of Black bodies provides insight into the embodied brilliance of Black athletes, in particular. Behind every technology lives an intelligence that anchors its auto- and/or allopoietic productivity. Technology, by definition, refers to the *way* a task is carried out more than the mere fact that it is. It is the practical application of knowledge—of intelligence—boiled down to a process that can be coded, or programmed. Technology is about harnessing intelligence. In this sense, technology is like the instruction manual meant to guide the neurophysiological process of muscle memory. It provides a blueprint that presumably anyone can follow. Consider the credence given to the role of *technique* in sports, which is a shorthand way to give authority to a technology that has already been created. Indirectly, however, such credence also grants authority to the intelligent design that is written into the technology based on the methodological process that was discovered and systematized for the sake of replication.[59] This suggests that even the most "gifted" Black athletes can never be reduced to their physicality. In fact, any recognition of "beast" that is based on extraordinary sport performance points beyond mere physicality to something inherently intellectual.

To the degree that any extraordinary sport performance relies on the mastery of a technique, or the creation of a new one, then it makes sense that its embodiment reflects an intelligence that lives behind the technology. Such brilliance is particularly bright when one's technological innovation has (r)evolutionary qualities that transform a field *and* the domain in which it exists. This is why "brilliant" is all Steve Kerr could come up with when trying to communicate Curry's significance during that 2017 championship press conference, because, by definition, "brilliance" cannot be contained, or controlled. It will find a way, regardless. Being in that close a proximity to Steph Curry on a daily basis allowed Kerr to realize the relational need to hold space for Curry to develop his range—not to control him based on the presumption that he knows best. It would have been unreasonable to try to force-fit Curry into schemes that were not designed for him. Kerr knew that the most reasonable thing—that which made the most sense given their relationship—was to let Curry cook. And the championships that ensued speak for themselves.

CHAPTER FOUR

Deion Sanders

Presence Beyond the Pull of Respectability

Sometimes you gotta pop out and show...
—Kendrick Lamar

PRESENCE IS AN intriguing phenomenon. In a mundane sense, it refers to the mere fact of one's appearance. If someone is present it means they are physically there, not somewhere else. It captures the materiality of their existence in time and space, literally how they take up space in time. But in a deeper sense, presence refers to the "more" that M. Shawn Copeland argues every person exists with.[1] That which is beyond mere material. This references the fact that someone can somehow be present *without* being physically "there." Hence, there is a spiritual dimension to presence that often eludes awareness even as it provokes it—because presence signifies poise. It is a performance that springs from the psychological balance one develops in relation to public space, wherever that might be. Presence actualizes range but does not exhaust it. It is both the materiality and mystery of one's appearance in the world. In this sense, presence is like a poker play in the way it strategically presents cards that will (hopefully) win the hand.

Presence is a mind game that we all participate in. As a psychological play, it cloaks the rest of the cards being held but does not hide the fact that they are there. Which is to say that behind every presence is a messy process that determines how someone will present themselves to the (political) world. Ask any athlete and they will tell you that what fans see on game day is merely the result of what they have done thousands of times on the practice field, albeit dressed up with a little more pizzazz to make it sexy—because fans love to be entertained. Ask any person and they will tell you that there is much that goes on behind the scenes of their public persona—that there is often a gap between the self they live with every day and the self the rest of us see. As a spiritual reality, presence is what happens as a result of seeing, smelling, or otherwise sensing the self someone shows up with when it's game time. Even if that game is everyday life. It is an aura that can be felt beyond the five senses too. The air that emanates from embodied performance, infectiously inhaled, even if ignored for lack of pungency. Or for fear of it.

Presence is a feat for any person who exists in a politically fraught world. To show up daily despite the variety of psychological traumas we face is an accomplishment, especially for people who have to deal with racial trauma. But for Black men, presence is especially tricky. Because Black men must know how to perform on two stages simultaneously. On one stage, they perform in relation to the stated audience of their activity—those gathered around social agreements meant to ensure that everyone participates equally. This is the more direct dimension of life, where following the formulaic "if, then" *narratives* of society pave the way for social advancement: "If you want to be successful, then work hard, go to college, etc."—in other words, those rules of the game that apply to everyone. The second stage is the unpredictable dimension of life, where the fictions that follow Black men make them move with the awareness that the mere appearance of their bodies complicates their capacity to follow the formula of the first dimension.

In ways that cannot be planned for, but must be accounted for, Black men modulate their **presence** in real time with a balance that is based on a keen ability to perceive political circumstances that have proven "real" in material ways. It is commonplace for Black men to show up strategically based on what they know about the power dynamics of a social space. This speaks to the second stage of presence, where too much of it can attract the wrong kinds of attention, but too little can get one looked through completely.[2] Black men live in this tension, under the constant pressure to perform with just enough pizzazz to be successful in a suspicious world, but not so much to be seen as a threat.

The creation of "Prime Time"

Enter Deion Sanders, whose pizzazz not only poses an *actual* threat to the psychospiritual social order, but more importantly, inspires young men to believe in themselves—which was always his point. Sanders has stated many times publicly that much of the reason he created "Prime Time" was to inspire Black youth, and specifically to show them that they could achieve, and secure all the accoutrements of being rich without needing to sell drugs or participate in other forms of illegal activity. In other words, "Prime" was always a ploy to counter the normalized images of drug dealers and pimps as written onto Black men. However, "Prime Time" also served a strategic business purpose in the NFL—it was Sanders's way of raising the price, so to speak, for defensive backs in the league. Hence, by the time Deion Sanders got drafted, he was already "Prime Time."

The legend began as a nickname he got early on in life as a result of a basketball performance that provoked a teammate to tell him he was "Prime Time." And the nickname resonated, so Sanders claimed it for himself as an anchor and a reminder as to who he was when the lights came on. And when it was his time to shine at the NFL Combine, he did just that. Sanders showed up in a limousine, fitted in a three-piece suit, and dripping with a kind of confidence—and probably curl grease—that left a mark on everyone he encountered, if not every couch he sat on. But his performance matched his appearance. He ran a 4.27 in the forty-yard dash—setting a combine record at the time—changed back into his suit, then left in his limousine. It should be noted that he declined participation in many of the "required" drills for players at his position. And Sanders is clear that even his decision to run the forty was based on a desire to show curious coaches that the legends were true—that Deion Sanders was really "Him," "Prime Time."

Sanders had so much swag at the combine that he told the first four teams picking in the draft that year that if they tried to draft him, he would just go play baseball. After all, Sanders did become the first athlete ever to score a touchdown in the NFL and hit a home run in the MLB *in the same week*. He is also remembered for being the first to play a football game and a baseball game *in the same day*. And arguably—though he has said there's no argument—Deion Sanders is the greatest athlete in the history of the NFL, if not one of the best male athletes of all time across sports.[3] Needless to say, the viability of playing baseball gave Sanders a bargaining chip that allowed him to sway his own destiny toward Atlanta, the "chocolate city" that blew his mind when he visited while playing at Florida State. Sanders talks openly about how a visit to Atlanta inspired him, specifically because it was the first time he had seen that many Black people in positions of power, and where the ***culture***[4] itself was held in high regard. Sanders cites the Black excellence he saw in Atlanta as the stimulus he needed to be(come) Prime with a level of freedom he did not previously know was available to people like him.[5]

More than his athleticism and his swag, however, Sanders's ace in the hole is his mindset. And there is one particular phrase that stands out among the many one-liners he is known for, which should be read for its psychospiritual brilliance:

> *You look good, you feel good,*
> *you feel good, you play good,*
> *you play good, they pay good ...*

He completes the circularity of his mantra by linking being "paid good" with two more measures that reinvigorate the ability to *look* and *feel* good, suggesting that "if they pay good" then you will also "eat good" and "live good." For Sanders, eating good and living good were accomplishments that his upbringing in Fort Myers, Florida, taught him not to take for granted. And yet, despite what they did not have in monetary value, he credits his mother for creating an environment that was abundant in love. Hence, Sanders has always rooted his motivation for

"Prime Time" in the deeper mission to create a life where his mother no longer had to work, and history demonstrates how he has acted himself (athletically) into a star role, and his mother's early retirement, on the biggest stages of the sports world. And his philosophy of performance has stuck with him well into his career as a college coach.

It is as if Deion Sanders knew then what neuroscientists would later discover about just how subject our psychologies are to the opinions of those around us, and how one's presence can shape their opinions too. In a real sense, his philosophy of performance speaks to the psychospiritual dimensions that play out in all of our lives. Despite how good it might feel to imagine we can develop and maintain confidence despite cultural messages to the contrary, we are designed to download those messages as a means of survival. This means that the selves *Homo sapiens* develop are shaped by the linguistic world of their becoming, even when that world insinuates their inferiority. Whether the language one hears about oneself, or the looks one receives from others, everything about our environments attunes us to our own subjectivity in ways that are productive. They shape how we show up.

At the same time, how we present ourselves—our presence—pushes back. How we perform matters because it literally materializes the mental structures in the minds of people we meet. We make imprints on each other based on the ways we act in relation. And sometimes those imprints cut against the grain of the ones that exist prior based on cultural messages. This was the reason Deion Sanders created "Prime Time." To change the narrative. Wrapped up in Sanders's slogan is a realization of the cyclical relationship between the way we are seen, the way we feel, and the way we show up. And "Prime Time" was the perfect strategy that allowed him to play the political game of presence proactively. This was his way of self-determining his reception based on his awareness of the ways Black men were typically received. Prime is the persona Deion Sanders created to give himself the mindset he needed to take on the political world of sport. The embodied brilliance embedded within Sanders's creation of "Prime Time" can be seen more clearly when considering the psychospiritual depth and complexity of personas.

Personas and the performance of identity

Personas are conscious deployments of self that are meant to constitute something in the world, even if another's worldview. It is a presentation of sorts, where one shows up strategically based on how one believes one will be received, or how one hopes to be. It takes the guesswork out of social interactions, and instead insinuates its own truth based on what it wants people to believe. In this sense, personas are a lot like acting, or role-playing, in that they work at the level of belief to create their reality. To *put on* a persona is an attempt to determine what narrative about oneself will live in other people's minds, and personas are born from the cultural awareness one has about the politics associated with one's embodiment. Personas, alter egos, and even the default selves we show up to the stage of everyday life with are all performances that are politically calibrated based on the relational dynamics we must navigate. And we are constantly performing roles in relation to one another—consciously and unconsciously—which shape our subjectivities as much as our presence pushes back on our cultural surround.

A persona is more than *just* an act, even while it *is* a performance. The word "perform" stems from the French "per," which means "completely," and "fornir," which means "to provide" or "furnish."[6] The connotation points to the process of bringing something to fruition, completely. In this sense, performance could be understood broadly as any act of accomplishing the most mundane movements of daily life: walking, bending one's arm, sitting, talking, and so on. Each of these actions is a performance in that they accomplish some specific task toward some predetermined (or hoped for) end. Such performances also participate in the plasticity of our brain–body connection. In one way, performance actualizes our hardwiring. It represents the process by which our brains send signals to our bodies to act in ways that support survival and seek flourishing, in all circumstances. In another way, however, performance *promotes* neuroplasticity. Novel or challenging performances in particular push the brain to remap itself, which provides the neurophysiological structures for new behavior. In either case, performance is central to *Homo sapiens*' existence. When conceptually linked with relationality, however, performance highlights our participation in the *synergistic*[7] formation of selves and society—the parts we play in the ongoing production of cultural realities. In this sense, performance could be understood as the mechanism through which *Homo sapiens* actualize relational existence—*how* we relate to ourselves, others, and the world. While being bound to relationships describes the *nature* of our existence, performance highlights the ways we *nurture* the relations that form us. And their mutuality can never be separated.

From the time a baby is born, they are wired to perform themselves in relational loops. Very quickly, they discover their agential power to act in ways that call forth the sustenance they need. Whether love and warmth, milk or a pacifier, or if they are simply tired of sitting in their own shit, a baby's cry is a call to caregivers for a particular kind of attention. And the relationality is illustrated by the constant back-and-forth communication of caregivers trying to respond to which particular kind of cry corresponds with cuddles, milk, or a new diaper. Eventually, the child and parent get a feel for each other's nonverbal cues—or performances—and a culture is created. At least until the "terrible twos" disrupts said culture, which invites a new kind of attention to be paid in service to establishing a new rhythm of performing in relation to each other. Cultural developmental theory suggests that the performative agency of infants illustrates the extent to which *Homo sapiens* are "biologically cultural," and "born with a self-regulating strategy for acquiring knowledge by human negotiation and cooperative action,"[8] which is essential for survival. In other words, every person is born ready to perform, culturally, and such cultural performances facilitate development as a means of survival. It is a constant creative exchange between nature and nurture, where existence extends in real time from relational performances. But they also construct our identities, which is a normalcy that adolescents demonstrate with their performative agency.

The formation of identities is one primary focus among early childhood psychologists, and the function of performance is well known—namely, the performance of playing roles as a means of constructing the *self*. *Pretend play* and *storytelling* in particular are two primary ways in which children develop their identities during early childhood. And this happens in at least two directions simultaneously. In one direction, pretend play allows children to explore social roles and aspects of their emerging selves *outside* the pressures of socialization, or the "rules" of their reality. In other words, they are free to fantasize and explore different selves without consequence, thus *putting on* possibilities as to who they can be(come). Storytelling, on the other hand, allows children to enact their imagined roles in ways that reflect involvement *with* the norms of social life. In other words, they can imagine and practice how they will apply their pretend selves *within* the culture they are being shaped by. This helps children become better oriented to the norms, policies, and rationalities in which they are developing, allowing them to imagine their future roles as adults operating within such spaces.

Such plasticity does not stop in early childhood, though. Performing oneself is an essential practice later in adolescence as well, albeit in service to developing a sense of coherence and stable identity. Researcher and game designer Sarah Bowman argues that role-playing can aid in the development of a stable and consistent sense of self, which is crucial for a child's ability to avoid identity confusion later in life.[9] A key distinction is in order, however, because it can be easy to conflate the coherent "sense of self" that is developmentally necessary for teenagers and the *multiplicity* of selves that exists in adults. Said differently, the coherent sense of self that "ideally" develops during adolescence is not antithetical to the presence and performance of multiple selves in adulthood, even if we do not acknowledge it as such. Bowman writes:

> Even if the mature adult achieves a sense of a stable ego identity, the "self" as a singular, coherent entity remains an untenable concept, especially in postmodernity. The self is a fragmented and contradictory mélange of images, concepts, and memories. Though the ego would like to believe that identity remains stable throughout the myriad of experiences and challenges faced in a lifetime, each presentation of self

represents an unconscious construction, pieced together through trial and error.[10]

Bowman is acknowledging here how the process of becoming a self—or selves—is never complete, despite how the plasticity of even adult brains gets ignored in favor of the egotistical affirmations of Western epistemology. The slippage of singularity is shown by the embodied brilliance of Black people who have always had to perform multiple selves strategically. By necessity, Black people regularly *put on* display the innate ability of all *Homo sapiens* to integrate the dynamic fragments of the self, blending life's disparate—if not despairing—parts into some meaningful and productive whole. The pressure to do so, however, is wholly unnatural. The very idea that we must integrate our selves into a singular whole, and be *certain* of who we are, is a product of a culture built around modern perspectives of the self, which prioritize singularity, certainty, and consistency. Such views are more deeply rooted in the assumption that *Homo sapiens* exist fundamentally as autonomous individuals who are separate from one another, which ignores our relational nature and contributes to pathologizing discourses about people and communities who embrace their multiplicity and perform it publicly.

Personas as the practice of self-regulation

The performative function of personas does not only establish one's presence in the political world, however. Personas also help to establish a fuller presence to oneself through self-regulation. For the last decade, psychologist and neuroscientist Ethan Kross has led a series of studies that demonstrate the psychological benefits of personas, or alter egos. In his bestselling book, *Chatter*, Kross lays out a plethora of neuroscientific research that identifies an "inner voice" that lives within each of us, locating its constant operation as the origin of identity in relation to cultural life. In effect, he argues that the self one knows as "I" in any given moment is born from, and marked by, an internal conversation that begins in early childhood and continuously shapes our first-person view of ourselves throughout our lives. And Kross is clear that this "chattering" voice can be our own worst inner critic or an inner superhero working on behalf of the (ever-emerging) self.[11]

One study, nicknamed the "Batman Effect," found that children were able to focus their attention for longer periods of time when they were given space to imagine and refer to themselves in the third person while performing a task. And the effects were even greater for the group that was invited to *name* themselves their favorite superhero during the study. Those children who got to imagine and name themselves as somebody else also reported happier emotional states associated with the otherwise boring tasks they were assigned to complete. In other words, the freedom to be "Dora the Explorer" was a more empowering option than having to be the version of oneself that already exists *within* one's social reality. More than attention, however, the study also found that this method helped children cope with difficult emotional traumas such as the loss of a parent.[12]

Across a series of studies in adults as well, Kross and his colleagues found that "distanced self-talk"—the practice of calling oneself by name—served a regulatory function that helped people manage stress and anxiety, modulate and balance emotional states, and maintain—or regain—fuller prefrontal control in the midst of otherwise anxiety-inducing circumstances. This is because the practice of talking to oneself as another entity allows one to effectively "zoom out," which opens our minds to alternative perspectives about challenging circumstances, delinking us from the debilitating emotional baggage that often comes with the "I" and its feeling of being bound by said circumstances.[13] Kross even tells a story about how calling himself by name provided the distance he needed to pull himself out of a debilitating anxiety episode that was triggered by a threat he received on account of his research.

Perhaps the most interesting feature of Kross's story is how the curiosity to pursue his groundbreaking research was inspired in the first place. Once he snapped out of his spiral and began to reflect on the psychological utility of talking to himself in the third person—by name—Kross mentions being reminded of one of the first instances where he witnessed someone utilizing this technique publicly:

> The threatening letter arrived in the spring of 2011, but the first case that caught my attention was actually a recollection I had of the basketball superstar LeBron James from the summer of 2010. As a lifelong Knicks fan, I had been holding out the naïve hope that he would come to New York to redeem my floundering team. Instead, he appeared on ESPN to announce that he was leaving the Cleveland Cavaliers, the hometown team that had nurtured his career from its inception, to play for the Miami Heat—a high-stakes and, by his own admission, difficult decision. "One thing I didn't want to do was make an emotional decision," LeBron explained to the ESPN commentator Michael Wilbon. A split second later, right after he articulated his goal to avoid making an emotional decision, he switched from talking about himself in the first person to talking about himself using his own name: "And I wanted to do what was best for LeBron James and what LeBron James is going to do to make him happy."[14]

It is hard to hear Kross account for the brilliance of James's deployment of a persona and not also be reminded of the regularity with which Black athletes have been chided for referring to themselves in the third person. Muhammed Ali, Shaquille O'Neal, and plenty other Black athletes have been criticized for employing this self-distancing technique, despite the subtle power and regularity of its use that Kross has demonstrated across people of all races. Deion Sanders too has been the recipient of accusations of "arrogance" due to the ways he deploys "Prime" strategically in relation to what he knows to be a culture that is biased against Black men. There is a deeper logic to such double standards, however, which becomes clear when "culture" is critically analyzed.

(White) culture and the pull of respectability

White is a color too, and whiteness a culture. This seemingly obvious point can be easy to forget given how prevalent "person" or "people *of color*" is in the United States. To consider someone a person "of color" has become one of the most common ways to categorize people based on cultural identity. It is a well-intentioned shift away from historical forms such as "colored," or "negro," popularized because its political correctness is more palatable to a society desperately trying to be post-racial. Such categorizations are misleading, however, because they assume white is not also a color. By functionally othering everyone who is not white, this linguistic play reinforces whiteness as the invisible norm around which everyone else is measured and made sense of. This is why it is so much easier to single out "Black" culture in this country, which usually comes with pathologizing connotations because of its comparison to the myth of what it means to be "white." Even the idea of a "white" culture may sound strange because of the extent to which it has been rendered synonymously with "society" at large. But what is society other than a multilayered conglomerate of cultures that compete under a banner that reads "American," which is really just a name meant to denote a national identity designed around the dominance of whiteness. Furthermore, what is a *culture*?

Culture here is defined as an *ongoing production born from the ritualized interplay of "policy" and performance*, which materializes (within) a field of shared meaning and material consequences. Culture is the pretend play of adults with power. It emerges in real time from ritualized enactments that are politically productive. While performance has been treated, "policy" here refers to the written and unwritten "rules" that determine what is and is not appropriate—or what will or will not be tolerated—as part of a given culture. Etymologically, "policy" shares the same root with *police* and refers to the variety of ways we police our own and each other's behavior in service to the culture being iterated. Conceptually, it refers to the full range of policing that happens within a culture, from suggestive looks that say "we don't do that here" to formal written policies that find expression in bylaws. Every culture polices the performances of its participants *in order to* direct their energies, because it is the performance of culture over and over again that makes it real.

The political dynamics of culture are always at work, insidiously iterated in loops that naturalize the feel we get for cultures simply by playing along with them. That *feeling* is not consistent for everyone, though. To the degree that a culture has been created around particular embodiments, those people will feel the most support while operating in it. The culture works in tandem with them because it presumes their priority. Protecting and propelling their embodiment is what forms the basis of the written (and unwritten) policies that direct the traffic of everyone's performance. It is their value systems that undergird the policies in the first place. But the *crux* of a culture is found in its imagination, which is like the mental (play) space from which the value systems that underwrite policies emerge. What one imagines about the world they are creating shapes the world that comes to be, particularly when the power dynamic works in their favor. The strength of a culture is found in its seemingly automatic function, and the invisibility that comes from it. Cultures operate on us and in us relationally in ways that reflect the neurophysiology of muscle memory. Culture is the muscle memory of collectives, developed and held together in much the same way that our bodies develop in relation to whatever we are downloading and doing in a loop.

It is important to note that creating cultures is a feature of *Homo sapiens'* existence that aids in survival. It is one of the ways we structure our movements so that we do not have to overexert the executive functioning needed to solve novel problems. To analyze cultures, however, is to deconstruct them. It is to peek behind the curtain of a production, seeking to understand how everything from imagination to the structures of society emerge from and contribute to the rationalities by which people relate. To analyze "white" culture, then, is to reflect the degree to which race factors into its interworking, creating a status quo around supremacist sensibilities in relation to Blackness. It is to acknowledge the extent to which white people—namely white men—enjoy the politically induced freedom to explore and express the full range of who they are (becoming) with impunity. Said differently, white culture is a play space for white people in that it grants them the privilege *to play* out their selves unencumbered.

The psychospiritual consequences of white (male) culture

Cultures are iterated based on the embodiments around which they are naturalized. This is why the image of the white man in control lives rent-free in American consciousness.[15] It has been woven into our minds as the quintessential reference point for *Homo sapiens'* existence, the zero point around which everyone else is measured. As a result, performing deference to that image is a default mode that all can identify with, because it is an image that has been iterated over time with such importance that even Jesus became a white man. And while many have worked to detract the default dominance associated with that image—and pictures of Jesus too—it still thickens the air we *all* breathe. Because its supposed supremacy reeks of racism's absurdity. And yet, its presence remains pungent. Yes, there are still plenty of people who are *actively* working to protect the supremacy of that image, because of the privileges that come with it. Their antics help us see its absurdity all the more clearly. But the comedy of it all is not enough to stave off the cultural consequences, especially for Black men, who have an intimately precarious relationship with white masculinity.

The image of the white man in control is part and parcel of the "politicized sense of history and memory" that Emilie Townes talks about in her description of the *fantastic hegemonic imagination*.[16] She demonstrates how worldviews are spun from "whirlwinds" of mythic images about Black women, which are used to shape the public's consciousness as a primary feature of the cultural production of evil. By redirecting attention to *imagination* as a site where racial evil is produced, Townes highlights the way racial stereotypes function as "cultural codes" that are structured into the pretend play that produces social realities in ways that land as normal. And she is explicit that the fantastic hegemonic imagination lives in "all of us," regardless of one's race, gender, sexuality, class, or age. While Townes's immediate goal is to deconstruct the mythic images that are used to marginalize Black women, her insight shines a light on all sides of this discussion. On one side is "beast," the insidious myth that lives behind the muscle memory of associating criminality with Black masculinity. On the hegemonic side of her analysis lives the image of the white man in control. For Townes, the power of such images *lies*—in both senses of the word—in their ability to (re)engineer everyone's imagination, which informs the ways people move in relation to each other, productively. She writes:

> We often operate out of structurally determined limits that do, at points, offer some creativity and autonomy—but these are controlled and managed by hegemonic forces. Selected individuals may prosper in conditions of domination, so would selected groups. However, this is a limited prosperity that never threatens the framework and structure of society. It only creates an austere marginal space that can lull many of us into a false but oh-so-deadly consciousness that contours our imagination.[17]

From a theoretical perspective, Townes is highlighting the way *Homo sapiens*' movement in the world is governed by structures of thought and practice that functionally restrict people based on the meaning associated with their embodiments. And she is clear that the privileged and oppressed alike are the governors, policing themselves and each other based on the presumed truths of the fantastic hegemonic imagination. The subtext of Townes's point, however, is that American society is still framed in such a way where Black achievement is actualized as an allowance. The fact that Black people are often made to feel that their achievements rely on opportunities *given* by white people—usually men—points to the prescriptive (pre)dominance of white power structures. And to the degree that this *does* capture how life plays out politically, it continually renders the dominance of white culture "real." Put differently, Townes indirectly articulates the ways white culture has been curated around the image of the white man in control, and how this presents "structurally determined limits" that Black people have to navigate.

It is often the case that Black men must move with a posture of humility in relation to white masculinity if they hope to have a spot on the roster. And this is the case across virtually every cultural domain. White men often hold the keys to the kinds of success Black men dream of. In a hopeful sense, the collaborative undertone to this idea *should* be seen as a mere fact of relational existence, assuming relational connectedness to be a starting point, and a space for regular check-ins, rather than an accusation of "socialist" propaganda. Because contrary to the cultural narratives of neoliberalism, there is no such thing as a "self-made man." Every person emerges from a community that, at different points throughout their life, has held and helped them. But in a real sense, it seems to always be white men with power that Black men must navigate in order to imagine and pursue flourishing. White men are often the gatekeepers in a sociopolitical reality constructed around their image. This creates a relational dynamic where Black men are coerced to perform their own subservience as a means of survival, or to pursue success. It is a subtle power play that targets the psychospiritual health of Black men on multiple levels.

On one level, white culture imposes an ever-present threat of violence against Black men based on the criminalizing assumptions that make "beast" land legible to society. This reveals an indirect dimension to the terroristic function of crucifixion—or lynching, whether by bullets or strangulation. It issues a warning that reads: "You might not be the one of the cross, but you damn sure look like him. So, you better act right." And white bodies are aware of this subtext too. Even if unconsciously, they perform insinuations of power that are backed by a structural reality tucked in the waistband, just in case. The normalcy of this relational dynamic is the reason Amy Cooper knew she could brandish her whiteness as a weapon in Central Park. Such cultural performances keep the question of "survival" lingering in the minds of

Black men, compelling them to carry themselves with a certain level of caution no matter how successful they become.[18] On another level, however, white culture coerces Black men to police themselves in service to the "success" they seek. By nature of the political hold white men still have on economic life in the United States, Black men are often positioned to need what they have, in a sense. This contributes to the relational dynamic where Black men are pressured to acquiesce to the written and unwritten policies of professional spaces, even when such policies require them to check their cultural identities at the door, thus foreclosing Black men's ability to live into the fullness of their being in ways that Greg Ellison highlights in his analysis of being *cut dead*.

Ellison captures in this concept the subtle, yet blatant psychological suffering Black men endure as a result of the "fragmenting portrayals"[19] that find expression in myriad media. Television depictions, statistical data, sociological practices, and the like create a cultural feedback loop where Black men must choose between countering the narratives that are told about them or playing along with them in a long game of survival and security. Perhaps the most "dignified" option would be to ignore the dynamics altogether, to the degree that this is even possible based on the reception of one's particular presentation. Regardless, Ellison exposes the absurdity of expecting Black men to resist psychospiritual violence without the resources that such narratives are designed to prevent them from developing in the first place. It is like cutting off someone's access to breath and then wondering why they can't breathe. For Ellison, stereotypes that create misrecognition have the effect of eroding Black men's ability to sustain themselves in relation to four fundamental needs that are foundational to the psychospiritual well-being of *all Homo sapiens*: (1) belonging, which allows persons to develop within a relatively stable community where affiliation and intimacy provide the psychological supports needed to stave off mental and physical illnesses that extend from being ostracized; (2) self-esteem, which is connected to belonging and references the ways not being acknowledged in one's fullness creates self-doubt and inner turmoil that cannot be course corrected without a community of reliable others due to isolation;

(3) control, or the belief that one has the capacity to change their circumstances, which empowers them to develop inner the resources to do so; and (4) meaningful existence, or the fact that having something to live for is foundational to psycho-emotional flourishing.[20]

More could be said about the psychosocial links between racism and fundamental needs, but their connection to white culture is most pressing at this point. It is well known that Black men are threatened by racial politics, targeted in ways that criminalize them and lead to various forms of containment, or death. This is a feature of white culture and the ways it polices Black men based on tropes like "beast." An element of white culture that is often missed, however, is the subtle psycho-emotional harm that comes from requiring someone to commodify themselves based on the awareness of not being welcome. Being forced to fit oneself into a culture that simultaneously exploits one's embodied intellectual energy while requiring them to bracket core aspects of their being has deleterious effects on the psycho-emotional and spiritual lives of Black men. It is like asking Black men to cut themselves dead as a prerequisite for pursing professional stability. This engenders scenarios where just enough felt success cloaks the internal harm being done, but only to a point, and only for so long. Eventually, the practice of cutting oneself (off) to fit cultural logics erodes even one's expectation of fullness, which in turn forecloses one's ability to develop more fully.

Code switching and the pull of respectability

White culture creates a pull for Black men to be respectable. If criminalization or containment are not viable options, then targeting the psychospiritual health of Black men by coercing them to commodify themselves is the best way forward. Hence, *respectability* becomes a game Black men must play to protect themselves and their pursuits of success. The *politics of respectability* is a concept that was coined by Black feminist writer Evelyn Brooks Higginbotham to capture Black women's early responses to what Black feminist writer Patricia Hill Collins calls the "controlling images"[21] that were meant to justify their mistreatment prior to and throughout integration. Respectability, according to Higginbotham, was a strategy whereby Black women would prove their inherent worth by disproving the assumptions embedded in the racist images that were inscribed onto them. Thus, Black women *performed* the "manners and morals" of hegemonic society even while they maintained a critical posture of protest toward it.[22] In this sense, respectability could be seen as a strategy to outwit a racist society by demonstrating Black people's capacity to embody the very traits that racial stereotypes assumed they *could not* possess. However, this performative strategy also includes a deferral to, and adoption of, those hegemonic values—even if for sport—in ways that support the maintenance of racist myths in the first place. Hence, playing (to) the politics of respectability has the effect of reinforcing many of the problematic assumptions of white culture, even while it allows Black people to successfully navigate it.

Code switching could be seen as a contemporary iteration of playing respectability politics. It is a performative strategy that Black people have often used to navigate the racial politics of contemporary life. Pastoral theologian Cedric Johnson suggests that Black people are in a "dialogical dance" with the market-driven forces of white supremacy. He argues that, in a neoliberal age, Black identities are born from a "transaction" between "black subjects shaped by the human psyche, mediating spaces, and market-driven structures and discourses," even as "these structures and discourses are transformed by struggling and resisting black subjects."[23] Johnson's critical engagement with the relational dimensions of racial politics discloses the extent to which white culture bears on the relational milieu out of which Black identities are formed. While Johnson does acknowledge that these forces do not overdetermine, he is also clear that racial politics *do* create a *unique* material struggle with which every Black American must contend. Hence, code switching foregrounds the *intentionality* with which Black people present themselves strategically for survival. He writes:

> The ability of African Americans to navigate multiple identity commitments in a matrix of market-driven systems in

> the neoliberal age is often referred to as *code switching*. Here, various identifications can emerge—various configurations of black subjectivity, various degrees of self-consciousness in relationship to political, economic, cultural, and social behaviors, and practices. Code switching signifies that in the neoliberal age, black subjects are composed of multiple "selves" positioned in relation to the different "worlds" they encounter.[24]

Highlighting Johnson's idea of code switching is important for two reasons. First, it underscores the agential aspect of relational human existence. This point may seem obvious, but claiming that *Homo sapiens* exist in mutually formative ways *with* their world can begin to sound like persons are caught in loops that are beyond their control—that the trajectory of who they can become, in a sense, is determined by circumstance. This would especially be the case when considering the politicized existence of Black women living under multiple forms of oppression. Code switching, however, highlights the creativity that spins from the *crux* of one's being. It reveals a performative brilliance that is occasioned by the problematic position of being routinely disempowered. To intentionally deploy aspects of oneself in strategic ways toward particular ends means one is always—to some degree—agential, and creative. It means the *crux* of their being has not crumbled in, and that the performative resources they draw from should be appreciated for their applicability to everyone. Second, code switching underscores the idea that *selves* are constantly being articulated in relation to the politics of everyday life. There is no fixed self, per se. Rather, *Homo sapiens* are multilayered, with identities that can be accentuated differently according to what a situation calls for. In other words, people are adept at performing their *selves* based on relational and political norms. As has been mentioned previously, but cannot be stressed enough, it is a common practice to essentially *put on* different aspects of oneself pragmatically, at times even without conscious awareness of doing so. This comes from the *feel* we get for the relational dynamics of culture.

To some, this idea of *putting on* different selves across situations may seem disingenuous, inauthentic even. But as E. Patrick Johnson notes in *Appropriating Blackness*, there is no such thing as authenticity in the context of identity.[25] That "authenticity" can only be considered as such based on an external authenticator—or authentication system—exposes the political play of the notion itself. In this sense, "authenticity" should be distinguished from *integrity*, which I would argue references the deeper sensibility at stake when someone appeals to "authenticity" as a signal that they are living according to their truth, outside the pressures of the political world, and in line with their deepest convictions as to who they are in any given moment in time. This would suggest that even the expectation that one should perform an "authentic" self extends from a privileged position in relation to culture, not its margins. Trying to fit in while also being marginalized means one must present oneself in a way that plays well within the dominant culture, which technically could be seen as "inauthentic" if the self they present does not reflect the person they feel themselves to be. This also means people who are a part of the dominant culture can merely play "themselves" in the production. Such selves are no less performative, though, and are just as productive—if not more, given the political privilege they enjoy. But the privilege of performing oneself uncritically makes the claim on "authenticity" easy because the culture itself authenticates it, reinforcing the meaning that comes with the ritualized practice of being catered to. This is not the case for persons who are denigrated by white culture— which is to say, Black people must play by different rules, strategically. Hence, code switching, and the absurdities of race it reveals, challenges even the idea of an "authentic" self. Rather it moves with an analysis that takes the power dynamics of culture seriously, with a focus on the performance of *all* selves that constitute it.

The fragmenting effects of having to code switch are further frustrated by a realization that the "self" was never meant to be singular, even while we exist with the capacity to synchronize multiple selves strategically. Outside the (subtle) psychosocial trauma one may experience from subscribing to culturally imposed norms related to a singular self—especially when that self is marginalized—the politics of race have also created a playground whereby persons who have to code switch develop (dimensions of) selves that can be deployed on a whim—embodied intelligences that are tested and translatable. In other words, what was meant to marginalize Black people actually made them more well-rounded in terms of sociopolitical performances that sustain. This puts a different spin on W. E. B. DuBois's understanding of "double consciousness," in the sense that such multiplicity helps one develop the kind of "second sight" that allows them to see deeper dimensions of life that are lost on someone who never has to reengineer themselves (in real time)—dimensions they are simply not trained to notice. Furthermore, theories of performance push us further by acknowledging "double consciousness" as evidence of *actual selves* that do not need to feel fragmented behind the false narratives of a society that says the self cannot be multiple.[26] This too is a remnant of Western colonial ways of thinking that exist in service to *capitalizing* at all costs.

The healing possibilities of countermemory

Prime is how Deion Sanders switches code, but spun (up) in the opposite direction. Rather than fit himself into the marginal spaces of a racist social order—thereby reproducing its rule(s)—Sanders's intentional deployment of self makes supremacist structures adjust to his tune. It is like when Neo flexed, and the hallway moved around him in the *Matrix*. After resurrecting himself from the dead, and subsequently realizing he was the One, Neo destroyed his formidable opponent—Agent Smith—by transcending the rules of the game they were playing. He infused his energy into Smith's digitized body and burst it at the seams. Emerging victoriously, Neo flexed, bending space and time, and proving to moviegoers that Morpheus's messianic hopes had finally come to fruition. In this sense, Prime's flexing should be read in the neurophysiological light of ***myokinesis***, which is the process by which exercise heals and transforms the body. This concept references the cognitive and physiological benefits of focused physical activity, and even more specifically, muscle contractions. Myokines represent the molecular wisdom that is developed and held in muscle tissue. They are molecules that help to regulate brain functions, including mood, learning, and locomotor activity. They also regulate glucose and metabolism, enhance insulin activity, and induce white adipose tissue (for storing energy). Myokines have also been shown to both repair brain injury and work as a protectant against neurodegenerative disease. Myokinesis—what happens when we contract developed muscle—is the process that releases myokines into the blood stream so they can work their magic.[27]

It is important to note that trauma is not held in muscle tissue. Suggesting that trauma lives in the body is helpful, but only tells part of the story. Trauma is downloaded and stored in the emotional memory centers of the brain, not in the materiality of the body, per se. However, muscle tissues do possess many (if not all) of the cytokines and peptides necessary to produce the plasticity and pharmacological cocktails needed to heal trauma, in addition to serving other reparative and preventative neurophysiological functions. There are many things that happen to *Homo sapiens* that threaten the body's health by assaulting key regions of the brain. In short, myokinesis is the process by which the body *talks back* to the brain, reminding it of its resilience and flooding it with the reparations it needs to maximize its capacity. So long as one keeps moving. Politically, myokinesis reflects Townes's concept of countermemory in that it *talks back to* the "politicized sense of history and memory" that is central to both the creation and maintenance of the fantastic hegemonic imagination.[28] She notes how narrow histories are told politically in support of the status quo, which occludes the *actual* histories and embodiments they purport to represent. Countermemories, then, are the reclamations that tell parts of the story that have always been present but not often narrated, because they tend to be subversive. What is particularly interesting about Townes's notion of countermemory is that she locates it *within* the status quo. She writes:

> The fantastic can also open up subversive spaces within the status quo rather than ghettoizing fantasy by encasing it within currish linear or deterministic thought or strategies.

The fantastic can retain its subversive qualities without capitulating to narrow categorization or classification designed to tame or make the fantastic sensible. One such subversive place/space is countermemory.[29]

Townes is arguing that, by nature of the systems—or cultures—that comprise the status quo being constructed based on fantasy, one should not assume they are fixed or inevitable. Rather, because it is all made up, there exists a perpetual readiness to recognize alternative stories around which new realities can be created, even against a default unwillingness. And if not a readiness, there is at least a possibility that remains open so long as realities are rooted in fantasy. To open up such spaces—and make legible their myokinetic possibilities—Townes suggests that countermemory "begins with the particular to move into the universal and it looks to the past for microhistories to force a reconsideration of flawed (incomplete or vastly circumscribed) histories."[30] In other words, countermemory calls upon embodiments to the contrary, those skeletal muscular holdouts that have ancient wisdom but have not had the space to exercise themselves, or have not been heard when they have.

In a deeper way, code switching functions to protect white comfort. It forecloses Black explorations of self and complicates social advancement. Code switching is a performance that functionally succumbs to the status quo as a means of survival. And to the degree that everyone switches code at times, this reflects the normalcy of deferring to the status quo. The difference is that the status quo across the majority of cultural spaces in the United States has been constructed around white comfort, which is a privilege with political consequences. This creates a scenario where Black people most often end up *downplaying* their range just to maintain the positions they have often worked twice as hard to get. In other words, white culture precludes Black people from embodying their fullness because it would cause white culture to heal, which would compel it to embrace the discomfort of necessary adjustment.

This is precisely why "Prime Time" is so important. He is not the respectable negro Black men are expected to be. By refusing to downplay himself, or his selves, Prime disrupts the supremacist logic by which Black men are coerced into performing their own subservience to white masculinity, and white culture—how, at the end of the day, bending a knee is the safest way to ensure survival. And even when one decides to stand in the face of it—which Black men always have—they do so with the awareness that they are venturing out, in a sense, "risking it all," as it were. They know they are performing against *policy*, so it is a fully embodied, conscious effort to disrupt. Such acts should be re-membered as examples of embodied brilliance that infuse the whole body with reparative wisdom that can heal and transform.

Prime *is* countermemory in that he opens new neural pathways into the far reaches of a racist society. Deion Sanders's *presence* demonstrates the healing and transformative potential that comes from exercising oneself against the hardwiring of culture, promoting its plasticity toward the possibility of change. Prime puts pressure on the muscle memory of the American mind. He disrupts the fantastic hegemonic imagination, especially as it relates to Black men. His refusal to play respectability politics makes legible a Black masculinity that redeems its own range through free expression. Hence, he widens the subversive spaces Townes speaks of, awakening the audacity Black men need in order to disrupt social conventions that are rooted in racist assumptions. In this sense, Deion Sanders lives in the history of Black men who have refused to perform the racial subtext of *staying in one's place*. He is cut from the same cloth as Cassius Clay, after the name change. If Steph Curry exemplifies agility, Prime typifies sprinting. He embodies the synchronization of self that one needs to propel oneself forward with a kind of reckless abandon that could only extend from a tight focus. And while such legendary performances can make one seem larger than life, the effervescence of their presence is grounded by breath and belief.

I breathe, therefore I am

Breath sustains all embodied performance. Whether one is sprinting or meditating, breath is both a prerequisite and the final exam. Breathing is how Denzel Washington is able to remain calm enough to remember his lines as he synchronizes himself into Academy Award–winning performances. It is how Steph Curry remains poised enough under pressure to sink that buzzer-beating shot when the game is on the line. Breathing is the only way marathoners are able to keep running for so long. If, at any point, they were to hold their breath, even for just a few seconds, their bodies would shut down pretty immediately—many of their bodies collapse from exhaustion even when they are breathing, regardless of what their V02 max might be.[31] And if Amy Cooper would have had the developed wherewithal to stop and breathe in that triggering moment, that interaction could have gone very differently. This is because breath sustains physiological function across the spectrum of embodied activity, in all directions.

Breath is life. It is both the baseline and bass line of embodied existence. It marks one's safe arrival into this world and at the same time carries the tune of a heartbeat that circulates the symphony of synchronicities that allow one to keep living, to keep oxygenating oneself. Every breath we take enchants our entire being. The ritualized practice energizes us at atomic levels in ways that are more vital than even water, whose elemental structure relies on oxygen for its existence too. All living things find life through breath. Fish find it using gills. Earthworms inhale through their skin. Even plants breathe through stomata, mouths that are hard to hear because they are not as loud as the ones *Homo sapiens* have. Respiration is a ubiquitous reality for all living beings. It is the mark of being, even prior to one's ability to think. Because breath, like all iterations of life, is sacred.

Sadly, the sacrality of breath has too often been taken for granted. As we tend to do with many other life forms, *Homo sapiens* are conditioned to look past breath because of the ease with which we can control it. We have secularized our own capacity to breathe because it is so easy to access. Perhaps this is because oxygen exists in such abundance, and so learning to appreciate it does not feel necessary because it has not been commoditized, yet. However, a closer look—if not a longer wait—reveals just how *in demand* the ability to breathe (easier) already is for far too many based on manufactured moralities. It is not enough to rest in easy explanations shrouded in moral sensibilities that can be relativized, if not trivialized to no end. Muscle memory reminds us that they are only easy because we are accustomed to them. And sometimes we are caught by them. New theological questions get raised when we learn to pay closer attention to the sacrality of breath—to our embodied interaction with life itself, regardless of race or religion. "What will we do with the life we have been given?" is one such question that is insinuated in the attention Philip Butler pays to the technology of Black bodies. His imagined inquiry is preceded, however, by two requisite questions he asks explicitly, both of which address the connection between the materiality and mystery of presence. He asks, "If the body is technology and there is no dualistic premise undermining the connection between body and mind, then what does the Black body carry? What is given access to the material world through the Black body? The short answer is vitality."[32]

Vitality is the last straw in Butler's theological leveling. It is that force (and source) of life that few acknowledge but all participate in, and have equal access to—the only (im)material evidence that there is a source of life beyond ourselves. Born from a conversation between African spiritualities and Eboni Marshall Turman's womanist ethic of incarnation—but grounded in the complex interworking of the (Black) body—Butler articulates a spirituality that conjoins the mysterious "insness of life" with the deepest materiality of embodiment. It is an embodied spirituality *because* it emanates from the life-giving interaction we have with vitality, actualized by the interworking that sustains embodied life. Stated plainly, Butler imagines a ***neurospirituality***[33] that emanates *from* the body. Distinguishing his view of vitality from ancient perspectives that, in their own way, are compartmentalized, he writes:

> The vitalism of Black transhuman liberation theology is not the vitalism of old. It calls for a radical extension of what can qualify as life force through an incorporation of mechanistic processes that were once denounced. It is a both and. It

is mystical in the sense that it refers to the immaterial phenomena not readily accessible. It functions as the thread of existence (ntu) which gives power to be (áse). But it is also mechanistic in that it relies on the materiality of the body; be it a person, animal, plant, or inanimate object to experience and possess the life force manifest within all existence. So, within Black transhuman liberation theology vitality is defined as the underlying force that enlivens and permeates all existence. More specifically, in *humans* it can be imagined as the electric current that powers the involuntary dialogue between sodium and potassium which sparks the human biological system, energizes it, and allows it to persist.[34]

Butler describes vitality as a life force that animates all existence. It is a force that cannot be contained even while it is always interacted with, consciously and unconsciously. His view not only posits the "human" body as "the conduit" for "God, or that which is beyond the perceptible self,"[35] he says, but it effectively disperses divinity across the ecological life of the universe. And while Butler does not use the language of "divine," it is apt in that it captures the overlooked power of something as subtle yet sustaining as breath. The vague profundity of his view of vitality can be seen in the way he locates divinity in the material depths of embodied existence, as connected to nature. In this sense, Butler's view is similar to panentheistic perspectives—such as process theology—that imagine the Divine to be imbued throughout the universe, even if also beyond it in some mysterious way. These views seek to capture more fully the collaborative, and tragic, nature of existence based largely on a critique of images of an omnipotent God that can, at any time, reach *into* time and space to intervene according to "His" moral agenda.

Bound to the process of breath(ing)

There are several problems that arise when God is viewed as simultaneously omnipotent, omniscient, and omnibenevolent, namely theodicy questions that seek to address the problem of suffering. If God is all-powerful, all-knowing, and always good, then God must—in some way—be responsible for all that happens in the world. This quandary has plagued Black faith communities for centuries and has been a sticking point for Black Christian thinkers of theodicy since (at least) the liberation theology of James Cone.[36] Process theology, such as in Monica Coleman's *Making a Way out of No Way*, removes omnipotence from the Divine based on a more functional understanding of how consequential *Homo sapiens'* behavior really is. That what we do in the world matters more than doctrines of destiny allow us to understand. Not only does Coleman's view better respond to the tragedy of suffering wrought by racism—centering *Homo sapiens'* history and activity as the culprit—but she also foregrounds the creative agency of Black people to perform their own salvation in collaboration *with* the Divine.[37] To challenge the interventionist assumptions of omnipotence, Coleman presents God as one who perpetually *lures* us toward better possibilities. "In every moment," she writes, "God is calling us," and she makes it clear that "we always have to choose."[38] What is particularly intriguing about Coleman's relational view of divinity is the way it imagines our participation with God as a constant creative exchange from which reality is produced into an open-ended field of possibilities. She effectively repositions God's benevolent omniscience as being the result of an intimate relationship, and incorporation of life, rather than foreknowledge of an end that is already written regardless of what we do.

The image of a God who breathes *with us* is not pronounced in Coleman's work, but it is palpable. Coleman variously describes God as "taking in," "feeling," or that God "gathers into God's self" the events of the world, which live on in God and change God's nature. This in turn influences the possibilities that God provides back into the world in real time, which we alone are responsible for bringing to fruition. Said differently, Coleman imagines a relational exchange wherein God *inhales* everything that happens in the world—the joys and the sufferings—metabolizes it, then breathes new possibilities back into the intimate connections we have with divinity. In this view, God is not all-powerful but rather relies on the participation of embodied beings for the performance of salvation *in* the world, not to mention of it. In this sense, Coleman and Butler articulate theological visions that root God in the relational intimacy of embodied existence, played out in the connections we have with each other and the cosmos. It is a view of God from the ground up, where any sense of being *beyond* is better understood to be "in here" rather than "out there" somewhere.

God *is* the abundance of life that imbues the soil from which plants grow, and breathe. God is found in the cosmic synchronicity of sun, soil, and skin, illustrated by the energizing effects of their interaction on and in our bodies. God is in the digestive details that allow us to extract energy from even the worst processed foods. God is energy, and Energy is divine. God is (in) the very air that we breathe. This is why the murder of George Floyd was particularly blasphemous. Breath is the most intimate way in which *Homo sapiens* participate in divinity. It is how we metabolize and are mobilized by God. Breath gives us Energy. To cut off another being's ability to breathe is to *directly* sever the mysterious but measurable tie they have with the Divine. Certainly, murder of all kinds is an abomination. Consciously actualizing one's ability to intentionally take life once incarnated is evil. But the fact of having such an ability should make us question our nature more deeply, especially considering the extent to which this capacity we wield can be linked to wisdom traditions (read: moral rationalities) that represent white supremacist ways of being in relation to the world, and each other. Taking seriously this participatory responsibility we have to breath raises related questions about belief.

To be "Him" and "human"

A tension arises when considering the regulatory function of belief in Black athleticism. It is a tension that Black athletes live with and illustrate publicly all the time. At the same time that Steph Curry bookends his acceptance speeches by "giving glory to God," the magic that wins awards is a result of *his* muscle memory. Marshawn Lynch too—on the rare occasions when the media has caught him talking in public—regularly cites God for his success even while *his* work ethic is largely the reason. And all throughout his career, across multiple sports, Deion Sanders is as forthright about his faith as he is *his* ability to flex. Each of these men exemplify a theological tension that lives at the intersection of their reliance on a force beyond themselves and the fact of embodied practices that actualize that force's *presence* in their lives, all bound together by the millions of breaths they have intentionally taken in service to their particular missions.

I'm really Him . . .

This tension is illustrated by a linguistic trend that is emerging from the cultural vernacular of Black athletes in the context of sport. "I'm Him" is a phrase that is gaining traction and signaling a reclamation of belief that "beast" is not designed to allow. Like "beast," it is also a mantra, but moves to a beat that gives off a different frequency. To be "Him" expresses the realization of feeling chosen. It is a way to stake one's claim as the One within the confines of a particular sport or social space. It is similar to "I'm a beast" in that it signals dominance, but it is shot through with the assurance of being more divine than animal. Usually exclaimed after making a big play, "I'm Him" is a proclamation of greatness grounded in the belief that one can also handle the responsibility that comes with it. It is like when Jesus responded "I am He" to the band of soldiers that approached his people after he was betrayed by Judas. There were two levels to this interaction worth noting, both of which relate to this tension as Black athletes embody it. On one level, Jesus was standing up for his people, his team. Wanting to protect them from any potential harm, he proclaimed "I'm Him" because he was ready to bear whatever brunt the soldiers were bringing. On another level, his proclamation was eerily, and strategically, similar to the Divine statement of identity found in Exodus 3 when Moses stood at the burning bush and wanted to know who he should tell the Israelites were coming to redeem them, to which God retorted "I am."[39]

Prime epitomizes both uses. On one hand, he is a fierce defender of the players he coaches, and of young Black men in general. Before moving to the ranks of college football, Prime made his coaching debut in youth leagues because he wanted to have a presence and provide structure in the lives of young Black men. In fact, he has dedicated his coaching career to the mission of developing young Black men in the ways he knows other institutions and sport organizations will not. Now, as the head coach for the Colorado Buffaloes, he is standing on the same business of raising young men while protecting them from the variety of assaults that Black male athletes invariably face.[40] He knows the strategies because he has lived it. On the other hand, Prime's belief in himself directly informs his god-like movement in relation to the white male culture of college football. In 2022, while coaching at Jackson State, an HBCU, Coach Prime successfully recruited and signed the #1 nationally ranked player in the country coming out of high school. This was unheard of for HBCUs because of the rationality of recruitment discussed in the previous chapter. PWIs[41] have so heavily (and hegemonically) imposed themselves into the pools of Black athletic talent that HBCUs—the only institutions Black players used to be allowed into—are reticent to even try recruiting the top athletes. They simply do not have the resources to make competitive offers to young athletes who are themselves trying to "make it."

The audacity of Deion Sanders to not only attempt, but to land Travis Hunter—when coaches like Nick Saban wanted him[42]—reflects the deep belief he has in himself and his mission. His confidence flies in the face of the "structurally determined limits" Emilie Townes speaks of in that he disrupts the cultural presumption that Coach Prime would *stay in his place*. The flashiness of his persona might still have been a bit surprising when he was player—because we are not used to seeing Black men boast in public—but it was not as problematic because he flourished *within* a space set aside and structured for Black men. But Black coaches at HBCUs are not supposed to move with this kind of self-assurance, or (athletic) ability in relation to the culture of college football. To add insult to injury, Hunter followed Coach Prime to Colorado along with his two sons, Shedeur and Shiloh, which sparked accusations of "nepotism" that Sanders rebuked with rebuttals that reveal the deep confidence he has in his boys as well: "Go watch the film."[43] And the film did not lie; Travis Hunter won the Heisman Trophy and Shedeur was named college football's best quarterback after a 2024 season in which Sanders's Colorado Buffaloes solidified themselves as a college football powerhouse. Coach Prime moves like a god in a collegiate football world where white men are the only ones who are supposed to. Yet, underneath the ways Coach Prime is intentionally—and successfully—*playing* this game, his movements are all grounded in a deeper belief that Prime is really "Him."

The (Black) magic of belief

Beliefs are more than mysterious. They are part and parcel of the embodied magic that is muscle memory. To believe in oneself as Prime does is to recruit one's *entire* being toward whatever outlook on life allows them to accomplish the task at hand. Beliefs function as the internal mechanisms by which *Homo sapiens* focus attention, attuning our minds according to whatever systems of meaning make up one's worldview. They act as psychospiritual filtration systems that shape not only one's experience of life, but also how they embody it. And this works at every level of existence. If one believes oneself to be under attack, their physiological response will testify to it—shortened breath, heightened hormonal vigilance, reptilian reasoning. In the same scenario, however, if one perceives such a threat as a challenge—yet another opportunity to overcome—their embodied response will act in kind. Rather than essentially shut down, studies have shown that persons who possess a "stress-is-enhancing" mindset, rather than one that assumes the nature of stress is debilitating, can functionally *turn on* their embodied systems in the face of various challenges.[44] These findings reflect recent studies that demonstrate the way subjective mindsets can shape objective reality.

To say that beliefs are magic is not an appeal to mystery. There is a materiality to this claim as well. In another study that investigated the neurophysiological power of the placebo effect, it was found that the mere perception of exercise triggered physiological changes that contributed to better health outcomes. Two groups of women working as hotel cleaning staff were compared over four weeks. At the onset of the study, one group was provided information from the CDC as to how much daily exercise was recommended for ideal health outcomes, *and* they were informed that their Energy expenditure during work exceeded those expectations. In other words, they were invited to shift their mindsets about how much daily exercise they were already doing. This information was not provided to the control group in the study. At the end of the study, the informed group showed decreases in weight, systolic and diastolic blood pressure, body fat percentage, waist-to-hip ratio, and BMI.[45] It is noteworthy that there were no changes in either group's activity, whether at work or outside of it. The only difference was the perception of exercise, which resulted in physiological changes to the body. This is not to suggest that beliefs are limitless. There are natural physiological processes that work to sustain life regardless of what one believes. To be sure, genetic reach can only go so far. But as an evolving species that has only just begun to understand the *neurospirituality* of its own circuitry, we do not yet know how far. Hence, such studies do provide a window into the embodied magic of belief, and invite us to consider how deeply we (all) materialize it despite its mysteriousness.

The productivity of belief is not politically neutral, however. Acknowledging that one's neurophysiological stress response is shaped by their mindset regarding the nature of stress implicates the cultures in which belief is formed. In other words, beliefs, like the performances they inspire, are subject to the power dynamics of their cultural surround. Beliefs are conspired (read: co-inspired) in cultures laden with racial politics, grounded by communities that either encourage or undermine them. And the depth of this mutuality can be seen when considering the etymology of "conspire," which literally means "to breathe together."[46] Communities breathe life into belief for better or for worse. This is why Donald Trump's delusions are so dangerous. The unwavering faith of his base bolstered the belief he had in himself, which shaped both his experience and embodiment of political performances that produced a reality in which many people suffered. Yet, any moral dispute one may have does not change the fact or productive function of his beliefs, or any belief for that matter. Delusions are only such when a belief is not shared in community. Kanye West is only considered "crazy" because everyone does not agree that he is a god. But Kanye's belief that he is (a god) certainly works in tandem with his ability to create music that is out of this world.

For Prime to believe himself to be "Him," then, should be understood as a (r)evolutionary feat that cuts across cultural fields designed to foreclose Black men's becoming. It speaks to a faith that simultaneously extends from and expands the beliefs of the community that supports him. His family, his peers, and his players all breathe life into his belief that he is "Him." This undergirds the myokinetic movement he embodies, which widens the space within which his community can also believe in themselves, and their cause. There was immeasurable excitement among HBCU supporters when Sanders *chose*[47] to coach at Jackson State, and even more elation when he recruited and signed the top athlete in the country. Now, all of a sudden, something that seemed impossible has become an option—a new neural pathway in the mind of a Black sports community that has had to forge belief against the currents of white culture. Questions remain as to whether and how those pathways will continue to be nurtured. But one thing that can be concluded with certainty is that if Prime did not believe he was the One (for this particular task), he would have been far less effective in carrying it out, assuming he even tried.

. . . and yet, only "human"

And yet, Deion Sanders knows he is not God. He regularly expresses humility in relation to God and is very open about how committed he is to his religious faith. In fact, he cites his commitment to his own faith as the primary reason for the confidence he has in himself. Sanders talks about how coaching is his calling. He also talks about how he has never been high or drunk alcohol a day in his life, and how he stopped cursing in the 1980s, actions that *for him* are centerpieces to *his* religious commitment. They are the signposts that help him measure how focused (read: synchronized) he is. And just as it might sound like he is boasting perfection, he backends such statements with, "All that stupidity . . . that was all me."[48] In other words, Deion Sanders knows he is only "human." He lives in the tension between created and creator, between personhood and the persona he uses to produce. It is a tension that grounds all *Homo sapiens* existence, and one that athletes have particular insight into by nature of the ways sport requires them to synchronize their selves for the sake of efficiency and productivity.

The implications of belief that live in this tension become especially interesting when considering that many of these athletes are competing against each other, praying to presumably the same God for conflicting results. And though most athletes at the elite level are not praying for results, necessarily, the gratitude they give (God) for winning reveals the hope they had for it the whole time. It is about more than winning, though. In a deeper way, prayers of preparation and thanksgiving are a way to express humility based on the recognition that the abilities athletes exercise and put on display are (genetic) gifts. Every interrelated piece of our being—from the breath of life to the ability to believe in oneself—are embodied capacities that are finite, even while they can be developed. And on any given day—whether at practice or in a game—one's body (or "mind") could fail them. Athletes know this. By nature of their intimate relationship with their bodies, athletes are aware of the finitude that grounds even the most extraordinary feats. And so, they are grateful for the ability to keep pushing themselves, and to keep finding out what they are capable of.

The moral ambiguity of (focused) Energy

This reflects a tacit awareness among athletes that vitality is no respecter of persons, a mindfulness that undergirds even the most confident articulations of religious belief. This also connects with one critical point worth underscoring in Butler's work, which is the nondeterministic nature of vitality. While Coleman's process view casts God as one who opposes all forms of oppression—exhaling alternatives in real time—Butler argues that there is no such direction to divinity. Rather, by nature of vitality's radical immanence in all living beings, God is ever present. "That is it."[49] God is already here, infusing life as it unfolds, and energizing our performances in ways that hold space for whatever we *choose* to do with our Energy. In other words, Butler argues that God does not act or intervene outside of imbuing creation with the life God keeps on giving. In this view, vitality is depicted as a pulsating power that we are intimately connected to, and ultimately responsible for—that life itself experiences an unfolding existence which is subject to the actions—the breathing and believing—of the living beings that embody it.

Stated plainly, God is not guided by a moral agenda that can be measured or manipulated by *Homo sapiens*, even if God does hope for, or *inspire*, better outcomes. Any moral agendas that exist are constructions which are designed and defined by "human" kind, and—by nature of relational existence—live in competition with each other. This tension extends to many of the moral conflicts in the United States but is perhaps best illustrated by the polarization that defines our political system. Politicians on all sides routinely reference "God" to support their respective agendas, and who is to say which side is right? Even the Bible has been subjected to so much proof texting that it is often of little help in moral debates about what is "right" or "wrong." This points again to the moral intractability at the center of our problem with race in the United States.

A vitalistic view might make sense when thinking of embodied spirituality, but politically it begs moral questions like, "Which side is God really on?" Unfortunately, the answers to such questions cannot escape the fundamental flaw of moral rationalities that are designed to function as feedback loops that work at the level of belief, shaping one's interpretation about everything from the nature of God to the meaning of one's own breath. Fortunately, one does not need to agree that vitality is all there is to acknowledge its existence or political productivity. This perspective provides a substrate of embodied spirituality on which articulated religion can still live, but it begs functional attention to be paid to the interactions that frame relational existence. Said differently, it invites us to recognize and take seriously the participatory responsibility we all have to breath, with particular attention to the consequences of our beliefs.

The urgency of this issue can be seen when considering the insurrection of January 6th, especially when taking seriously the consequences of focused Energy within the context of belief. Even more telling, however, was the rally that led up to riots. The very existence of this rally was occasioned by the constant call-and-response of Trump's rhetoric in relation to a community that believed (in) him. The content of his rhetoric functioned as the messages that calibrated the commitments of this group, which focused their Energy and motivated their attendance at this rally. While at the rally—finally in the presence of someone they worshipped—Trump's supporters chanted together, generating more Energy in the name of whatever "truths" they believed themselves to be proclaiming. And he stoked the flames until the communal effects of his delusion became an ecstatic spiritual experience that could be linked to what neuroscientists have begun to refer to as *group flow*.

Group (or "team") flow[50] is a phenomenon whereby groups of people who are collectively focused on the same thing are able to create a cohesiveness that allows them to move in unison toward possibilities that would be impossible individually. While the concept has been studied in relation to Navy Seals, work teams, or other groups trying to accomplish specific tasks in controlled environments, descriptions of the phenomenon suggest an interpretive possibility in environments that are less controlled, and far more political. This is especially the case when considering the findings of more recent studies into group flow, which have discovered that "inter-brain synchrony" occurs concomitantly with the coordination of the interrelated movements (and focus) that kicks groups into a higher-functioning gear that is measurable, and matched, in the circuitry of their brains. In other words, the research reveals the extent to which *Homo sapiens* possess an ability to literally link their minds together in ways that produce an exponential energetic effect, which heightens their ability to carry out the collective task at hand.[51]

There is a cultural familiarity with this phenomenon that Black people of (Christian) faith might recognize, whether in a rereading of the Acts of the Apostles or experiences growing up in the Black Church. Born from the call-and-response of worship, one might remember those moments when the rhythmic movement of energetic bodies that are collectively focused, chanting in unison, all of a sudden ends up *creating* an ecstatic experience of spirituality that can often only be explained by "you had to be there." It seems to be the same phenomenon that Luke, the author of Acts, was trying to capture when describing the ecstasy that the apostolic community experienced when the Holy Spirit "filled the entire house where they were sitting" during Pentecost.[52] After emphasizing that the people were "all together in one place"—which sounds redundant only because of the English language's attempt to capture Luke's emphasis (in Greek) on the embodied focus they exhibited—Luke further mentions that they were "filled with the Holy Spirit," and that the Spirit "gave them ability."[53] What Luke does not mention, but what a theological consideration of neuroscientific discoveries might suggest, is that the movement of this "Spirit" could also be read as a *result* of the rhythm in their gathering.

This reading points back to Jesus's exhortation in Matthew 18, where he reminds the disciples not to cause anyone who believes in him—especially children—to "sin," or stumble (read: be distracted from their belief), which culminates in Jesus offering the oft-quoted, "for where two or three are gathered in my name, I am there among them."[54] And as Western tradition would have it, most of us have assumed this means that the "spirit" of the Lord joins our gatherings from the outside. But this is not what Jesus says, nor does it seem to be what Luke was trying to communicate. Could it be that the performative act of gathering "in Jesus's name" is the conduit that allows his spirit to emerge from within the community? Could it also be that the collective focus around Donald Trump's delusions is also what allows his spirit to continue to animate the embodied performances of people who believe he is their savior? This alternative reading would make sense when considering Jesus was still physically present when he offered this exhortation, prior to any ascension that would become an invitation to read this text through a disembodied spiritual lens. Taking seriously the Energy we embody invites us to recognize that whatever we focus on in community breathes life into political realities that reflect the "names" of the religions we articulate.

Deion Sanders thus reappears as Dwight Hopkins's conjurer because of the way he is able to rouse breath and belief, both within himself and on behalf of a community, based on a calling to cut against the grain of racist cultural wiring. And the communal significance of "Prime Time"—the persona he created to simultaneously protect and propel himself in this mission—can be seen in the ways he both represents and reinvigorates a community of Black belief that also pays homage to a power higher than he, which keeps him humble too. The conjurer, Hopkins argues,

> instructs us to tune into the latent and too-often underutilized resources offered by nature to the human realm. Conjuring intimates that human daily survival is a consequence of the presence of animals, plants, air, water, and the earth. To be human, in the fullest sense imaginable, derives from attending to the gifts of nature or all of creation.[55]

In speaking of the political importance of the conjurer's performance, Hopkins highlights:

> The potency of nature and its esoteric wisdom allow the conjurer to facilitate a balance of ethics and morality among the folk as well as have an impact on the structural powers of domination outside of black culture. Conjuring works on the individual within a racial culture and has the potential to reconfigure the stubborn minds and callous hearts of oppressors.[56]

In other words, for Hopkins, the conjurer is one whose performance promotes the plasticity of society by pushing at its boundaries. And the only technology used is that of the body in its connection with vitality, in community, which points to the ways spirituality—wrought by breath and belief—emanates from embodiment in whatever direction it is focused. This picture of embodied brilliance emerges from the recognition, and warning, that there is a moral ambiguity to sacred Energy that can be pointed in any direction. Prime awakens an audacity that activates our deepest potential to be found in the mundane fac(e)ts of embodied existence, which *induces* an embodied spirituality that is politically productive. And when considering the roles we play as performers of rituals that bring social and political realities to fruition, it brings Butler's insinuated question even closer to home and asks it explicitly: "How will we focus our Energy?"

CHAPTER FIVE

Embodied Brilliance Beyond the Myth

> Free at last, free at last...
> —Dr. Martin Luther King Jr.

THE SUBTLE SHIFT from "beast" to "brilliant" that Raible *could* have made in that moment might seem insignificant until one considers all that can happen in contexts of play. Sport stadiums are regularly filled with fans who show up in their most plastic selves for the purpose of cheering their favorite team on to victory. They come with faces painted, jerseys on, and (good luck) charms of choice in hand, ready to chant incantations that invigorate their team with the Energy they need to win. All throughout the game they participate in rituals specific to the identity of their team, conjuring its spirit in ways that move back and forth between fans in the stands and players on the field. For some this is an explicitly religious experience, while for others it is only tacitly so. But it is spiritual for everyone. Even fans watching from home have their rituals. They gather around television devices in community, ready to imbibe the experience in a dimension once removed, but still "there" *in spirit*—not to mention the spirits that flow through their physical space, loosening them for the sake of the shared experience. Each time a good play happens they clap and scream, emanating positive Energy as reinforcement. When bad plays happen, they groan together, bonding over their discontents, and occasionally curse players for letting them down. Across the spectrum of involvement and investment, people participate in the spiritual experience of sport. They (re)create it as such.

To question what Raible could have done in that moment is to understand the perpetual pregnancy of play (space), particularly as it relates to the energetic intimacy with which we exist. For it is only in a play space that one can galvanize the heightened attention of more than sixty thousand high-energy people focused on the same thing, bathing together in affect, and ready to download new and exciting material. It is even more rare when this dynamic is created among people who represent different cultural identities, political viewpoints, and religions, reasons for which many of them would not otherwise gather, especially with such positivity in mind. But this is what play occasions. Play invites us to temporarily suspend the rules by which we typically relate. It brings the world of fantasy to bear on reality as we know it, meeting imagination with malleability to fund the practice of performing alternative possibilities.

Play spaces are like little sanctuaries we set aside *from* reality—or open in the midst of it—for the purpose of exploring dimensions of life that are typically off limits. This is why play is referred to as *recreation*. It provides the space within which people can *re-create* alternative worlds (of meaning) that allow them the freedom to explore and perform different versions of themselves in spaces unencumbered by political constraint. Consider the play space of a stand-up comedy show. A comedian stands before an audience and tells jokes that functionally expose aspects of the shared reality that they all participate in. The best comedians are able to make people see the absurdities of daily life, exposing rituals of behavior that—when the curtain is pulled, and we are invited to laugh—seem downright silly. In "reality," the content of a comedian's jokes would be the kind of thing that might land someone in a human resources office. Fired. But in contexts of play, such content is welcome and often accounts for the funniest jokes. Because play reminds us that this is all made up anyway.

Play also softens us. It arises from an evolutionary impulse that creates a neurophysiological cocktail designed to make us more flexible (read: plastic) in our embodied state of being. It has been shown that regular visits to such embodied states are essential in the healthy developmental unfolding that is "human" existence.[1] This is why *Homo sapiens* play so frequently. We know intuitively that play helps us stave off the rigor mortis that comes with taking life too seriously, or being sedentary for too long. We have a feel for the flexibility play provides, and it feels good for a reason. The health benefits of play have been the subject of a number of studies that enumerate the immeasurable positive effects of play on the neurophysiology of *Homo sapiens* across the lifespan. Fortunately, for the sake of this project, the reparative effects of sport spectating in particular—as a form of play—*have* been measured, and the research suggests that "beast quake" is better understood as a big bang explosion of positive emotions that loosened the soil of minds rather than merely an earthquake that registered on nearby Richter scales. Three specific findings illustrate just one of the interrelated processes that provide evidence of this effect.

First, it is well documented that sport participation—including spectating—increases levels of ***dopamine*** in the brain. Dopamine is most commonly known as a "feel good" hormone that is induced by, and largely responsible for the feeling of pleasure and the motivation to find more of it. But dopamine also serves a range of other functions, such as supporting short- and long-term memory, motor learning and movement, and the ability to seek reward as a function of survival, to name just a few. As a neurotransmitter that links to all major regions of the brain, dopamine also plays an essential role in promoting neuroplasticity—that intellectual quality that allows *Homo sapiens* to adapt to, learn from, and successfully navigate both familiar and novel, even challenging, circumstances.[2] Greater amounts of dopamine in the brain can be associated with greater mental flexibility and capacity for learning, while dopamine deficiencies are known to produce *stiffness* that manifests in movement disorders like Parkinson's disease.[3]

Second, even for viewers who may find themselves stressed out on account of their team losing—hypothetically lowering dopamine levels—the practice of watching sports has also been shown to induce a range of other mental health benefits. Researchers have variously linked sport spectating with higher self-esteem,[4] lower rates of depression,[5] and greater life expectancy.[6] However, each of these findings have been more deeply linked to the practice of ***social bonding*** that (live) sporting events occasion. In other words, it is the communal experience itself that induces the healing and sustaining effects of playing in community.

Social bonding over sport in particular supports mental well-being in at least two additional ways beyond what has already been named. In one way, the act of collectively cheering for a team provides a sense of identity that is connected to a greater whole. This taps into our fundamental need for belonging, and even more deeply our relational nature, which supports personal flourishing *and* promotes communal accountability. In another way, the social bonds of sport occasion experiences of *collective joy*, which are exponentially greater than the joy one can experience alone. This is because the emotion of joy extends from and is compounded energetically in community to degrees that individuals cannot conjure by themselves.[7]

Lastly, and in ways connected to the first two, the practice of watching and listening to sports commentary has been shown to enhance one's ability for **_language comprehension_**, both specific to sports and in general. It might seem obvious that someone would learn more about a given sport the more they watched and listened to its narration. We know intuitively that we exercise an ability to adapt to the linguistic worlds in which we must survive. Perhaps there is even a working awareness that constantly listening to sports would help a person become more adept at understanding and embodying the movement patterns that are closely associated. While recent research supports both of these conclusions, it also demonstrates how the act of listening to sports *enhances* the neurological structures necessary for language acquisition, even unrelated to sport.[8] This is because the complexity of athletic movements—whether making them or needing to understand them—recruits more regions of the brain that are involved in the interrelated tasks that make up one's ability to "read and react" in a split second the way an athlete would. In effect, sport causes one to pay closer attention to something, from multiple sides, and in ways that are conscious of temporal constraints, all of which creates a more holistic understanding of a thing *and* an enhanced capacity to understand in general.

Stated plainly, "beast quake" would have been the perfect time to link "brilliance" with somebody typically thought of as "beast." Assuming his belief system already registered "brilliance" when thinking of Black athletes, Raible's reversal would have landed on freshly tilled psychological soil, and with it, a greater ability to act on new insights and/or reconstitute previous conclusions. The play space of sport abounds with moments ripe for commentary that could insinuate new scripts into minds made malleable by both the expectation and healing experience of witnessing the embodied brilliance of Black athletes. It is only right that people be given the opportunity to appreciate the depth of what they unknowingly draw from. There could not be a more opportune time to begin this counternarrative than in a context of play. Furthermore, this reveals how a word play in particular can redirect tragic trajectories of thought toward more redeeming, truthful, and measurable conclusions that have consequences for social life. And this does not even account for inspiration.

Inspiration (and energetic intimacy)

It would be hard to overstate the impact that Black athletes have had on children in the United States. The regularity of seeing kids dodging phantom defenders and scoring touchdowns, shooting imaginary buzzer-beating three-pointers, or doing the Griddy[9] at school after a nice play on the playground all testify to the ways Black athletes have inspired youth. In many cases, such inspiration turns into aspiration, creating a "call" within children toward sport participation in youth leagues and, for some, eventual careers as athletes. However, it would be equally difficult to overstate the impact of Black athleticism on adults as well. Beyond the physiological health benefits already named, it is not a stretch to see grown men and women winning the imaginary championship in the kitchen by shooting that slightly damp wad of paper towels into the trash while cleaning up after the party they hosted to watch Steph Curry. Even for those who are better at hiding their inner child, watching sports has a way of motivating children and adults to become more physically active. And this makes sense when considering the health benefits associated with seeing brilliant displays of athleticism, especially in community. The ritual of watching sports shakes us from sedentary lives that sediment neurophysiological function—because movement is life, and athletes motivate us to move.

But to use the language of *inspiration* is to look deeper than mere motivation. Motivation entails providing someone with a motive to do something, which can operate at a mechanistic level regardless of mental or material well-being. One can be motivated to act against their own belief systems—and well-being—such as in code-switching scenarios wherein playing along with a racial game forecloses one's ability to show up fully, even while it might prevent the political consequences of such. One can also be motivated to work a job they hate because of financial circumstances, or stay in a relationship for fear of loneliness. *Homo sapiens* have manufactured all manner of ways to motivate ourselves toward the maintenance of status quos that are comfortable because we are accustomed to them. However, such rituals of playing along are the practices that calcify our creativity. They deaden the **crux** of a person so that their enactments are more akin to automatons than beings who embody divine Energy. Yet, such motivated movements remain politically productive in that they still exercise divine Energy, which extends into realities made or maintained.

Inspiration is different. It energizes the very **crux** of a person, enhancing both the hold and hope they have relative to their movements. Inspiration operates in a spiritual dimension that connects us through our ability to sense one another. In other words, its spirituality is both mysterious and material. We could think of the relationship between inspiration and embodied existence moving in two directions. In one direction, inspiration *enhances* embodied existence, enlivening our performances across the spectrum of activity. This is the kind of inspiration artists and musicians identify with, where an idea happens upon them in a way that could not have been predicted but is certainly appreciated, both for the sake of the art itself and for the ways it energizes the creative process. This is the same kind of inspiration that we all experience in life, where an insight about something hits us seemingly from out of nowhere, infusing whatever we were doing with passion and purpose.

This kind of inspiration functions like spirit possession. To the degree that a person can be taken by an idea, and then feel "called" to apply it practically, one could think of them as possessed, in a sense. Of course, they are still the ones embodying their artistic version of the idea, bringing it to life in ways that are unique to their experience, and their genetic reach. But the idea itself remains the reference point that enlivens their embodied activity. This is also the same inspiration that happens when one witnesses the seemingly extrahuman feats of (Black) athletes who defy the laws of time and space and *possess* us with a "spirit of Steph Curry" in ways that spill over into daily life. Now, not only am I shooting that wad of paper towels with a different Energy, but more importantly moving with the intention to apply that Energy to everything I do, especially in relation to whatever specific kind of spiritual nudge I needed at the time. This captures the way inspiration works, or at least the ways we experience it as an *inbreaking* that enlivens the very *crux* of our creative being.

But inspiration also *emanates from* embodied performances across the same spectrums of activity. This is to say that the immateriality of inspiration flows in the other direction as well, from the material. Buried within Merriam-Webster's metaphorical presentation of "impel, motivate or affect" and "bring about, occasion," and right after "incite"—in their attempt to capture "inspire"—is a single "inhale."[10] Every single breath we take, technically, is inspiration. Etymologically, "To breathe, or blow into" was originally meant to capture the spiritual dimensions of inspiration. However, it also captures the materiality of breathing in the form of an exhale. This takes seriously the idea that I share in chapter 4, that "every breath we take enchants our entire being," but applies it to the other position. To inhale, or be "inspired," is to be the recipient of life given. But to inspire is to be the one breathing life that others are taking in. Literally. It is to embody and exercise Energy in a way that energizes others, and sometimes possesses them with ideas that they then relate to their felt purpose in life. This more fully captures the energetic intimacy with which we exist and navigate daily life. We feed off of each other's Energy in ways that are largely overlooked but deeply consequential. Beyond the intimacy of breathing shared air in community—a material dimension of relationality that COVID-19 confronted us with—we rely on the respiration of the relational interactions that sustain us. They give us Energy; literally, they give us life.

This brings the inspiration wrought by Black athletes a lot closer to home. It means that all those energizing moments of awe that cause one to take in more air and then move with a new zest for life, which then spills over into revitalized interactions that in turn give life, have the markings of Black athletes all over them. The very (f)act of inspiration induced by Black athleticism raises theological questions regarding the intimate depths of racial conditioning in the United States. That politicized messages about Black men can create belief systems that are designed to prove themselves right in the name of survival—or "Jesus"—speaks to the depths with which white supremacy is embodied. Such is how our brains use belief to filter and focus attention toward the construction and maintenance of worldviews that make sense with regard to whatever rationalities are their reference point. Sadly, the rationalities of race continue to be funded by messages that demean Black athletes, which creates a cultural hyperfocus on finding whatever evidence proves such messaging right. This is why even well-intentioned people who express their appreciation of Black athleticism often still cannot recognize the spiritual depth or intellectual complexity of Black athletes themselves. A culture around such commentary does not yet exist.

However, Black athletic inspiration also reveals a theological depth of the discrepancy between "beast" and "brilliance." Brilliance is revealed by the mere fact of its breaking forth. By definition, it is too multifaceted to be contained because its nature is to be free. Moreover, brilliance exercises itself intellectually. It finds expression even when most of the openings have been covered. And where there are none, it bursts through the seams of constructed realities, exploiting cracks that are invariably there by nature of being manufactured, built by racial beliefs designed to colonize. But belief systems are reconstituted by counternarratives, plotlines that are strategically planted and then nurtured over time until the story *they* tell becomes muscle memory.

And every expression of Black athletic brilliance is a potential starting point for a new story to be told. Every time a Black athlete mesmerizes onlookers, inviting them to look more deeply at themselves, brilliance has broken through. Every life-giving dunk that dazzles, or world record that produces wonder, or explosive run that touches down in the *crux* of a person's being and ignites ecstatic experiences of joy are expressions of brilliance that heal even if they have not been heard. We can manufacture a new mind for Black athletes – and Black people – simply by using language that is truer to form.

The embodied brilliance of "beast mode"

Marshawn Lynch is resurrected by the (im)material life he has given to millions of people, many of whom can only see him as a "beast"— or "thug"—who exists for public consumption. But buried within the machinery of the animal, and behind the curtain of curtailing narratives, lives a divinity expressed as embodied brilliance that enchants even as it disrupts. Lynch is redeemed by the realization that no amount of criminalizing can contain ***imago DNA***—the divinity that exists in the very ***crux*** of *his* creative being and is exercised in the materiality of his body. To say "beast quake" was a spiritual experience acknowledges the messianic ways in which Lynch's iconic run produced healing physiological effects that fans benefit from. It highlights the pharmacological markings of *his* (Black) athleticism in the bodies of those he has touched. But it also accounts for the broader ritual of Black athletes breathing life into people looking for it in contexts of play. To acknowledge the spirituality of sport in this way reveals the extent to which the embodied brilliance of Black athletes inspires the energetic intimacy that binds us together even beyond the ways it can be measured in the body—how even the protracted act of inhaling the memory of such awe-inspiring moments testifies to a lingering presence that provides a slow release of medicine that people continue to draw from well after they leave the stadium, or turn off the TV. And to the degree that such energetic intimacy emanates *from* Black athletes performing in the context of their profession, it speaks to the inherent intellectual significance of Black athleticism.

To suggest that it was Lynch's intellect in particular that incited the ecstasy of this spiritual experience is to recognize that Lynch himself was possessed during his iconic run, high on his own (divine) supply. Lynch's ability to master his own machinery had the effect of inspiring his embodied performance in a way that spilled over into arguably the greatest touchdown run of all time. In short, Marshawn Lynch was in *flow*. When asked about his experience of "beast quake" during an NFL Films interview, and whether or not he heard the seismic noise of the crowd, Lynch replied, "You don't hear nothing. All I heard was the ruffle of my shoulder pads, and breathing." Later in the interview, after narrating the finer details of the play he made, Lynch stated that at the time all he could think was, "What the hell just happened? Did this really just happen?"[11] In another interview with Conan O'Brien, Lynch is asked about the origins of his nickname, and how people he has encountered off the field have found *inspiration* to bring their own versions of "beast mode" into their professions. In response, Lynch recounts an interaction he had with a barista at Starbucks, wherein the employee recognizes him standing in the line, states that he is a big fan, and then—as Lynch puts it—"he just flipped the switch like, 'I'm going beast mode,' then he made like four of 'em," as Lynch playfully acted out the seamless movements of making a latte.[12]

Lynch's intuitive estimation of the barista's 400 percent productivity increase as a result of going "beast mode" is not far off from the 500 percent productivity boost that flow researcher Steven Kotler and the Flow Research Collective advertise to sell their services to private corporations and the public.[13] "Peak performance," as they call it, is based on research into the neurophysiological phenomenon called "flow," which has been defined as an altered state of consciousness wherein a person becomes so fully absorbed in the performance of a task that they are able to bridge effectiveness and effortlessness.[14] It describes the experience of being "in the zone" or "caught up in the spirit," where one seemingly loses oneself in the midst of mastering an activity without having to think much about it. It is when the game slows down and we feel like we are flowing, or moving fluidly through whatever obstacle is before us. This feeling of a difficult task becoming second nature is precisely the appeal of flow research to the public. Gamers refer to flow as going into "god mode" because it is like playing with a cheat code that makes the usual difficulty of a task disappear. Flow is like acquiring a star on *Super Mario Bros*, or being "on fire" in *NBA Jam*. It is when one experiences a certain synchronicity between self and whatever task one is engaged in. And athletes epitomize this synchronicity in ways that are reflected physiologically.[15]

Phenomenologically, there are six core characteristics that distinguish a flow state from similarly altered states of consciousness such as meditation, traumatic stress, or other experiences of personal or group ecstasy:[16] (1) complete concentration; (2) merger of action and awareness; (3) time dilation; (4) loss of a sense of self; (5) a heightened sense of control; and (6) a deep sense of intrinsic motivation. Together these factors tell a story of poetry in motion that is usually associated with artists, musicians, or other professions for whom "genius" is a common ascription. This is because such professions are recognized for their acuity in terms of possessing many, if not most, of flow's causal triggers, which include a blend of internal and external conditions that all assume a level of *skill* that can meet and potentially master even the most difficult challenges. Which begs the question, how, and to what degree can anyone access flow? Is it a state that can be induced by focusing intently, regardless of specialization or IQ? Or are there prerequisites to flow states that are specific to a person or their training? According to Lynch, it is the latter, "I don't know if you can like, get into it. You know, this ain't something you can go home and be like, 'I wanna get in beast mode, I wanna get in beast mode.' Nah, that ain't the way it works. Beast mode is already inside of you."[17]

Neuroscientists would agree with Lynch's assessment. Until recently, researchers have been torn as to whether the phenomenon of flow is induced by one's ability to focus tightly on a task in a moment, or if its magic relies on a more mundane kind of expertise. In other words, they wondered if flow registers more closely with the activity of the prefrontal cortex, or if it is associated with the brain's default mode network, which aligns more closely with muscle memory than executive function. By measuring the brain activity of jazz musicians experiencing flow states, it was discovered that the phenomenon extends from, and exists within, the specific domains of deep expertise. It shows up in the brain as a quieted prefrontal cortex and an active default mode network.[18] In other words, flow cannot be forced based on one's ability to focus in a moment, but rather extends from a previous regime of focus (read: expertise, or training) that lives behind the ritualized recruitment of the neurophysiological interworking necessary to function automatically. Stated plainly, flow can only exist within the field of developed expertise. This conclusion effectively locates "beast mode" within the same faculties (of "mind") that make Beethoven land as a genius. The process is neurophysiological, the prerequisite is expertise, and the experience is spiritual in that the *trance* Lynch was in during "beast quake" not only possessed people in the stadium that day but continues to inspire everyone from ball players to baristas with a divine brilliance that possesses them to perfect their crafts as well.

Drawing out the satirical thread

But play has another side. Connected to its rehabilitating nature is a disruptive dimension that occasions it. Play in this sense is a double entendre because it references the way in which wit factors *into* the softening of neuroplasticity. This is the kind of play that constitutes those initial reaches into uncharted, or "off-limits," dimensions of the mind. Well captured by the phrase "you got played," this is the one that refuses to *play along*. This is the play that promotes plasticity by provoking the system—disrupting its status quo, whether muscle memory or white supremacy, or the muscle memory *of* white supremacy. It is the ***satirical*** side of play, which exists to challenge power by exposing the absurdities that support it. Consider again the stand-up comedian, who playfully softens the audience with humor that releases feel-good hormones that give laughter its life-giving feel. And this heals, in that it reveals a physiological truth to the intuitive exclamation, "this is giving me life." But its healing is connected to content that breaks rules, which is what provides the break *from* "reality." And the only reason HR even cares is because it goes against policy. Satirical play is fundamentally political, then, in that it is designed to disrupt. Bringing chaos is in its nature. Satire, in this sense, is like Deebo riding Red's stolen bike around – from the movie *Friday* – just looking for a fight, but more *explicitly*[19] intellectual in its violence. However, satire would be Craig in this scenario, the unlikely victor who wins by outwitting the stronger opponent.[20] Because by definition, satire punches up. It bobs and weaves by nature of being marginalized, sneaking uppercuts at the absurdities around which power has been calibrated *because* of where it lives in relation to that power. In other words, it must maintain some sense of deniability if it is going to "live to fight another day."[21]

Yet, the real power of satire can be seen both in its ability to creatively expose the cultural logics of coloniality and at the same time sustain marginalized people by helping them laugh to keep from crying. Or, according to Danielle Fuentes Morgan, from dying. In *Laughing to Keep from Dying*, Morgan captures the simultaneity of satire's healing and liberating functions in relation to the particular struggles of Black people in the United States. She argues that satire is a strategic impulse that has emerged from the unique experience and history of African Americans trying to survive and develop in a cauldron of colonial dominance predicated on control and, where necessary, violence. From antebellum slavery up through the contemporary moment, Morgan alludes, the ability to laugh at that which is absurd provides the salve of psychic survival for Black people, while at the same time occasions moments that invite society to recalibrate itself based on the same realized stupidity of racism. She writes:

> satire creates new realms in which social justice *might* be enacted by disrupting social expectations and demonstrating the connection between laughter and ethical beliefs. Through a clear focus on questions of racial essentialism, either by disavowing or ironically embracing racial performativity,

> satire creates a tension that opens up a hidden interior into kaleidoscopic Blackness, those multifaceted, private recesses of black identity and selfhood that are often unknown to or overlooked by those who would simplify Blackness to render it consumable and commodifiable.[22]

Satire, for Morgan, is more than just a way to make people laugh. Rather, it is a particular brand of comedy that serves a destabilizing function which aids in the development of healthy selfhood and societal balance. In this sense, satire could be understood for the way it occasions the brain's plasticity. Satirical performances expose glitches that invite reconsideration, which can open into all kinds of new directions that remap our sensibilities. In terms of theological sensibilities, the subversiveness of satire should also be seen for its salvific quality, in that it opens up (play) spaces for healing and the potential for performing new social paradigms. This is why satire is so threatening. What is especially inviting about the way Morgan connects the "hidden interior" of kaleidoscopic Blackness to the political possibility for new realms of relationship to be created is how it can be read in terms of the *neurospirituality* of embodiment.

Satire occasions energetic exchanges that depart from "reality" and register in the circuitry of bodies that give off Energy, Energy that is politically productive in whatever direction it is focused. It is a spiritual miracle for any person to be mesmerized, and a potential revolution if it were millions, because it signals an opening in the mind whereby the seeds of a perspectival shift are planted. Moreover, Morgan's analysis of the ways satire *creates* space for kaleidoscopic Blackness is also inviting because it alludes to its own possibility to be read backwards. Not only does satire create space for flourishing, but its very appearance could also be understood more deeply as an *expression of* kaleidoscopic Blackness, breaking through *because* it is divine. This would suggest that satire is an exercise of that which already is, even as its performance creates space for one to more fully be(come). In other words, many of those inspiring moments that we so mindlessly metabolize are occasioned by "those multifaceted, private recesses of black identity and selfhood"[23] that find intellectual expression in the form of flipping the script.

In this sense, a kaleidoscope is the perfect metaphor to capture the divine brilliance of Black interiority, which lives behind Black athletes' ability to mesmerize millions, and discloses the broader ability, and regularity, with which *Homo sapiens* mesmerize one another. But the multivalence of a kaleidoscope can only be seen when looking closer. It makes sense, then, that a closer look at the satirical disruptions of Black athletes would reveal a kaleidoscopic brilliance that points not only to the existence of a multivalent intellect that emerges from within Black people, but also highlights alternative possibilities for the political world as it relates to the (ir)rationality of race. Hence, by reading the contributions of Marshawn Lynch, Steph Curry, and Deion Sanders *as satire*, we are invited to see more clearly the absurdity of white supremacy as it gets *played* by Black athletes across three dimensions within the context of sport.

Marshawn Lynch's creative *resistance* exposes the **moral dimensions** of white supremacy as illustrated in the dehumanizing logic of criminalization. His embodiment of the outlaw subverts cultural expectations of compliance, which has historically been used to police Black men, and to justify their crucifixion when they say "no." But Lynch found a way to refuse—both in the sense of saying "no" and shitting on the underlying logic itself—in a language that was allowed, exploiting an opening within the rule book. This gave him the plausible deniability necessary to bring attention to the common practice of demeaning Black athletes based on cultural narratives outside of sport, which is occasioned by the requirement that athletes *must* talk to the media. He exposed a gap in the logic, creating space for a more robust conversation about the content of questioning that *all* athletes must field in sports. Marshawn Lynch may never be "human" but by nature of being *Homo sapiens*, he is akin to a god—a kind of Christ given the way he inspires.

The salvific quality of Steph Curry can be seen in the ways his *range* exposes the **economic dimensions** of white supremacy, which is illustrated by his disruption of the exploitative logic of neoliberalism and its rituals of recruitment. His embodiment of the trickster makes legible an innovative intelligence that compels league offices to nuance their conversations based on the unforeseen ways in which skill can stretch a court beyond imaginations which are bound by a (Black) body logic that is further narrowed by the felt need to boast a labor force that looks the part. Curry epitomizes the neurophysiology of muscle memory, which brings the intellectual magic of athleticism to the fore in ways that widen our scope of understanding what brilliance looks like at play. Inasmuch as sport is a cultural domain comprised of fields that accentuate particular intelligences, athleticism is revealed as an intellectual blend akin to that which is necessary in other domains, such as medicine, engineering, or music. Sport just so happens to require more fully embodied rituals of practice that make it more difficult to recognize its myriad intellectual functions.

Deion Sanders's *presence* exposes the **psychospiritual dimensions** of white supremacy as illustrated in the subtle cultural assault of respectability. His embodiment of the conjurer makes legible a confidence that catalyzes belief among (young) Black men. And as we have seen, belief—one's mindset—is a communally informed orientation toward life that can alter one's experience of even their breath. To believe in oneself is a revolutionary accomplishment for any person or community that is marginalized by the culture in which they operate. It requires a cadence of self-talk that cuts against the grain of messages meant to diminish, creating an interior space that can imagine alternatives outside of what seems allowable. Based in the belief that "I'm Him," Prime is to Deion Sanders what "Christ" is to Jesus. The very appearance of Prime epitomizes the self-determination that is available to Black men, and Black people, despite persistent expectations that they will bend toward the cultural rule of whiteness.

Brilliant with a blind spot

As an element of the embodied brilliance that makes them excel in their respective domains, each of these figures move with a satirical bent that functionally exposes cultural expectations and thereby creates space for new ways of reading Black athletes. But only to a point, because Black men benefit from white supremacy's patriarchal logic. Black men may have a precarious relationship with masculinity as defined by dominant culture, but the mere fact of having a penis in a political world created for men affords us privileges that undercut our access to satirical power. Certainly, being a man occasions (if not coerces) audiences who stand ready to receive our wisdom, to celebrate our accomplishments, even in underhanded ways. Patriarchal privilege grants men's voices access to a listening world that is trained to assume masculine wisdom can be trusted, even when it comes from the mouth of a Black man—assuming he is "articulate." But the real power of satire is predicated on being trained to see power dynamics that privilege is designed to ignore. So, while being a man in a patriarchal world comes with perks that occasion a certain openness among listeners, it also comes with blind spots that can cause misused satirical opportunities.

Wit is a dangerous thing because it can manipulate power. Too often, in our attempts to outsmart the "man," Black men have participated in *his* patriarchy. We have often succumbed to the slipperiness of masculine privilege based on the desire to be all that it says we should, or could, be. But to the degree that colonial conceptions of masculinity reflect the toxicity of **whitemalegod**,[24] Black men's attempts to "be a man" have often taken the bait and switch of over-rotating in our resistance to "boy," thus falling victim to performances of hypermasculinity that have become muscle memory in the name of not showing weakness. In reality, however, meekness—the quiet confidence of being strong without having to prove it—should be our goal. Meekness can be understood as measured "weakness" for the sake of the situation. It emerges from a checked ego, which is based more deeply in the relational recognition that one does not know it all—because we were never meant to (know everything). Rather, men are because women have been, and vice versa. Queer people know this very well, and Black queer folx have an even more intimate understanding of the energetic fluidity that we all rely on in life.

A host of problems come with the privilege of patriarchy, but eschewing vulnerability lies at the root. Boasting solitary strength is a key element of the lie white supremacy tells men in a patriarchal society. It is both a symptom and signifier of the scripted distrust of women, especially Black women, and even more deeply the feminine Energy embedded within our bodies and being, not to mention across the cosmos. According to Christena Cleveland, the fundamental flaw of patriarchy is that it takes the *intrinsic beauty of masculine wisdom* and renders it supreme in much the same way that whiteness has been constructed in relation to Blackness.[25] In other words, there is a fundamental imbalance to fashioning any political world based only on half of who we are, and how we are created to be . . . in mutually life-giving relationship. No wonder even the phenomenon of flow assumes an openness to vulnerability, evidenced by the balance between the *strength* of internal preparation and *surrender* in relation to external circumstances. In other words, it is not an energetic accident that flow cannot be born from the attempt to control, but rather it is induced by being fully present with . . .

Patriarchy enjoys a perichoretic relationship with racism and capitalism that creates scenarios where Black men must be strong all the time. This erodes our capacity for vulnerability. In this sense, Black men suffer from the burden of strength similarly to what Chanequa Walker-Barnes highlights in *Too Heavy a Yoke*, albeit to degrees of depth that pale in comparison to the triple oppression Black women experience.[26] Black men are patted on the back and paid well for embodying such impenetrability. Black women are called "Mammy" and punished for it. But everyone is expected to play along with white masculinity's toxic history, and its overidentification with the heroic, because it reproduces the myth of individualism on which neoliberal capitalism relies. Embracing vulnerability not only challenges toxic histories of the heroic, but more importantly allows Black men to recognize and reclaim the feminine wisdom in our lives, and ourselves—including our bodies. This acknowledges the satirical near-sightedness wrought by the blind spot that comes with male privilege, reminding us that there is no such thing as a "self-made" Black man either. Hence, embracing vulnerability not only reinstates Black men's agency to choose a more abundant emotional life, but it also acknowledges the satirical advantage of feminine wisdom in a way that better positions us to hear, and hopefully heed, the wit of Black women.

Witnessing (to) the wit of Black women

Taking seriously the subaltern nature of satire exposes the patriarchal field on which the foregoing analysis of Marshawn Lynch, Steph Curry, and Deion Sanders has played thus far, which suggests that this reading is limited by nature of the privilege they each enjoy as male athletes competing in a society where the cultural domain of sport is marked, if not marred, by a patriarchal logic that plays out in the very design of the games athletes play,[27] and the amounts they pay. So, while a particular focus on "beast" and its foreclosure of Black men's fullness might reveal critical insights into the ways white supremacy threatens Black male athletes, and how they disrupt its cultural logic, delineations of any kind keep us from understanding the underlying truths that undergird even the best patriarchal analyses of race, regardless of how mindful they might try to be. Furthermore, to the degree that satire is a distinguishing feature of Black athleticism, one cannot even begin to talk about the disruptive nature of embodied brilliance without mentioning a few of the greatest athletes of all time, who also happen to be Black women.

Arguably the greatest tennis player, if not athlete, of all time, Serena Williams has made legible the expectation of Black female dominance in sports. And she has accomplished this while having to repeatedly return a barrage of insults that have served her femininity up to the public as "manly," which is revealed by the ways her "abnormal" prowess has been rendered the stuff of steroid use.[28] Simply by nature of how she blends beauty, brains, and brawn, "beast" has also been inscribed onto her Black female body in ways that are meant to police her based on the presumption that a (Black) woman cannot be both strong and sexy, and certainly not smart. Despite attacks on her body and brains—on her very being—however, Williams embodies a presence that provokes a cultural discomfort akin to the effects of "Prime Time." Her brilliance emerges from the divine kaleidoscope within her and shines forth in a way that has created space for Coco Gauff and others to chase their dreams and step into the spotlight of a sport that, if not for the legacy of Althea Gibson, Black women may not have taken over. Similarly, any conversation about the embodied brilliance of Black athletes would be remiss to not completely bend to the innovative intelligence of Simone Biles. To have performed skills that can only be named "The Biles" is to epitomize the embodiment of technological advances that literally break through the limits of consciousness and demand their own category.

But deeper than both of these examples, the wit of Black women is revealed in the example set by the Atlanta Dream during the nation's shutdown during COVID-19. Born from the vulnerable space of the WNBA bubble—both in the sense of safety and the politics that still make Title IX necessary—Black women demonstrated the communal power of protest, which produced not only a heightened awareness, but moved the needle in relation to the politics of the sport they play.[29] In a real sense, the Atlanta Dream actualized what could have become more than the momentary pause that kneeling during the National Anthem incited. Which is to say—in part—that Colin Kaepernick's protest was undone before it began by the economic power of the NFL, and the fact that even if one thousand players from across the league were willing to risk their livelihoods to follow his lead, there would be a million more hungry athletes ready to step into their place. Certainly, this level of protest would have been inconvenient, but ultimately workable, because of a political reality that renders male sports—and Black male athletes—a centerpiece in the appetite of American society. Female athletes do not live with such privilege and have often had to consider other forms of financial viability even while competing at professional levels, especially if they play sports that do not feature femininity in ways that can be easily fetishized. In other words, the financial impact of losing one's spot on a roster hurts in the same proportion as the financial privilege one enjoys by nature of competing with either a penis or a vagina. And in a political economy predicated on dick swinging, satirical privilege is granted to the one without.

To take satire seriously is to acknowledge the presence and pre-eminence of womanist wisdom even as it is buried within the bodies of Black male athletes. And attending to Black women's wit in particular invites us to summon the fourth and final folk hero that Hopkins highlights, framed as the One who bats cleanup after the trickster, the conjurer, and the outlaw have done their bidding. For Hopkins, it is the Christian *witness* who "effects empowerment and thereby yields a spirituality of compassion for the poor."[30] He casts this archetype closest to the model of Jesus, understood to be a savior—enlivened by a divine spirit of liberation—who identifies and works collaboratively *with* the least among communities for the purpose of saving *everyone* from the dehumanizing forces of empire. While it can be tempting to rest in the assumption that Hopkins's proposal for theological anthropology culminates in "Christ," the critical difference between this figure and the other archetypes is how the *witness* embodies *with* as the primary method for enacting salvation.

Rather than assume one needs be the lone hero working on behalf of the community, but without their participation, the witness moves with a relational sensibility that presumes the involvement of the least in order to ensure that nobody gets lost or left behind—to realize the truth spoken by the late Maya Angelou, which echoes across the work of Black feminists and womanist theologians: that "no one of us are free until everybody is free."[31] Every single sheep. In this sense, Hopkins's rereading of Harriett Tubman and Denmark Vesey through the lens of the *witness*—examples he gives for people who embody "Christ" in this collaborative way—is similar to Monica Coleman's reading of "saviors," people who emerge from within the community and deploy a satirical brilliance that cuts across narrative histories of the heroic and instead foregrounds the relationality from which all real revolution emerges. In this sense, the satirical wit of Black women invites a reinterpretation of patriarchal conclusions, which reveals the collaborative thread that cuts through the contributions of Lynch, Curry, and Sanders.

Re-telling the (w)hol-istic truth *with* womanist wisdom

When considered through the lens of Black women's wit, it is revealed that Marshawn Lynch's creative resistance is undergirded by a ***legibility of listening***. As brilliant as it was, Marshawn Lynch did not come up with the idea for his media protest in isolation. While the commitment to protest was his alone, and he trademarked the viral phrase, the brilliance of "I'm just here so I won't get fined" was born from Lynch's *relationship* with Dave Pearson, who at the time was the Seahawks' public relations director, and the person who pestered Lynch to do interviews during his tenure in Seattle.[32] Pearson acted as a liaison between Lynch and the NFL, simultaneously urging him to comply while listening to his concerns and finding ways to support his conviction not to. In a sense, Pearson was Lynch's accomplice in cocreating a way for him to resist without continued financial penalty. And the brilliance of the phrase itself was born from the constant give and take of talking and listening—and struggling—in a relationship bound together by the bonds of a shared commitment, which helped Lynch find the words for his *technical* availability.

The satirical brilliance of ***with*** also provides a rereading of Steph Curry's range that reveals the ***relationality of (being) reason(able)***. Contrary to what Kant or Descartes may have said, what is most *reasonable* is decided by the rationalizing community. In community. And the best chance any community has at precision is linked directly to adequate representation, which ensures that the pool from which "policy" is pulled reflects the variety of perspectives therein. Steph Curry would not have been able to develop his world-record-breaking range without his coach, Steve Kerr, who—like Pearson—co-conspired (read: breathed) with Curry to create something new. And while Kerr has proven himself to be both genuinely kind and concerned for justice in his own right, it was his contrarian willingness to recognize Curry's potential despite the predominant rationality—or Reason—that was operative in the NBA, which allowed him to create space, and a culture, for Curry to cook like only a Chef can.

And finally, taking seriously the satire revealed by womanist wit invites a reinterpretation of "Prime Time" that reveals the relational *politics of presence*. That Deion Sanders credits the very creation of "Prime Time" to a visit he took to Atlanta, Georgia, while a senior at Florida State, where for the first time this young Black man from Fort Myers, Florida, witnessed what he calls a "chocolate city," which understood his Blackness and emboldened him to believe in himself, speaks to the political power that comes from community. This is precisely why Sanders told the four teams who had picks before the Atlanta Falcons in the 1989 NFL Draft that if they tried to pick him, he would go play baseball. He felt, and wanted to continue to feel, the support of a community that both showed him who he was and held space for him to become more fully himself, however he wanted to be. "Prime" is because they were.

But even more immediately than coaches or chocolate cities, each of these exemplars point back to Black mothers who nurtured them from boys to men in ways that only a Black mother can. It is the wit of *with* revealed by the embodied brilliance of Black women that not only undergirds Black men's satirical disruption of white supremacy's cultural logic, but also keeps Black masculinity honest in its own tendency to reproduce white male patriarchy. And this has been the case theologically as well. From the formal beginnings of womanist theology until today, Black women have responded to the quandaries that have hamstrung Black (male) liberation theologians by re-membering and reclaiming dimensions of African spirituality that colonial Christianity coerced us to forget. By nature of existing on the outskirts of an already marginalized political existence—oppressed within oppression—womanist standpoints have been satirically positioned to help us all see more clearly the kinds of (r)evolutionary ideas that can return Black people to themselves spiritually, embodied, even when this has meant dispensing with categories previously understood to be sacred.

Whether Delores Williams listening to the cries of her *Sisters in the Wilderness* and critiquing notions of redemptive suffering in the doctrine of atonement,[33] or Monica Coleman casting off the traditional notion of "Christ" and calling us to *Make a Way Out of No Way* by collaboratively saving ourselves, and our communities, through creative transformation,[34] or Christena Cleveland dispensing with the *whitemalegod* of colonial Christianity and inviting us to receive the feminine wisdom that comes with realizing that *God Is a Black Woman*,[35] womanist theologians have satirically disrupted colonial notions of salvation in ways that are salvific because they recognize—no, summon— the ancestral brilliance of Black people, which begins and ends with the whole **body** in mind. There is a depth and breadth to the satirical wit of womanism that is to be found in the theme of ***with***, which more deeply references the relational sensibility that has grounded Pan-African spirituality even when Black theologians have forgotten. Because some insights only Black women can embody. Hence, paying particular attention to the embodied brilliance of Black women can help us—Black men—do the *root work* necessary to understand how we can resist white supremacy more responsibly, with community.

Reckoning with "religious" experience

The play of satire is reflected in spiritual dimensions that womanist theologians continue to point us back to. For the last several decades, Black thinkers have wrestled with theological questions that emerge from the plight of Black people in the United States, and around the globe. Theodicy questions, quandaries about salvation in relation to the sin of racism, and even the question of God abound in Black theologies seeking to provide answers that assuage the suffering of Black people across the spectrum of gender expressions, sexualities, and other politicized dimensions of existence, namely as they intersect with the politics of race. The tapestry of theological perspectives that has been woven by Black liberation theology, womanist theology, Black humanism, and even Black naturalist ways of making sense of ecological existence have variously—and increasingly—contributed to a necessary distancing from the commitments that have grounded colonial Christianity, and with it many of the categories that continue to bind Black faith communities, especially the Black Church. And to varying degrees these theological perspectives have been shot through—sustained even—by African spiritualities that move satirically based on cosmological understandings that beat just beneath the surface but have been buried because they are not wired for control like their colonial competitors. The very cloth from which the variety of Black religions have been cut reflects a pastiche of Pan-African spiritualities that have been nurtured despite naming practices that were designed to cut these ties.

Unfortunately, the asphyxiating nomenclatures of Western Christianity have made it difficult, and sometimes impossible, to investigate and intentionally nurture this spiritual (im)pulse. As a political play, Western Christianity—with its epistemological categories—*has been used* as a ploy to disembody Black people. It has functioned as the predominant moral apparatus used in a centuries-long attempt to dig all Africanity out of people who exist in Black bodies. To crumble our ***crux***, as it were. And if not crumble, this ploy certainly commodifies, which is more insidious because it utilizes our Energy to support missions that misuse. This is not to suggest that Christianity, or any religion for that matter, is inherently anti-Black. However, as Willie Jennings and Kelly Brown Douglas both demonstrate in their work, the very foundation of *Western* Christianity in the United States has been politically calibrated to colonize African cosmologies. And one way it has accomplished this is by prioritizing a racial story that has coerced religious sensibilities into fetishizing our finitude to such a degree that we could miss, or perhaps even muzzle, what Jesus himself was trying to tell us about who we are and what *all Homo sapiens* are capable of, if they "just believe."

He shared stories that allude to the health effects of love on the bodies of other beings; he waxed eloquent on the neurophysiology of belief before it was a discipline; he outwitted the gatekeepers of sedentary ways of thinking, even when they were based on the religion they both articulated. Jesus of Nazareth painted portraits of embodied brilliance that are captured in red letters that still cut through canonization, empowering stories that continue to enliven the least among us, satirical stories that still challenge power. But the political canopies of colonization—via capitalism—have worked over centuries to suppress beliefs that would threaten the social and religious order of white supremacy. Hence, the rule(s) of religion have too often been written with theologies that splinter—people and communities—which undermines our relational nature and the material beauty of our (Black) bodies. Such religious *rites* contribute to the (re)creation of a reality whereby Black subjects must rely on racist structures for their own survival. And *everyone* is coerced to play along with this game, thereby reproducing white culture's dominance through ritualized performances that bring racist scripts to life, in the name of Jesus.

But Black people keep breathing and believing, which begs the question, "How?". How have we exhibited such religious resilience in a political reality that bends toward whiteness? How are Black people able to keep laughing in the midst of a cultural assault that makes it virtually impossible to see any evidence that the moral arc of the universe bends toward justice? How has white supremacy not been able to destroy the *crux* of Black being already? It is because we are divine—conscious Energy connected to a common source but exercised in bodies of all kinds, in all directions. We are embodiments of the Divine living an enchanted existence. And we have been gifted with machinery that makes magic possible. Every manifestation of *Homo sapiens* who breathes is an expression of divinity, an iteration of the Divine, equipped with Energy that we direct based on our beliefs. We are spiritual beings not in spite of the body but *because* of it, realized in the ways we materialize our existence into an open-ended field of (r)evolutionary possibilities in **uni**son *with **imago DNA***.

The satirical play of African spirituality

The resilience and satirical plot twist of embodied spirituality can be seen most clearly in Emmanuel Lartey's identification of a latent spirituality, which he argues continues to sustain Black people of all faiths. In *Postcolonializing God*, Lartey, a Ghanaian scholar, tells a story about attending a Black Church in Atlanta, Georgia, shortly after his arrival in the United States in 2001. He shares how an associate of his, who was also from continental Africa, was turned off by her visit to this Black

Church because of the similarities to religious practices she wanted to distance herself from. Seeking to understand her reaction, Lartey reflects:

> I wished to know why. Her response was telling. "It's just like a session of the traditional fetish shrine back home in my traditional African community," she said. "When the drumming takes a particularly exuberant form, and they begin to dance, shout and sway, I feel just like I did at the fetish shrine—not at Christian worship. It's just as if the spirits are being invoked and possessions are about to occur—just like the shrine. It's all so pagan and traditional. It transports me back to and re-enacts that from which I thought I had been liberated in Christ!"[36]

But even Jesus never asked anyone to throw away their religion, so long as it compels them to love. Philosopher and musical artist Frank Ocean says any religion that brings one to their knees—in a subservient sense—is a "bad religion," and he cites "unrequited love" as the prevailing symptom. Ocean's description of what it is like to participate in a "bad religion" is even more telling:

> *To me, it's nothing but a one-man cult*
> *And cyanide in my Styrofoam cup*
>
> *I can never him love me,*
> *Never make 'em love me,*
> *Love me, love me...*[37]

Ocean caps off his metaphorical theology by saying outright that trying to live a "bad religion" can be like balancing "three lives on one's head like steak knives," concluding with the realization that there is a direct link between the unrequited love of "bad religion" and the feeling of being fragmented. Lewis Gordon calls this "bad faith," but athletes know it as cheating in a game. It is like promising love but giving whips and chains instead, then promising freedom but finding new ways to police based on the same assumptions, or paying millions and expecting that to muzzle messianic truth. Western Christianity, inasmuch as it has been used as technology of empire, has been the driving force that made it all morally permissible. It has provided the narratives needed to explain away the persistent political extraction of Black vitality in service to the (re)creation of a world that Black people have too often not been able to name for themselves.

And we've played along with this game. Whether duped by the threat of death or doctrine, Black people have our part to play in this cultural production. We've fought over made-up categories like any *Homo sapiens* trying to make sense of a marginalized existence would. But as we claimed Western Christianity, we also inherited an epistemological cosmos that has coerced us to code switch *off* a religious sensibility that lives in the very materiality of our bodies, which has engendered an accumulative denial of the kinds of spirituality that was muscle memory for our ancestors—that embodied spiritual pulse that just won't go away. Over time, very natural dimensions of African spirituality were written off as "superstitious," or charged as "demonic," which seduced Black people of faith to articulate themselves, and increasingly believe, on the terms set by European thinkers whose primary concern was to control Black being. In this sense, Western Christianity has targeted what Yvonne Chireau calls the "vernacular religions"[38] of African people, which was a colonial method of control and a way to preemptively squelch the possibility of revolt based on the political need to utilize Black muscle to construct a reality based on a capitalist fantasy. Hence, any religious expressions that were wired for the empowerment of Africans, and which prioritized their bodies in connection to nature, were cast as evidence contrary to civility, which was believed, and sold, to only be correctable through (Western) Christian conversion. And this legacy continues.

Still, Black people of all faiths continue to embody the rhythms that have sustained us over centuries, rhythms that can dance to any beat, whether Catholic, Protestant, or "spiritual but not religious."

The divine brilliance we embody breaks through, regardless of names given. As a species, *Homo sapiens* embody and emit spiritualities prior to their articulation, and often in spite of. That said, the fragmenting effects of "bad religion" do create doubt, which can functionally derail any person's ability to focus their Energy. Consider the trepidation of trying to walk forward while being unsure of your direction, or whether the way you are walking is appropriate, not to mention if this particular path(way) is a choice you made for yourself or merely the muscle memory of cultural upbringing. Either way, "bad religion" speaks to the disembodying discrepancies that are designed to derail Black being through dismemberment. It shines a light on the subjugation of those feelings that emerge when one's embodied reality bleeds the linguistic containers given by their cultural religion—when religion fails to support a life of love and instead constricts its capacity.

By extension, "good religion" is one where love is shared mutually, freely, and where all embodied parts, and parties involved, can enjoy the freedom to synchronize themselves in ways that re-member, which heals *and* makes sense. This perspectival shift allows persons and communities to refocus their Energy with confidence, because apparently good religion does not move based on fear, but rather love. And this applies whether one is taking on empire or taking out the trash. The *love* of good religion is literally life-giving in all directions. It is good for the nervous system and the heart. In this sense, it seems that neuroscientists are starting to discover that Jesus was in fact onto something. Moreover, dancing, shouting, and swaying in community are all embodied spiritual practices that give life. They energize us, which means they literally heal and transform. Such ritualized exercise contributes the very vital signs on which good religions come up from the ground and can be articulated. How much more benefit might we get from the realization—the belief—that we in fact intuit more good religion than we have learned to articulate?

According to Ocean, the discrepancy this woman felt—the feeling of being fractured—is a sign of "bad religion." Unfortunately, her diagnosis as to which one was "bad" led her to deny her spiritual roots—her training—and with it dimensions of her own body that, because of this denial, cannot be appreciated for its inherent sacred worth. In other words, she participated in her own fragmentation at the behest of a colonizing interpretation of her embodied spirituality. For embodied spirituality can only technically be controlled if a person controls it themselves. And even then, I wouldn't put money on it. A *better* religion would at least hold space for integration—for synchronicity, based on the spiritual priority of being embodied. The worst kind of religion is one that forecloses the fullness of one's embodiment based on race or any other phenotypical expression of ***imago DNA***. It seems that the best chance we have at good religion is to learn how to play. Because to *play* the game—in the sense of seeing through it—recognizes that no amount of colonial reengineering can sever the ties Black people have with breath, even while it has tried to bind our beliefs.

The best religions are flexible, playful in their seriousness. They allow us to love deeply while holding loosely because they understand that there may always be a separation between embodied spirituality and articulated religion. Religion is understood here as the attempt to make sense of what is—to capture the ways we embody spirituality, and bind ourselves together in community. Though closely related, the two are not twins. Their genealogical gap will exist as long as "humans" rely on their ability to apply fixed names to an unfolding existence. To *play* the game is to speak of spirituality based on our deepening understanding of embodiment. It redirects attention to the spirituality of Energy, grounded in our participation with vitality for the purpose of increasing said Energy, and bound to the responsibility this includes to collaboratively direct it toward the re-creation of a world in a more holistic image. An image that we know is still unfolding, not just because science says so, but because we can feel it in our bones.

To *play* the game

To *play* the game is to take seriously the ***contingent divinity*** of *Homo sapiens*. This is not to claim that we are God in any kind of supreme sense. We are not. The last few centuries have demonstrated the dangers of what can happen when people feel they can monopolize meaning, or create cultures that claim superiority, or supremacy, in relation to other beings. Such attempts to control that which is essentially free deal death by design, contributing to a depressive state of being that we all get caught up in. Rather, **contingent divinity** understands that Energy is sacred, and productive, and it takes these twin realities seriously. In a creative sense, it acknowledges that we bear the responsibility to cocreate this life with God, whose creativity sets things in motion and whose immanence continues to breathe life into our bodies to oxygenate a network of muscles meant to expand our creative capacities. And this is meant as expansively as possible, but still grounded in embodiment. "Muscles," in this sense, refer to all embodied capacities that can be trained, or—within genetic reason—reprogrammed. However, it is important to understand that *Homo sapiens* embody divine Energy for good or for ill. We have been gifted with the capacity to heal and transform, which comes with a cautionary tale that compels us to take responsibility for such. That we also have the capacity to destroy based on the same embodied Energy is precisely the reason to remember that such divinity is always contingent, linked to systems and species across the spectrum of beings that also embody vitality. To be sure, there are consequences in either direction. In every moment, we can give life or deal death. And Monica Coleman is right, the choice is ours.

Lartey rightly notes that there are *pervasive* and *discernible* characteristics of a latent African spirituality "which are manifest in different ways among particular peoples and cultures."[39] Whether Black churches in the United States, or other diasporic religions in the Caribbean or South America, he argues, "African religions survived and have been *recreated*[40] in the 'New World' partly because one of the crucial functions of religion in the African mind is to provide the power by which people are enabled to cope with life successfully."[41] To the degree that such an African *mind* represents a fully embodied presence, and process, and (Black) athleticism an intellectual proclivity oriented toward success, and survival, then *Sport* should be added to *Church* as a unique space where latent African spirituality exercises itself. Sport provides the perfect play space (read: practice field) where the spiritualities of Black athletes can play out productively through intellectual embodiments that create new pathways of racial understanding. If we listen—but the language we have been given forecloses this kind of legibility.

Hence, to play the game is to propose a ***spirituality of Energy*** as an attempt to make legible a new language by which we can begin to notice the embodied spirituality of Black athletes, and by extension, *Homo sapiens* across a variety of contexts and cultural expressions. It invites us to focus on the Energy we embody in order to understand the magic that is found in the mundane crevices of communal life. It is an embodied spirituality that is necessarily pragmatic, which is to say, it is more concerned with shedding light on the relational dynamics of everyday life than creedal commitments that may or may not influence how one shows up to everyday life. A spirituality of Energy sees everyday life as a stage and invites us to pay closer attention to the productivity of the ritualized performances we participate in, because they create reality. It understands that Energy extends from but ultimately builds on the breath, because breath gives us Energy, and our bodies hold the capacity to generate more of it, especially in community. Hence, its course of study includes breathing and believing bodies as its primary texts. And it asks Black athletes to be our instructors.

While a case could be made for all seven of Lartey's discernible characteristics, four are especially pronounced in the context of sport and will function as frames for this final section:

The sacredness of all of life

Hardly any word exists in most African languages for "religion" per se. Most often the word "religion" has been translated by African words for "ritual" or "ceremony" or "service". The reason lies not in the absence of religion but rather in its pervasiveness. All of life pulsates with the rhythms of the spiritual realm. Mbiti's "incurably religious" is not to be interpreted in western categories of religiosity divorced from everyday life, or as some narrow innate penchant for superstition, but rather in terms of the pervasive and encompassing zest for life in its multidimensional complexity which often finds expression in very humanistic forms.[42]

Mystical connectivity through communal ritual

African religion is not so much a matter of "beliefs, dogmas and creeds" as it is of the performance of powerful rituals and the expression of communal solidarity through participation in such rituals.... The rhythmic language of the drum creates and mediates the liminal space between the visible and the unseen world enabling beings to traverse this space in both directions.[43]

Creativity and adaptability

African religion is demonstrably flexible, pliable, pluralistic and adaptable. The rituals and practices, while maintaining their essential form, have been re-invented in different ways and forms throughout the world. Wherever Africans have gone, willingly or unwillingly, in the world they have formed communities of faith and practice drawing creatively and synthetically on their heritage, as well as upon features of their current context and other realities they have found.[44]

Affirmation of life

The values adumbrated through ritual and practice in African religion are all directed towards the flourishing of human community. Fecundity, bountiful harvests and peaceful communal relations are key prayers in each ritual of libation. Religion is powerfully present in the drum, rhythmic movement of the body and dance not merely through contemplation, reflection or other mental calisthenics. African traditional theology is not only thought out but also expressed in bodily form. Doctrine and ethics revolve around this central thesis, that religious rite and activity needs to promote the well-being of the human community.[45]

The beatitudes of beast mode

Lartey's cosmological assumptions set the stage for a rereading of three rituals that are uniquely embodied by (Black) athletes in the context of sport, and which provide instruction for the first steps in what can become a new rhythm for taking seriously our Energy.

Prayer (and plasticity)

Prayer is how we focus attention. It brings Energy to center for the purpose of (re)directing it. But it also changes the brain.[46] Prayer, meditation, or any concerted study of something promotes neuroplasticity even as they connect us to a wisdom beyond ourselves. It has been shown that prayer serves a regulatory emotional function that shapes the brain and is marked in the body.[47] Embedded in the ritual itself is a recognition that we do not own Energy, or the vitality from which it comes. We merely participate with it, trusting our ability to develop it and call it forth, but grounded in a humility that comes from being bound to bodies that can fail us at any time. Prayer entails a process of synchronizing oneself—breath, body, and belief—in preparation for performance, or to express gratitude afterwards. It is a bookend that keeps us grounded. Built within a posture of prayer is a humility that comes from the understanding that regardless of how much talent we have, or how much we exercise our Energy, we are still finite. Our divinity is always contingent. Sometimes no amount of prayer can prevent one from pulling a hamstring during a competition, or making microaggressive statements based on ignorance. However, prayer is also the mechanism by which we can become mindful enough to take the necessary steps to prevent injury (i.e., warming up before, strengthening surrounding muscles, stretching after, etc.). It is also the mechanism that can sustain the reparative process when we misstep, providing hope that healing can happen once the hamstring or relationship is frayed.

The embodied spirituality of prayer can also be thought of more broadly, however. Visualization is a ritual practice that functions like mental rehearsal for athletes. It is the mental practice that informs how they will show up in the game. Visualization—the practice of using mental imagery—promotes neuroplasticity in much the same ways that physical exercise does. In other words, we can develop muscle memory around mental imagery, which works in unison with the embodiment of a task in "real" life. However, visualization is also connected to belief in that it provides a mental playground where someone can convince themself of their own ability to successfully achieve a goal—every athlete has seen themself winning before it actually happens, and the act of winning itself contributes to the ever-moving target as to how lofty one's aspiration becomes. That is why the ritual of prayer—reconceived (also) as a training modality—is so productive in bridging the gap between imagination and embodied practice. It provides the rehearsal necessary to ready the body for performance.

Even in team sports, prayer is meant to focus the collective Energy of the community toward unifying beliefs and practices. Whether pregame, postgame, or those that bookend practices, the spiritual function of "team" prayer is to bind together different embodiments around a synchronized self, even if that "self" is the identity of the collective and not a specific person. However, even among teams that do not formally pray, there are ritualized mechanisms in place that are designed to synchronize the attention of players toward a common goal. One such mechanism in the context of sport is film study. Most sports, and certainly all team sports, watch film *religiously*. "The eye in the sky don't lie" is a popular saying in team sports because it signals the authority of film study. It is a ritual for teams to watch the recordings of their practices and games together, then to watch them again based on the respective positions they play, and even to study film of their individual performances. This reflexive method of mental rehearsal—or praxis—allows athletes to critically examine everything from their overall performance to their specific technique, which provides the basis for enhancing themselves in real time. Not all teams are religious, per se, but they all embody a spirituality of prayer that connects to a functional and purposeful engagement with their respective and collective Energy.

Practice (and muscle memory)

Practice is the process of focusing our Energy on developing ourselves in particular directions based on the demands of a cultural domain, in line with the direction that prayer provides. Whether solo[48] or as a team, practice is where muscle memory is developed. It is the embodied activity that establishes rhythm. In this sense, practice is the ritualized movement of bodies in unison with the expressed purpose of using collective Energy to form a community toward a reality not yet realized but hoped for. In a solo sense, this is where the interrelated pieces that make up the larger movements of one's performance are enhanced based on position. Resistance training, agility work, overload days for track athletes who need to condition their bodies to run a little longer than whatever the distance of the race will be, even rest days, are all part of the process of honing oneself toward the tasks that have been chosen, or assigned. Practice is Steph Curry working incessantly on skill combinations that he knows he will use in games—a brilliant creative process. It is Denzel Washington rehearsing lines for a new role, downloading them until he has such a *feel* for the character that it becomes synchronized as part of his personality wheelhouse. Practice engages the neurophysiology of motor learning as an intentionally directed ritual based on the understanding that it "makes perfect." In other words, how we practice (life) is how we will play *because* the brilliance of the body can be directed.

Team practice is similar, but more complex. It contributes to cultures in that solo participation is integrated into a greater whole, and the communality of the ritual is seen more explicitly. This signals the way cultural participation both emerges from the culture that exists and contributes to its re-creation. A review of any cadence of practice in a team sport will reveal a ritualized structure whereby the Energy of each participant is synchronized in particular ways that fit the larger movements deemed necessary by the culture, wrought through coaching. All of these movements are based on strategies designed to put the players in positions to win, and they are drawn from the wealth of knowledge that has been accumulated about what "winning" requires. Even for track and field, or other solo sports that do not directly apply to the team dynamics, orienting one's Energy toward something like the Olympics—where they are now a team representing a larger whole—adds a different level of religious meaning (and pressure) to the performances.

Performance (as play with intention)

Performance is when it's game time. It is when the lights come on and we get to flex all the muscle we have developed throughout our training—when the truth of that training is revealed. Game day is when teams put the rhythms of their practice to the test with the hopes of winning a competition. And even if not necessarily a competition against another "team"—so, less gladiator-like in its complexity—track athletes or gymnasts will tell you that the real competition is with(in) oneself. In this sense, performance is when preparation meets circumstance, and we find out what we are made of – what we have made of ourselves.

Daily life is the real game, though. That is when we all get to find out what kind of work we've been putting in. It is both the practice field and the stadium, where we train and test, exercise and expose, practice and perform tasks that reveal as much as they produce. It is when the person who claims to be "not racist" finds out that they have been conditioned otherwise, unintentionally, and often in spaces they believed were benign. It is when one realizes that they have developed muscle memory around racist beliefs that they would have never chosen, and yet have still been shaped by—when the reality of white supremacy is revealed in spaces one thought provided a break from the political game of race. Daily life might seem like a grand stage at times, but it can be boiled down to moments-in-time when we learn to be more mindful, and more fully present. In other words, we can learn to be *athletic* in our attentiveness to the power of our Energy, and in our relationships, especially when we recognize how deeply bound together we are in a relational web of life that simultaneously occasions and extends from the ways we act in relation to each other.

Conjuring the athlete within

Sport represents one of the largest stages where racialized bodies can clash in a controlled environment, and we can all be mesmerized. In this sense, it does provide a *break from* the reality of race—if we listen, and if we learn to articulate the truths as they play out in front of us, even if this means creating a language we do not yet have. Sporting competitions create a unique environment where everyone is invited to witness the big bangs of *Homo sapiens* Energy. This is precisely the reason millions of people show up to watch athletes of all races compete, and especially why Black athletes have such an appeal in a supremacist society. We need the novelty. We feed off the inspiration, the hope. Deeper than the desire to be entertained, we can feel the effects that witnessing god-like feats have on us at a spiritual level, even when the commentary is fraught in ways we are not trained to notice. It is the same appeal that music may have for the non-sports fan who loves to dance, or a blank canvas and blocked-off time for an artist. Sport performance taps into the felt need to be reminded that we are more than merely "human." We know intuitively that something is wrong with the category, which is why we keep questioning it. And this is why we show up to witness the embodied brilliance of (Black) athletes who tell a different story. So, we assign ourselves games in order to put our learnings to what often feel like the ultimate tests; to be studied in a controlled environment; to be consummated in moments of play, then incorporated into our being as we return to the "reality" of daily life. Hopefully at this point we can acknowledge the brilliance of the test subjects who have taught us all so much about the resilience, creativity, and beauty of our species.

But perhaps the most important thing we can learn from Black athletes is that we are all athletes at heart, in body (read: "mind"), and in (embodied) spirit. From the very *crux* of our being to the phenotypical reach of our bodies, Black athletes—by nature of being people—demonstrate the depth of our embodied capacities to manipulate ourselves for survival *and* (r)evolutionary action. They put on a master class for *Homo sapiens* to learn about being "human," and they have done it from outside the technicality of the category itself. Unacknowledged but vital. Like Energy. Or breath. Black athletes demonstrate our connection to the earth and its many sources of vitality. In this sense, athleticism could be defined as a developed state of enhanced readiness to respond with playful intention to whatever demands one may face in a situation, whether a stadium filled with sixty thousand fans or a tough conversation with a loved one. To be an athlete is about honing the art of paying full-bodied attention to oneself for the purpose of showing up fully to the game of everyday life.

In the ultimate plot twist, it is the embodied brilliance of Black athletes that provides much of the inspiration we need in order to find within ourselves the wherewithal to disrupt the messages that are often associated with Black bodies—especially in the context of sport. Fortunately, Black athletes also provide a training program we can follow to recondition ourselves based on a renewed commitment to take seriously the Energy we embody. First of all, they would remind us to *play* (the game): to perform with playful intention based on a recognition that all this is made up, which means we can show up flexibly and ready to enjoy the collective process of *recreating* the realities of race as they play out in our lives. But knowing that mistakes will always be made, they would also encourage us to *practice*: to hone ourselves in communities of belief with people who can hold us accountable to our role in relation to the whole, and to stay there until new rhythms that redeem the lives of the least become muscle memory. Then they would tell us to *pray*: to incessantly employ the full range of the various ways we "put our minds to" the tasks of healing and reconciling, transforming the relationships and systems we participate in, respective to the cultural domains of our expertise. And in a final word of encouragement, they would remind us to "be an athlete" – to pay attention, because we both know you are better than this.

Just remember to do it *with* . . . love.

NOTES

PREFACE

1. Barbara J. McClure, "Pastoral Theology as the Art of Paying Attention: Widening the Horizons," *International Journal of Practical Theology* 12, no. 2 (October 2008): 189–210.

CHAPTER 1: THE MYTH OF LEVEL PLAYING FIELDS

1. My emphasis on Black male athletes in this book should not indicate that these racial politics do not also converge on the bodies of Black women, whether athletes or otherwise. Rather, my emphasis reflects the depth I explore around the particular trope, "beast," and the ways it uniquely reflects and reproduces politics that visit Black men. I strongly believe another book could, and should, be written that addresses the ways racial politics converge on Black women's bodies in sport, which could also reference "beast" but would focus more immediately on the trafficking of tropes that are specific to Black women's embodiments.
2. A full exposé of the systems and interlocking institutions that comprise the "complex" of sport is outside the scope of this project. Later in this chapter, I provide an analysis that connects sport to neoliberal capitalism, and throughout the book I detail the interworking of this association as it sheds light on the ways sport occasions expressions of racialized capitalism to the detriment of Black men in particular. Ultimately, however, Black male athletes disrupt this exploitative logic in ways that also are unique to their experience. Hence, my analysis is only focused on responding to the problem of race as it intersects with the politics of Black masculinity.
3. "Iconic Calls: Seattle Seahawks Beastquake," accessed October 28, 2024, https://www.seahawks.com/video/iconic-calls-seattle-seahawks-beastquake.

4. Andrew C. Billings, "Depicting the Quarterback in Black and White: A Content Analysis of College and Professional Football Broadcast Commentary," *Howard Journal of Communications* 15, no. 4 (October 1, 2004): 201–210, https://doi.org/10.1080/10646170490521158.
5. There are several public reports that demonstrate this based on recent studies about sports commentary. For an analysis of results based on one recent study, see Dimitrije Curcic, "Racial Bias in NBA Commentary (Analysis)," RunRepeat, March 25, 2024, https://runrepeat.com/racial-bias-in-nba-commentary.
6. Paul Ian Campbell and Louis Bebb, "'He Is Like a Gazelle (When He Runs)': (Re)Constructing Race and Nation in Match-Day Commentary at the Men's 2018 FIFA World Cup," *Sport in Society* 25, no. 1 (December 27, 2021): 144–162, https://doi.org/10.1080/17430437.2020.1777102.
7. This reflects both my everyday conversations with peers and recorded interview data from my dissertation, which approached this issue with the disciplinary concerns of pastoral theology in mind. See Gary F. Green II, "Playing the Game: Unmarking 'Beast' from the Bodies of Young Black Men," PhD diss., Brite Divinity School, June 2020, 164ff., https://repository.tcu.edu/handle/116099117/40353.
8. This discrepancy can also be seen in a series of tweets wherein Tom Brady himself referred to Lamar Jackson, current quarterback for the Baltimore Ravens, as a "beast" when he was preparing for the draft coming out of college, to which Jackson responded online by saying, "the GOAT has spoken." See Mike Reiss, "Tom Brady on Louisville QB Lamar Jackson: 'He's a Beast!,'" ESPN.com, April 12, 2018, https://www.espn.com/blog/boston/new-england-patriots/post/_/id/4812827/tom-brady-on-louisville-qb-lamar-jackson-hes-a-beast.
9. Contrasting this segment with a more recent one entitled "The Himmy Awards" signals an intriguing shift wrought by younger Black sports analysts, and beloved ESPN anchor Scott Van Pelt. Rather than celebrate phenomenal performances as animalistic acts of talent, The Himmy Awards extend from the phrase, "I'm Him," which is a more contemporary confession of one's own prowess. It is theologically intriguing to explore the ways this newer iteration of self-conscious greatness doubles as a reclamation of one's own divinity, even if unintentionally. I take this up in chapter 5.
10. "Giannis Gets Freaky, Warriors New Reality, NFL Week Preview and More!!! From Jalen & Jacoby," ESPN podcasts, October 25, 2019, https://www.stitcher.com/s?eid=64850700.
11. "Giannis Gets Freaky."

Notes

12. The more explicit phrase "freak of nature" is often used instead of "beast" and was perhaps more prevalent before Marshawn Lynch's persona as "Beast Mode" became common parlance.
13. Denzel Washington's son.
14. "'He's a BEAST!' Spike Lee on Adam Driver Owning *BlacKkKlansman*," BBC Radio 1, August 24, 2018, https://www.youtube.com/watch?v=xkeNEZ-G-Rw.
15. "Marshawn Lynch: Actor, Producer, Writer," IMDb, accessed October 28, 2024, https://www.imdb.com/name/nm2834234/.
16. The use of these terms is often preceded by the qualifier "my" in order to signal relational intimacy and trust, which is more deeply grounded by the recognition of a shared cultural experience.
17. Dwight N. Hopkins, *Black Theology: Essays on Gender Perspectives* (Cascade Books, 2017), chap. 4.
18. Associated Press, "Vogue Cover with LeBron Stirs Up Controversy," TODAY.com, March 25, 2008, https://www.today.com/news/vogue-cover-lebron-stirs-controversy-wbna23797883.
19. Because this commercial was also taken down, and presumably still owned under Adidas's copyright, a credible citation is not available. However, searching "Patrick Ewing Adidas Conductor Commercial" on YouTube will turn up results one can explore and verify oneself.
20. Patrick Ewing's former college coach recounts the regular occurrences of racism that Ewing faced while at Georgetown, as well as the commercial being referenced here. To hear the full interview and read an opinion piece about it, see "Patrick Ewing's Former Coach Writes Script About Racism NBA Icon Endured," Audacy, March 30, 2023, https://www.audacy.com/cbssportsradio/sports/nba/mike-jarvis-writes-script-about-racism-patrick-ewing-endured.
21. There is an argument to be made regarding the racist origins of the King Kong story itself, which one could argue extended from the "Black man as a 'beast'" narrative even as it reproduced it. This certainly reflects the historical association between Black people and monkeys, and tracks eerily through historical depictions of the sexualized fear of Black men in relation to white women. Walt Disney's depiction of *Beauty and the Beast* is strangely similar to renowned author Mackinlay Kantor's *Beauty Beast*, which was published in 1969 and reflects a resurgence of popular "fiction" portrayals of Black men—like Mandingo—that would have monopolized the media in that time. However, verifying racial intent of an author or filmmaker is beyond the scope of this project. That said, my argument

in this book is that intent doesn't matter. This project analyzes race as a matter of conditioning that exists prior to and/or underneath motivation. Hence, the only "proof" one needs is to look at the cultural milieu surrounding the story and development of King Kong to recognize the coherence, convenience, and the cultural impact of this racist association.
22. Mark Anthony Neal, *Looking for Leroy: Illegible Black Masculinities* (New York University Press, 2013), 4.
23. Neal, *Looking for Leroy*, 4.
24. Neal, *Looking for Leroy*, 8.
25. Gregory C. Ellison, *Cut Dead but Still Alive: Caring for African American Young Men* (Abingdon Press, 2013), 1–11.
26. Ellison, *Cut Dead*, 14–19.
27. A Google or social media search will turn up a variety of videos that reflect the virality of this incident. For a more detailed news report of the details, and for an example of the video see "Amy Cooper Made 2nd Call To 911 About Black Birdwatcher, Prosecutors Say," *Today*, October 15, 2020, https://www.youtube.com/watch?v=L3662COVmn8.
28. William C. Rhoden, *Forty Million Dollar Slaves: The Rise, Fall, and Redemption of the Black Athlete*, reprint ed. (Broadway Books, 2007).
29. For official NCAA data that is regularly updated, see "Estimated Probability of Competing in College Athletics," NCAA.org, accessed October 28, 2024, https://www.ncaa.org/sports/2015/3/2/estimated-probability-of-competing-in-college-athletics.aspx.
30. The Pro Bowl represents the annual all-star game and festivities that the best players from the league are selected for and participate in. The Super Bowl is the championship game that crowns the best team in the league. Because the Pro Bowl takes place the week before the Super Bowl, players who are selected but who play for one of the Super Bowl contending teams do not participate in Pro Bowl activities, as a safety feature to protect against injury before the championship game. However, qualifying for either (or both) of these games reflects positively on the careers of those who get to participate.
31. Most of the reports that are published about this reflect heteronormative (read: homophobic) analyses that I do not feel comfortable citing, and there are no official reports about this from the NFL Combine or NFL Network. That said, the popularity of this, and other instances, can be seen by searching online, and a YouTube search in particular does provide a few opportunities to witness this specific example.
32. I would still argue that the NFL is unique in the extent to which such explicitly exploitative language is allowed, if not expected, given the physical brutality of the sport.

33. Louis Moore, *We Will Win the Day: The Civil Rights Movement, the Black Athlete, and the Quest for Equality* (The University Press of Kentucky, 2021), 1–20.
34. Moore, *We Will Win the Day*, 1–20. This entire chapter demonstrates Moore's point about the civil rights significance that sport held in service to racial integration.
35. Bruce Rogers-Vaughn, *Caring for Souls in a Neoliberal Age* (Palgrave Macmillan, 2016), 42–46.
36. Rogers-Vaughn, *Caring for Souls*, 90–95.
37. See specifically Rogers-Vaughn's analysis of "third order" suffering, Rogers-Vaughn, *Caring for Souls*, 125–128.
38. For a fuller analysis of this myth and its historical construction, see Stephen J. McNamee, *The Meritocracy Myth*, 5th ed. (Rowman & Littlefield, 2023).
39. Cedric C. Johnson, *Race, Religion, and Resilience in the Neoliberal Age* (Palgrave Macmillan, 2015), 30–34.
40. Johnson, *Race, Religion, and Resilience*, 48–54.
41. Johnson, *Race, Religion, and Resilience*, 48.
42. Johnson, *Race, Religion, and Resilience*, 48–49.
43. Emilie Maureen Townes, *Womanist Ethics and the Cultural Production of Evil* (Palgrave Macmillan, 2006), 18–22.
44. Townes, *Womanist Ethics*, 18.
45. Townes, *Womanist Ethics*, 21.
46. Townes, *Womanist Ethics*, 37–55.

CHAPTER 2: MARSHAWN LYNCH

1. I remember firsthand on several occasions hearing sports reports using that language to characterize Marshawn Lynch. Beyond my own experience, however, a simple Google search of "Marshawn Lynch" and "thug" demonstrates the traction on this topic. For an example of one of his former teammates—Donald Penn—challenging this narrative and instead talking about how Lynch is one of the nicest, most genuine people he knows, see Peter King, "The Peter King Podcast," accessed October 27, 2024, https://www.nbcsports.com/nfl/the-peter-king-podcasts.
2. "Super Bowl LVIII Is Most-Watched Telecast in History," NFL Football Operations, February 13, 2024, https://operations.nfl.com/updates/the-game/super-bowl-lviii-is-most-watched-telecast-in-history/.
3. In a recent interview with Hall of Fame tight end, turned journalist and podcast mogul, Shannon Sharpe, Lynch cites the treatment of the media in Buffalo as the primary reason he decided to stop giving interviews.

He notes how some of the same people who were congratulating him on dominant performances were also the reporters calling him a "thug" in response to mistakes he made—after he had publicly taken responsibility for them—early in his career. For the full interview, see "Club Shay Shay: Marshawn Lynch Part 1," Apple Podcasts, October 4, 2023, https://podcasts.apple.com/us/podcast/marshawn-lynch-part-1/id1531023690?i=1000630127547.
4. "Shoot" is a euphemism for asking questions in this context. It has a connotation of "feel free to try, if you want to." For an ABC report and footage of this interview, see ABC7 San Francisco, "Marshawn Lynch at Super Bowl Media Day: 'I'm Just Here so I Won't Get Fined,'" ABC7 News, January 27, 2015, https://abc7news.com/marshawn-lynch-beastmode-seattle-seahawks-new-england-patriots/493651/.
5. Lynch recounts the situation and shares more intimate details about the politics at play during this podcast conversation about Black athletes and mental health: "Marshawn Lynch on Mental Health, Pete Carroll & More," I AM ATHLETE, February 20, 2023, https://www.iamathletetv.com/show/marshawn-lynch-lendale-white-on-their-mental-health-pete-carroll-more.
6. "NFL Media Access Policy," PFWA, accessed April 30, 2024, https://www.profootballwriters.org/nfl-media-access-policy/, my italics.
7. The entire video of this press conference is no longer available online, but the Seahawks have kept records of them and feature a good portion of this particular interview here: "Marshawn Lynch's Best Press Conference Moments," accessed October 27, 2024, https://www.seahawks.com/video/marshawn-lynch-press-conference-best-moments.
8. Sambo is another racist caricature that was used to infantilize Black men, and portray them as ultimately happy (go lucky) in their oppression. For a brief description and history of this trope, see "The Coon Caricature—Anti-Black Imagery," Jim Crow Museum website, accessed October 27, 2024, https://jimcrowmuseum.ferris.edu/coon/homepage.htm.
9. For a helpful explanation, see "How Your Brain Creates Reality, Explained by a Neuroscientist," *Big Think* (blog), accessed October 27, 2024, https://bigthink.com/the-well/what-is-reality/. Lisa Feldman Barrett has done extensive research in this area. The thrust of her academic work in brain science is captured in *How Emotions Are Made* (Houghton Mifflin Harcourt, 2017) and *Seven and a Half Lessons About the Brain* (Houghton Mifflin Harcourt, 2021).
10. Townes, *Womanist Ethics*, 18.
11. Kelly Brown Douglas, *Stand Your Ground: Black Bodies and the Justice of God* (Orbis Books, 2015), chap. 1.

12. Ibram X. Kendi, *How to Be an Antiracist*, updated ed. (One World, 2023).
13. Willie James Jennings, *The Christian Imagination: Theology and the Origins of Race* (Yale University Press, 2010), 6.
14. Jennings, *The Christian Imagination*, 24.
15. For a fuller explanation of this concept, see "zero point epistemology" in Walter Mignolo, *The Darker Side of Western Modernity: Global Futures, Decolonial Options* (Duke University Press, 2011). By beginning in the index, one will find links to the thoroughgoing ways in which thinkers like René Descartes both benefitted from, and reproduced, the idea of a "zero point," which bolstered the felt humanity that European colonizers assumed was unique to themselves, and antithetical to Africans.
16. Jennings, *The Christian Imagination*, 25.
17. Jennings, *The Christian Imagination*, chap. 2.
18. Douglas, *Stand Your Ground*.
19. Douglas, *Stand Your Ground*, 44.
20. This conception of "property" is not to be confused with the ways Black people were construed as chattel, property to be owned and exploited for free labor. To be cherished white "property," in this sense, is to be protected at all costs.
21. "What Is the Doctrine of Discovery?," The Coalition to Dismantle the Doctrine of Discovery, June 29, 2015, https://dismantlediscovery.org/about/doctrine-of-discovery-basics/.
22. Kelly Brown Douglas, *Sexuality and the Black Church: A Womanist Perspective* (Orbis Books, 1999), 45.
23. Hopkins, *Black Theology*, 48.
24. "Super predator" is a racist myth that was popular during the late 1980s and 1990s, which was used to target young Black men by casting them as the ultimate menaces to society.
25. Mark S. Roberts, *The Mark of the Beast: Animality and Human Oppression* (Purdue University Press, 2008), 3–7.
26. Mignolo, *The Darker Side of Western Modernity*, 194–202.
27. Roberts, *The Mark of the Beast*, 7–12.
28. "Marshawn Lynch/Cheated/USA Rugby/A Survivor's March," *60 Minutes Sports*, June 7, 2016, https://www.imdb.com/title/tt6573364/?ref_=ttep_ep6.
29. Rate coding and motor unit recruitment are well-known processes in the athletic training world, which refer to the process by which the brain sends signals that "recruit" more muscle tissue in the creation and maintenance of new muscle fibers. This neurophysiological process is central to all muscular adaptations, but is especially central to the process by which resistance training builds strength. I treat motor unit recruitment

in relation to "muscle memory" in chapter 4, but for an analysis of "rate coding" and its involvement in the process, see Roger M. Enoka and Jacques Duchateau, "Rate Coding and the Control of Muscle Force," *Cold Spring Harbor Perspectives in Medicine* 7, no. 10 (October 2017): a029702, https://doi.org/10.1101/cshperspect.a029702.
30. Billie Holiday, "Strange Fruit," lyrics, Genius.com, accessed October 29, 2024, https://genius.com/Billie-holiday-strange-fruit-lyrics.
31. See James H. Cone, *The Cross and the Lynching Tree* (Orbis Books, 2011), chaps. 1–2.
32. Douglas, *Stand Your Ground*, chap. 2.
33. Philip Butler, *Black Transhuman Liberation Theology: Technology and Spirituality* (Bloomsbury Academic, 2020), 27–31.
34. Butler, *Black Transhuman Liberation Theology*, 27–31.
35. Butler, *Black Transhuman Liberation Theology*, 30.
36. See M. Shawn Copeland, *Enfleshing Freedom: Body, Race, and Being*, 2nd ed. (Fortress Press, 2023), chap. 1.
37. Copeland, *Enfleshing Freedom*, 1.
38. I prefer the term *biotechnology* as opposed to *biomechanics* because of the former's focus on "living" organisms as the interrelated pieces of *Homo sapiens* embodiment that are oriented toward the creation or maintenance of embodied systems. However, biomechanics *is* an underlying focus inasmuch as it informs my constructive engagement with kinesiology and theological anthropology in service to a redefinition of (Black) athleticism as embodied brilliance.
39. I have conceptualized it this way to capture the simultaneous ways in which policies are designed and enforced in a loop that reinscribes their legibility, which also illustrates the formal and informal ways Black men are policed in a racist society. I treat *policy* more fully in chapter 4.
40. From this point forward, I will use *Homo sapiens* to replace the term *human*, unless I am making a specific point about the political limitations of the latter.

CHAPTER 3: STEPH CURRY

1. "Bodied" is a Black cultural euphemism for an extraordinary performance, but one in which the actor has so thoroughly absorbed the role/task into themselves that it reflects their own flavor. To "body" a performance means one has made it their own, exceeding the minimum expectations called for by the script. It is Denzel Washington as the Equalizer,

or Health Ledger as the Joker in *The Dark Knight*. As a result of these performances, it is difficult to imagine these roles without these actors ... because they *bodied* the roles so well.
2. More on performance in chapter 4.
3. He actually measured at 6'2" with shoes off, making him even more of a long shot—no pun intended—to make it in the NBA.
4. "Stephen Curry Draft Report: Actions Speak Louder Than Words," CoachUp Presents, September 22, 2015, https://www.youtube.com/watch?v=WLb8AwuZ7N8, my italics.
5. With the exception of a "full court press," which is a strategic break from the norm that is only used when a defense wants to put more pressure on an offense. However, this strategy is used sparingly due to how physically taxing it is on defenders.
6. The "paint" is that area directly under the basket where the highest percentage of shots were taken. This is where taller players—usually "centers"—dominate, and where shorter players typically struggle to score.
7. In a real sense, Steph Curry creates the kind of pressure that is akin to the "full court press" strategy defenses used to disrupt offenses, but flipped where the burden of maintaining stability amid the chaos he creates is on the defense.
8. My italics.
9. Usain Bolt remains the world record holder in both.
10. Certainly, there are factors beyond his play that have made this possible. Even Usain Bolt credits those around him for much of his success, so it is understood that an accomplishment like this in a team sport is to be held more communally. But there are also elements to Steph Curry's range that only he can take credit for, and that speaks to the brilliance of his athleticism.
11. For a critical analysis of "mass incarceration," and its interrelated political dimensions, see Michelle Alexander, *The New Jim Crow: Mass Incarceration in the Age of Colorblindness* (The New Press, 2012).
12. I can remember the feeling of being simultaneously excited and anxious when college coaches would come to my practices in high school, or even walk through the locker room to get a closer glimpse at me or my teammates' physiques as part of the recruitment process.
13. Rhoden, *Forty Million Dollar Slaves*, chap. 7.
14. Rhoden, *Forty Million Dollar Slaves*, 174–175.
15. David Epstein, *The Sports Gene: Inside the Science of Extraordinary Athletic Performance* (Portfolio, 2014), 115–117.

16. Epstein, *The Sports Gene*, chap. 7.
17. And to a certain degree, team sports are unique in the ways they invite people with different social identities to suspend their typical commitments for the sake of a common goal. However, the uniqueness of this opportunity does not guarantee "progress" in any direction, nor should it be taken as proof as such. More on this in chapter 5.
18. "Stephen Curry (ft. Golden State Warriors)—2014–15 MVP Acceptance Speech," speech delivered at the NBA Season Awards, May 4, 2015, https://genius.com/Stephen-curry-2014-15-mvp-acceptance-speech-annotated, my italics.
19. While Curry's contributions to youth outside the NBA are well known, he is also widely recognized for his investment into the lives of Black youth in particular, which is a commitment he has spoken about publicly on numerous occasions. He has partnered with Snoop Dogg to develop youth basketball players, created a junior golf tour for disadvantaged youth, and he and his wife, Ayesha, started a foundation called Eat.Learn.Play., which exists to support and raise funds for Oakland public schools. To get involved, visit https://www.eatlearnplay.org.
20. NIL represents recent changes that now allow college athletes to benefit financially from the use of their name, image, and likeness to sell merchandise, to feature them on video games, or to otherwise market their participation to the public on behalf of the institutions they represent. When I was in college, the NIL did not exist. This meant that we were not compensated for the use of our names, images, or likenesses, which resulted in a multimillion-dollar lawsuit in which the NCAA and EA Sports had to settle with former players whose names, images, and likeness were used in the college football video game at the time. I was one of these athletes. For a fuller description of NIL and some of its features, see "What Is NIL? NCAA Name, Image, Likeness Rule Explained," accessed October 22, 2024, https://www.ncsasports.org/name-image-likeness.
21. "Estimated Probability of Competing in College Athletics."
22. "NBA Players by Ethnicity 2023," Statista, accessed June 24, 2024, https://www.statista.com/statistics/1167867/nba-players-ethnicity/.
23. "Share of NFL Players by Race 2023," Statista, accessed October 29, 2024, https://www.statista.com/statistics/1167935/racial-diversity-nfl-players/.
24. "Employed Persons by Detailed Occupation, Sex, Race, and Hispanic or Latino Ethnicity," Bureau of Labor Statistics, accessed October 29, 2024, https://www.bls.gov/cps/cpsaat11.htm.
25. Most notable among the many commentators in this film who speak to the political dynamics of race in hip-hop are Michael Eric Dyson, who analyzes specifically the lack of control Black artists have in the

music industry, particularly when white male CEOs are overrepresented among executive leadership. Byron Hurt, dir., *Hip-Hop: Beyond Beats and Rhymes*, PBS, 2007, https://www.pbs.org/independentlens/documentaries/hiphop/.
26. According to the CDC, Black males continue to lead in homicide statistics and rates of imprisonment.
27. bell hooks, *Where We Stand: Class Matters* (Routledge, 2000), 70–79.
28. Felecia Lee et al., "Promoting Positive Youth Development by Examining the Career and Educational Aspirations of African American Males: Implications for Designing Educational Programs," *Journal of Prevention & Intervention in the Community* 39 (October 1, 2011): 299–309, https://doi.org/10.1080/10852352.2011.606402.
29. "The Educational Opportunity Monitoring Project: Racial and Ethnic Achievement Gaps," accessed July 1, 2024, https://cepa.stanford.edu/educational-opportunity-monitoring-project/achievement-gaps/race/.
30. Jennifer D. Turner, "Freedom to Aspire: Black Children's Career Dreams, Perceived Aspirational Supports, and Africentric Values," *Race Ethnicity and Education* 25, no. 1 (January 2, 2022): 128–153, https://doi.org/10.1080/13613324.2020.1718074.
31. Butler, *Black Transhuman Liberation Theology*, 42–45. Also see Epstein, *The Sports Gene*, chap. 9.
32. Butler, *Black Transhuman Liberation Theology*, 27.
33. Mignolo, *The Darker Side of Western Modernity*, 194–202.
34. Copeland, *Enfleshing Freedom*, 1–14.
35. Copeland, *Enfleshing Freedom*, 2.
36. Victor Anderson, *Beyond Ontological Blackness: An Essay on African American Religious and Cultural Criticism* (Continuum, 1995).
37. Archie Smith, *The Relational Self: Ethics & Therapy from a Black Church Perspective* (Abingdon, 1982), 59.
38. Smith, *The Relational Self*, 57.
39. Smith, *The Relational Self*, 57–58.
40. I am referring here to the default mode wherein "white" is blindly assumed, and thereby prioritized.
41. Barbara J. McClure, *Moving Beyond Individualism in Pastoral Care and Counseling: Reflections on Theory, Theology and Practice* (Cascade Books, 2010), 187.
42. Barbara J. McClure, *Emotions: Problems and Promise for Human Flourishing* (Baylor University Press, 2019), chap. 5.
43. Ryan Wagner et al., "Race and Concussion: An Emerging Relationship," *Ochsner Journal* 20, no. 4 (2020): 348–349, https://doi.org/10.31486/toj.20.0145.

44. Michael L. Alosco et al., "Interactive Effects of Racial Identity and Repetitive Head Impacts on Cognitive Function, Structural MRI-Derived Volumetric Measures, and Cerebrospinal Fluid Tau and Aβ," *Frontiers in Human Neuroscience* 13 (December 20, 2019): 440, https://doi.org/10.3389/fnhum.2019.00440.
45. My father was part of this lawsuit and was among the many Black former players who were invited to be tested again for brain trauma at no cost. For a public report of this legislative change, see Associated Press, "NFL Agrees to End Race-Based Brain Testing in $1B Settlement on Concussions," NPR, October 20, 2021, https://www.npr.org/2021/10/20/1047793751/nfl-concussion-settlement-race-norming-cte.
46. Wendy Farley, *Tragic Vision and Divine Compassion: A Contemporary Theodicy* (Westminster John Knox Press, 1990), 54.
47. Fuu-Jiun Hwang et al., "Motor Learning Selectively Strengthens Cortical and Striatal Synapses of Motor Engram Neurons," *Neuron* 110, no. 17 (September 7, 2022): 2790–2801.e5, https://doi.org/10.1016/j.neuron.2022.06.006.
48. Hwang et al., "Motor Learning."
49. Onaje X. O. Woodbine, *Black Gods of the Asphalt: Religion, Hip-Hop, and Street Basketball*, reprint ed. (Columbia University Press, 2018), 29–30.
50. Woodbine, *Black Gods of the Asphalt*, 29–30, my italics.
51. Hwang et al., "Motor Learning."
52. Dwight N. Hopkins, *Being Human: Race, Culture, and Religion* (Fortress Press, 2005), 171.
53. Curry breaks down his creative process in a podcast conversation with former NBA player, and now coach of the Los Angeles Lakers, JJ Redick. To hear the interview, see JJ Redick and Tommy Alter, "Stephen Curry," Apple podcasts, November 22, 2022, https://podcasts.apple.com/us/podcast/stephen-curry/id1525281746?i=1000587042299.
54. For a fuller analysis of the neurophysiological processes at work during Steph Curry's training as it relates to "muscle memory," or the "triple extension," see Prue Cormie et al., "Developing Maximal Neuromuscular Power: Part 1—Biological Basis of Maximal Power Production," *Sports Medicine (Auckland, N.Z.)* 41, no. 1 (January 1, 2011): 17–38, https://doi.org/10.2165/11537690-000000000-00000.
55. Sadly, the addition of Breaking was short lived, as the Olympic committee announced that it would not return for the 2028 Olympic Games—one wonders how much this decision was shaped by the controversy sparked by the performance of Raygun, a self-proclaimed "expert" from Australia who could not *embody* the intelligence she claimed to have. Beyond social

Notes

media mimicry, much of the cultural concern fueling the backlash was based in the feeling that Rachel Gunn—the dancer's real name—was appropriating Black and Latine culture in a way that made a mockery of it.

56. Howard E. Gardner, *Frames of Mind: The Theory of Multiple Intelligences*, 3rd ed. (Basic Books, 2011), 3–9.
57. Gardner argues that the bidirectionality of being able to "resolve difficulties" and "finding or creating problems" is a prerequisite to identifying an intelligence. See Gardner, *Frames of Mind*, 64–65.
58. The "cultural domain" and "field" are sociological concepts that Gardner uses to distinguish an intelligence from (1) the space within which it operates and is recognized or defined (cultural domain); and (2) the people, institutions, and award mechanisms used to assess competence (field). See Gardner, *Frames of Mind*, xxxiv–xxxvi.
59. Interestingly, this sheds light on many of the racial problems of artificial intelligence, in the sense that it unmasks the political dimensions behind technologies that have already been created. Hence, it makes sense that AI systems could be racist because they are designed based on programs that extend technical intelligences that are circumscribed by the perspective of their creator.

CHAPTER 4: DEION SANDERS

1. Copeland, *Enfleshing Freedom*, 1.
2. See Ralph Ellison, *Invisible Man*, 2nd ed. (Vintage, 1995).
3. Many commentators debate this, but most agree that Deion Sanders is in a category alone with Bo Jackson.
4. This is not to suggest that Black culture is a monolith, but it is to reference a cultural ethos that is embodied by cities like Atlanta, Washington, DC, and others where Black populations and political leadership are not in question. There is a very real feeling of "home" associated with such places, particularly for Black people who move with a racial consciousness that they desire to connect with intentionally.
5. While Sanders has shared his story in many interviews, this podcast conversation with Hall of Fame tight end, Shannon Sharpe, provides a unique opportunity to hear the more intimate details and motivations behind his persona and strategic moves: "Deion Sanders," Club Shay Shay, December 20, 2022, https://omny.fm/shows/club-shay-shay/deion-sanders.
6. "Perform," Online Etymology Dictionary, accessed September 6, 2018, https://www.etymonline.com/word/perform.

7. McClure, *Moving Beyond Individualism*, 186–187.
8. Barbara Rogoff, *The Cultural Nature of Human Development* (Oxford University Press, 2003), 63ff., 68.
9. Sarah Lynne Bowman, *The Functions of Role-Playing Games: How Participants Create Community, Solve Problems and Explore Identity* (McFarland & Company, 2010), 61.
10. Bowman, *The Functions of Role-Playing Games*, 136.
11. See Ethan Kross, *Chatter: The Voice in Our Head, Why It Matters, and How to Harness It*, reprint ed. (Crown, 2022).
12. Rachel E. White et al., "The 'Batman Effect': Improving Perseverance in Young Children," *Child Development* 88, no. 5 (2017): 1563–1571, https://doi.org/10.1111/cdev.12695.
13. Kross, *Chatter*, chap. 3. See also Ethan Kross et al., "Self-Talk as a Regulatory Mechanism: How You Do It Matters," *Journal of Personality and Social Psychology* 106, no. 2 (2014): 304–324, https://doi.org/10.1037/a0035173.
14. Kross, *Chatter*, 69.
15. I would argue globally, but my immediate focus is on the US context.
16. Townes, *Womanist Ethics*, 21.
17. Townes, *Womanist Ethics*, 19–20.
18. I am reminded of the instance when Henry Louis Gates Jr. was arrested in Cambridge, Massachusetts, after being mistakenly accused of trying to break into his own house.
19. Ellison, *Cut Dead but Still Alive*, 3.
20. Ellison, *Cut Dead but Still Alive*, 19–25.
21. Patricia Hill Collins, *Black Feminist Thought: Knowledge, Consciousness, and the Politics of Empowerment*, rev. 10th anniversary ed. (Routledge, 2000), chap. 4.
22. Evelyn Brooks Higginbotham, *Righteous Discontent: The Women's Movement in the Black Baptist Church, 1880–1920* (Harvard University Press, 1994), 186–188.
23. Cedric C. Johnson, *Race, Religion, and Resilience in the Neoliberal Age* (Palgrave Macmillan, 2016), 56.
24. Johnson, *Race, Religion, and Resilience*, 64.
25. Johnson arrives at this conclusion based on an analysis of appropriation, namely how widely Blackness is appropriated and performed culturally. See E. Patrick Johnson, *Appropriating Blackness: Performance and the Politics of Authenticity* (Duke University Press, 2003), 14–15.
26. While my perspective is informed by the works of Judith Butler in *Gender Trouble* (Routledge, 1990), *Bodies That Matter* (Routledge, 1993), and

Undoing Gender (Routledge, 2004), I draw more heavily on theorists who conceive of performance more expansively than in specific relation to the politics of gender. In this sense, E. Patrick Johnson is a primary source, in addition to the performance theory of Richard Schechner, inasmuch as he draws on social psychology and cultural anthropology to inform the depth of his work. See Richard Schechner, *Performance Studies: An Introduction*, 2nd ed. (Routledge, 2006).

27. Lucia Scisciola et al., "Sarcopenia and Cognitive Function: Role of Myokines in Muscle Brain Cross-Talk," *Life* 11, no. 2 (February 23, 2021): 173, https://doi.org/10.3390/life11020173.
28. Townes, *Womanist Ethics*, 21.
29. Townes, *Womanist Ethics*, 22.
30. Townes, *Womanist Ethics*, 22–23.
31. V02 max is a measure of how much oxygen the body uses during exercise and is usually associated with endurance athletes whose V02 max is much higher than sedentary persons who do not train in the same ways.
32. Butler, *Black Transhuman Liberation Theology*, 45.
33. I use this concept in much the same way that Butler talks about the "neurophysiological components of spiritual experience," which he reads through what he suggests are the four realms of experience: physiological, psychological, neurological, and somatic. See Butler, *Black Transhuman Liberation Theology*, 73–80.
34. Butler, *Black Transhuman Liberation Theology*, 51, my italics.
35. Butler, *Black Transhuman Liberation Theology*, 54.
36. I say "at least" because other Christian thinkers like Howard Thurman, as well as Black thinkers outside the field of theology, like Zora Neale Hurston and James Baldwin, take up similar questions related to being human and the politics of race prior to Cone. However, Cone is credited as the father of Black theology and was one of the earliest to engage questions of suffering within the formality of systematic theology. Hence, I highlight him as a way to reference a theological point in time where "theodicy" took center stage among Black theological thinkers.
37. Monica A. Coleman, *Making a Way Out of No Way: A Womanist Theology* (Fortress Press, 2008), chaps. 3 and 5.
38. Coleman, *Making a Way Out of No Way*, 54–55, 57.
39. "Exodus 3: 13–14 NRSVUE—The Divine Name Revealed—But Moses," Bible Gateway, accessed October 30, 2024, https://www.biblegateway.com/passage/?search=Exodus%203%3A%2013-14&version=NRSVUE.
40. Coach Prime makes it clear that he is for all young men, regardless of race. However, I highlight this particularity because his attention to the

challenges his athletes will face has been honed by his experience as a Black male athlete, and his subsequent insight into the dynamics of race as they visit his players. In this way, *all* his players benefit from a coach who is more mindful about racial dynamics that other (white) coaches may be aloof to, and certainly not able to identify with personally.
41. PWI stands for "predominantly white institutions."
42. I include this reference because Nick Saban was at the center of the controversy which ensued after Sanders signed Travis Hunter while at Jackson State, which resulted from Saban's accusation that Sanders paid Hunter to come play for him. Given Saban's prominence as a college coach, and the finger he had on the cultural pulse among college football coaches, his accusation could be seen as one major catalyst that created the shitstorm that Coach Prime had to deal with. It also proves the point I am making about how Coach Prime has shaken the college football world up in ways that the established culture was not comfortable with.
43. "Deion Sanders."
44. Alia J. Crum, Peter Salovey, and Shawn Achor, "Rethinking Stress: The Role of Mindsets in Determining the Stress Response," *Journal of Personality and Social Psychology* 104, no. 4 (April 2013): 716–733, https://doi.org/10.1037/a0031201.
45. Alia J. Crum and Ellen J. Langer, "Mind-Set Matters: Exercise and the Placebo Effect," *Psychological Science* 18, no. 2 (February 1, 2007): 165–171, https://doi.org/10.1111/j.1467-9280.2007.01867.x.
46. "Conspire," Online Etymology Dictionary, accessed October 30, 2024, https://www.etymonline.com/word/conspire.
47. A choice that he understands as a call from God.
48. Deion Sanders participated in a live interview with Matt Sapaula of the 7 Figure Squad in which he shared about his faith. The full interview is available here: "CU Head Coach Deion Sanders on the UNFAIR Treatment of HBCUs, Travis Hunter, and Life in The NFL," 7 Figure Squad, September 30, 2022, https://www.youtube.com/watch?v=Bt0w9x2c7Ts.
49. Butler, *Black Transhuman Liberation Theology*, 53.
50. For a helpful review of definitions, different theoretical approaches, and significant findings, see Fabian Pels et al., "Group Flow: A Scoping Review of Definitions, Theoretical Approaches, Measures and Findings," *PLOS ONE* 13, no. 12 (December 31, 2018): e0210117, https://doi.org/10.1371/journal.pone.0210117.
51. Mohammad Shehata et al., "Team Flow Is a Unique Brain State Associated with Enhanced Information Integration and Interbrain Synchrony," *eNeuro* 8, no. 5 (September 1, 2021), https://doi.org/10.1523/ENEURO.0133-21.2021.

52. "Acts 2:1–2 NRSVUE—The Coming of the Holy Spirit—When," Bible Gateway, accessed October 30, 2024, https://www.biblegateway.com/passage/?search=Acts%202%3A1-2&version=NRSVUE.
53. "Acts 2:4 NRSVUE—All of Them Were Filled with the Holy," Bible Gateway, accessed October 30, 2024, https://www.biblegateway.com/passage/?search=Acts%202%3A4&version=NRSVUE.
54. "Matthew 18:6-20—New Revised Standard Version Updated Edition," Bible Gateway, accessed October 30, 2024, https://www.biblegateway.com/passage/?search=Matthew%2018%3A6-20&version=NRSVUE.
55. Hopkins, *Being Human*, 175.
56. Hopkins, *Being Human*, 175.

CHAPTER 5: EMBODIED BRILLIANCE BEYOND THE MYTH

1. The late Jaak Panksepp is renowned for his work on affective neuroscience, and, more specifically, his argument that play possesses its own emotional operating system that is largely responsible for joy. Panksepp thus argues that there is a homeostasis to play that lives behind the urges that we all have for recreation and supports the evolutionary process. In other words, if too much time has passed without play, we will find ourselves doing it because we literally need it to survive. See Jaak Panksepp, *Affective Neuroscience: The Foundations of Human and Animal Emotions* (Oxford University Press, 2004). For a brief article introducing Panksepp's core arguments and principles, see Kenneth L. Davis and Christian Montag, "Selected Principles of Pankseppian Affective Neuroscience," *Frontiers in Neuroscience* 12 (January 17, 2019), https://doi.org/10.3389/fnins.2018.01025.
2. Luisa Speranza et al., "Dopamine: The Neuromodulator of Long-Term Synaptic Plasticity, Reward and Movement Control," *Cells* 10, no. 4 (March 26, 2021): 735, https://doi.org/10.3390/cells10040735.
3. Mojtaba Madadi Asl, Abdol-Hossein Vahabie, and Alireza Valizadeh, "Dopaminergic Modulation of Synaptic Plasticity, Its Role in Neuropsychiatric Disorders, and Its Computational Modeling," *Basic and Clinical Neuroscience* 10, no. 1 (2019): 1–12, https://doi.org/10.32598/bcn.9.10.125.
4. Silvia Knobloch-Westerwick, J. C. Abdallah, and Andrew C. Billings, "The Football Boost? Testing Three Models on Impacts on Sports Spectators' Self-Esteem," *Communication & Sport* 8, no. 2 (April 1, 2020): 236–261, https://doi.org/10.1177/2167479519830359.

5. Taishi Tsuji et al., "Watching Sports and Depressive Symptoms Among Older Adults: A Cross-Sectional Study from the JAGES 2019 Survey," *Scientific Reports* 11, no. 1 (May 19, 2021): 10612, https://doi.org/10.1038/s41598-021-89994-8.
6. Jaime Vila, "Social Support and Longevity: Meta-Analysis-Based Evidence and Psychobiological Mechanisms," *Frontiers in Psychology* 12 (September 13, 2021), https://doi.org/10.3389/fpsyg.2021.717164. When considering these results in connection with the association between lower rates of depression and longevity, the connection becomes clear. See also Stephen E. Gilman et al., "Depression and Mortality in a Longitudinal Study: 1952–2011," *Canadian Medical Association Journal* 189, no. 42 (October 23, 2017): E1304–1310, https://doi.org/10.1503/cmaj.170125.
7. Helen Keyes et al., "Attending Live Sporting Events Predicts Subjective Wellbeing and Reduces Loneliness," *Frontiers in Public Health* 10 (January 4, 2023), https://doi.org/10.3389/fpubh.2022.989706. See also social psychologist Carrie Wylands's comments featured in this brief article: Jocelyn Solis-Moreira, "5 Ways Cheering for Your Favorite World Cup Team Improves Your Health," Popular Science, December 2, 2022, https://www.popsci.com/health/world-cup-sports-cheering-mental-health/.
8. Sian L. Beilock et al., "Sports Experience Changes the Neural Processing of Action Language," *Proceedings of the National Academy of Sciences of the United States of America* 105, no. 36 (September 9, 2008): 13269–13273, https://doi.org/10.1073/pnas.0803424105.
9. The Griddy is a touchdown dance that was popularized by Justin Jefferson of the Minnesota Vikings. The dance went viral on social media and featured videos of children (and adults) across the country trying to emulate it in a variety of settings. My daughter was one of them, and as a result of the Griddy's popularity, Justin Jefferson is now one of her favorite football players.
10. "Inspire," Merriam-Webster.com, accessed September 11, 2024, https://www.merriam-webster.com/dictionary/inspire.
11. "Classic NFL Films Presents: Marshawn Lynch," accessed October 31, 2024, https://www.seahawks.com/video/classic-nfl-films-presents-marshawn-lynch-108371.
12. "Marshawn Lynch on the Origins of 'Beast Mode,'" CONAN on TBS, June 30, 2015, https://www.youtube.com/watch?v=tocg16sQkwk.

13. This productivity boost in particular can be seen when viewing the fourth item under "what to expect" as part of their description of what consumers will gain from the "Zero to Dangerous" training, which can be found on their website: https://www.flowresearchcollective.com/.
14. Steven Kotler et al., "First Few Seconds for Flow: A Comprehensive Proposal of the Neurobiology and Neurodynamics of State Onset," *Neuroscience & Biobehavioral Reviews* 143 (December 2022): 104956, https://doi.org/10.1016/j.neubiorev.2022.104956.
15. Longxi Li and Daniel M. Smith, "Neural Efficiency in Athletes: A Systematic Review," *Frontiers in Behavioral Neuroscience* 15 (August 5, 2021), https://doi.org/10.3389/fnbeh.2021.698555.
16. Kotler et al., "First Few Seconds for Flow."
17. "Classic NFL Films Presents."
18. David Rosen et al., "Creative Flow as Optimized Processing: Evidence from Brain Oscillations During Jazz Improvisations by Expert and Non-Expert Musicians," *Neuropsychologia* 196 (April 15, 2024): 108824, https://doi.org/10.1016/j.neuropsychologia.2024.108824.
19. One could technically argue that even Deebo was exercising his own brand of embodied intelligence, albeit not in culturally acceptable ways.
20. Craig hit him with a brick, then a trash can, before delivering the final right hook that put Deebo to sleep—because sometimes you have to use the master's tools . . .
21. This is a reference to the wisdom Craig's father gave him earlier in the film after realizing Craig had a gun. He encouraged him to "be a man" by putting the gun down and, if need be, fighting hand to hand without the intent to kill one another. And "living to fight another day" was "Pop's" rationale for offering this advice.
22. Danielle Fuentes Morgan, *Laughing to Keep from Dying: African American Satire in the Twenty-First Century* (University of Illinois Press, 2020), 2, my italics.
23. Morgan, *Laughing to Keep from Dying*, 2.
24. I borrow this term from Christena Cleveland, coined in her groundbreaking work *God Is a Black Woman*. For a constructive analysis of her concept, see Christena Cleveland, *God Is a Black Woman* (HarperOne, 2022), 27–43.
25. Cleveland, *God Is a Black Woman*, 34.
26. Chanequa Walker-Barnes, *Too Heavy a Yoke: Black Women and the Burden of Strength* (Cascade Books, 2014).

27. Brian Pronger, "Outta My Endzone: Sport and the Territorial Anus," *Journal of Sport and Social Issues* 23, no. 4 (November 1, 1999): 373–389, https://doi.org/10.1177/0193723599234002.
28. Katie Kindelan, "Serena Williams Alleges 'Discrimination' in How Often She Is Tested for Drugs," ABC News, July 25, 2018, https://abcnews.go.com/GMA/Culture/serena-williams-alleges-discrimination-tested-drugs/story?id=56804801.
29. Candace Buckner, "WNBA Players Helped Oust Kelly Loeffler from the Senate: Will She Last in the League?," *Washington Post*, January 7, 2021, https://www.washingtonpost.com/sports/2021/01/07/wnba-loeffler-warnock-senate-atlanta-dream/.
30. Hopkins, *Being Human*, 180.
31. Maya Angelou, during a CNN interview with Anderson Cooper while talking about the legacy of Dr. Martin Luther King Jr. on the 50th anniversary of the March on Washington. "Angelou: 'No One of Us Can Be Free Until Everybody I . . .,'" CNN, August 29, 2013, https://www.youtube.com/watch?v=UxkTd6BFL1o. For the full transcript of this interview, see "CNN.Com—Transcripts," August 28, 2013, https://transcripts.cnn.com/show/acd/date/2013-08-28/segment/02.
32. "Da Get Got Pod with Marshawn Lynch & Mike Robinson," Apple Podcasts, accessed October 31, 2024, https://podcasts.apple.com/us/podcast/da-get-got-pod-with-marshawn-lynch-mike-robinson/id1765564684.
33. Delores S. Williams, *Sisters in the Wilderness: The Challenge of Womanist God*, anniversary ed. (Orbis Books, 2013), 161–167.
34. Coleman, *Making a Way Out of No Way*, 93–100.
35. Cleveland, *God Is a Black Woman*.
36. Emmanuel Lartey, *Postcolonializing God: An African Practical Theology* (SCM Press, 2013), 15.
37. Frank Ocean, "Bad Religion," lyrics, Genius.com, accessed October 31, 2024, https://genius.com/Frank-ocean-bad-religion-lyrics.
38. Yvonne P. Chireau, *Black Magic: Religion and the African American Conjuring Tradition* (University of California Press, 2006), 3.
39. Lartey, *Postcolonializing God*, 25.
40. My italics.
41. Lartey, *Postcolonializing God*, 25.
42. Lartey, *Postcolonializing God*, 26–27.
43. Lartey, *Postcolonializing God*, 28.
44. Lartey, *Postcolonializing God*, 29.
45. Lartey, *Postcolonializing God*, 30.

46. Anna Lardone et al., "Mindfulness Meditation Is Related to Long-Lasting Changes in Hippocampal Functional Topology During Resting State: A Magnetoencephalography Study," *Neural Plasticity* 2018 (2018): 5340717, https://doi.org/10.1155/2018/5340717.
47. Simón Guendelman et al., "Mindfulness and Emotion Regulation: Insights from Neurobiological, Psychological, and Clinical Studies," *Frontiers in Psychology* 8 (March 6, 2017): 220, https://doi.org/10.3389/fpsyg.2017.00220.
48. I use *solo* here based on the recognition that there is no such thing as an individual. *Solo* better captures the relationality of beginning as part of a whole and separating oneself for the sake of performing a solo—such as in a jazz band—before returning to the whole from which we all come.

BIBLIOGRAPHY

ABC7 San Francisco. "Marshawn Lynch at Super Bowl Media Day: 'I'm Just Here so I Won't Get Fined.'" ABC7 News, January 27, 2015. https://abc7news.com/marshawn-lynch-beast-mode-seattle-seahawks-new-england-patriots/493651/.

Alameda, Clara, Daniel Sanabria, and Luis F. Ciria. "The Brain in Flow: A Systematic Review on the Neural Basis of the Flow State." *Cortex* 154 (September 1, 2022): 348–364. https://doi.org/10.1016/j.cortex.2022.06.005.

Alexander, Michelle. *The New Jim Crow: Mass Incarceration in the Age of Colorblindness*. The New Press, 2012.

Alosco, Michael L., Yorghos Tripodis, Inga K. Koerte, et al. "Interactive Effects of Racial Identity and Repetitive Head Impacts on Cognitive Function, Structural MRI-Derived Volumetric Measures, and Cerebrospinal Fluid Tau and Aβ." *Frontiers in Human Neuroscience* 13 (December 20, 2019): 440. https://doi.org/10.3389/fnhum.2019.00440.

"Amy Cooper Made 2nd Call to 911 About Black Birdwatcher, Prosecutors Say." *Today*, October 15, 2020. https://www.youtube.com/watch?v=L3662COVmn8.

"Angelou: 'No One of Us Can Be Free Until Everybody I . . .,'" CNN, August 29, 2013. https://www.youtube.com/watch?v=UxkTd6BFL1o.

Associated Press. "NFL Agrees to End Race-Based Brain Testing in $1B Settlement on Concussions." NPR, October 20, 2021. https://www.npr.org/2021/10/20/1047793751/nfl-concussion-settlement-race-norming-cte.

Associated Press. "Vogue Cover with LeBron Stirs Up Controversy." TODAY.com, March 25, 2008. https://www.today.com/news/vogue-cover-lebron-stirs-controversy-wbna23797883.

Beilock, Sian L., Ian M. Lyons, Andrew Mattarella-Micke, Howard C. Nusbaum, and Steven L. Small. "Sports Experience Changes the Neural

Processing of Action Language." *Proceedings of the National Academy of Sciences of the United States of America* 105, no. 36 (September 9, 2008): 13269–13273. https://doi.org/10.1073/pnas.0803424105.

Big Think. "How Your Brain Creates Reality, Explained by a Neuroscientist." Accessed October 27, 2024. https://bigthink.com/the-well/what-is-reality/.

Billings, Andrew C. "Depicting the Quarterback in Black and White: A Content Analysis of College and Professional Football Broadcast Commentary." *Howard Journal of Communications* 15, no. 4 (October 1, 2004): 201–210. https://doi.org/10.1080/10646170490521158.

Bowman, Sarah Lynne. *The Functions of Role-Playing Games: How Participants Create Community, Solve Problems and Explore Identity*. McFarland & Company, 2010.

Buckner, Candace. "WNBA Players Helped Oust Kelly Loeffler from the Senate: Will She Last in the League?" *Washington Post*, January 7, 2021. https://www.washingtonpost.com/sports/2021/01/07/wnba-loeffler-warnock-senate-atlanta-dream/.

Bureau of Labor Statistics. "Employed Persons by Detailed Occupation, Sex, Race, and Hispanic or Latino Ethnicity." Accessed October 29, 2024. https://www.bls.gov/cps/cpsaat11.htm.

Butler, Philip. *Black Transhuman Liberation Theology: Technology and Spirituality*. Bloomsbury Academic, 2020.

Campbell, Paul Ian, and Louis Bebb. "'He Is Like a Gazelle (When He Runs)': (Re)Constructing Race and Nation in Match-Day Commentary at the Men's 2018 FIFA World Cup." *Sport in Society* 25, no. 1 (December 27, 2021): 144–162. https://doi.org/10.1080/17430437.2020.1777102.

"Classic NFL Films Presents: Marshawn Lynch." Accessed October 31, 2024. https://www.seahawks.com/video/classic-nfl-films-presents-marshawn-lynch-108371.

Cleveland, Christena. *God Is a Black Woman*. HarperOne, 2022.

"Club Shay Shay: Marshawn Lynch Part 1." Apple Podcasts, October 4, 2023. https://podcasts.apple.com/us/podcast/marshawn-lynch-part-1/id1531023690?i=1000630127547.

"CNN.Com—Transcripts." CNN, August 28, 2013. https://transcripts.cnn.com/show/acd/date/2013-08-28/segment/02.

Coalition to Dismantle the Doctrine of Discovery. "What Is the Doctrine of Discovery?" June 29, 2015. https://dismantlediscovery.org/about/doctrine-of-discovery-basics/.

Coleman, Monica A. *Making a Way Out of No Way: A Womanist Theology*. Fortress Press, 2008.

Cone, James H. *The Cross and the Lynching Tree*. Orbis Books, 2011.
"Coon Caricature, the: Anti-Black Imagery." Jim Crow Museum website. Accessed October 27, 2024. https://jimcrowmuseum.ferris.edu/coon/homepage.htm.
Copeland, M. Shawn. *Enfleshing Freedom: Body, Race, and Being*. 2nd ed. Fortress Press, 2023.
Cormie, Prue, Michael R. McGuigan, and Robert U. Newton. "Developing Maximal Neuromuscular Power: Part 1—Biological Basis of Maximal Power Production." *Sports Medicine (Auckland, N.Z.)* 41, no. 1 (January 1, 2011): 17–38. https://doi.org/10.2165/11537690-000000000-00000.
Crum, Alia J., and Ellen J. Langer. "Mind-Set Matters: Exercise and the Placebo Effect." *Psychological Science* 18, no. 2 (February 1, 2007): 165–171. https://doi.org/10.1111/j.1467-9280.2007.01867.x.
Crum, Alia J., Peter Salovey, and Shawn Achor. "Rethinking Stress: The Role of Mindsets in Determining the Stress Response." *Journal of Personality and Social Psychology* 104, no. 4 (April 2013): 716–733. https://doi.org/10.1037/a0031201.
"CU Head Coach Deion Sanders on the UNFAIR Treatment of HBCUs, Travis Hunter, and Life in the NFL." 7 Figure Squad, September 30, 2022. https://www.youtube.com/watch?v=Bt0w9x2c7Ts.
Curcic, Dimitrije. "Racial Bias in NBA Commentary (Analysis)." RunRepeat, March 25, 2024. https://runrepeat.com/racial-bias-in-nba-commentary.
"Da Get Got Pod with Marshawn Lynch & Mike Robinson." Apple Podcasts. Accessed October 31, 2024. https://podcasts.apple.com/us/podcast/da-get-got-pod-with-marshawn-lynch-mike-robinson/id1765564684.
Davis, Kenneth L., and Christian Montag. "Selected Principles of Pankseppian Affective Neuroscience." *Frontiers in Neuroscience* 12 (January 17, 2019). https://doi.org/10.3389/fnins.2018.01025.
"Deion Sanders." Club Shay Shay, December 20, 2022. https://omny.fm/shows/club-shay-shay/deion-sanders.
Douglas, Kelly Brown. *Sexuality and the Black Church: A Womanist Perspective*. Orbis Books, 1999.
Douglas, Kelly Brown. *Stand Your Ground: Black Bodies and the Justice of God*. Orbis Books, 2015.
DuBois, W. E. B. *The Souls of Black Folk*. CreateSpace Independent Publishing Platform, 2014.
DuBois, W. E. B., and Norman Harris. *The Souls of Black Folk*. Pocket Books, 2005.
Eat.Learn.Play. Foundation. "Eat.Learn.Play. Foundation." Accessed October 9, 2024. https://www.eatlearnplay.org.

Ellison, Gregory C. *Cut Dead but Still Alive: Caring for African American Young Men.* Abingdon Press, 2013.
Ellison, Ralph. *Invisible Man.* 2nd ed. Vintage, 1995.
Enoka, Roger M., and Jacques Duchateau. "Rate Coding and the Control of Muscle Force." *Cold Spring Harbor Perspectives in Medicine* 7, no. 10 (October 2017): a029702. https://doi.org/10.1101/cshperspect.a029702.
"Estimated Probability of Competing in College Athletics." NCAA.org. Accessed October 28, 2024. https://www.ncaa.org/sports/2015/3/2/estimated-probability-of-competing-in-college-athletics.aspx.
Farley, Wendy. *Tragic Vision and Divine Compassion: A Contemporary Theodicy.* Westminster John Knox Press, 1990.
"Giannis Gets Freaky, Warriors New Reality, NFL Week Preview and More!!! From Jalen & Jacoby." ESPN podcasts, October 25, 2019. https://www.espn.co.uk/radio/play?id=27928512.
Gilman, Stephen E., Ewa Sucha, Mila Kingsbury, Nicholas J. Horton, Jane M. Murphy, and Ian Colman. "Depression and Mortality in a Longitudinal Study: 1952–2011." *CMAJ: Canadian Medical Association Journal = Journal de l'Association Medicale Canadienne* 189, no. 42 (October 23, 2017): E1304–E1310. https://doi.org/10.1503/cmaj.170125.
Green II, Gary F. "Playing the Game: Unmarking 'Beast' from the Bodies of Young Black Men." PhD diss., Brite Divinity School, June 2020. https://repository.tcu.edu/handle/116099117/40353.
Guendelman, Simón, Sebastián Medeiros, and Hagen Rampes. "Mindfulness and Emotion Regulation: Insights from Neurobiological, Psychological, and Clinical Studies." *Frontiers in Psychology* 8 (March 6, 2017): 220. https://doi.org/10.3389/fpsyg.2017.00220.
Guthrie, Steven R. *Creator Spirit: The Holy Spirit and the Art of Becoming Human.* Baker Academic, 2011.
"'He's a BEAST!' Spike Lee on Adam Driver Owning BlacKKKlansman." BBC Radio 1, August 24, 2018. https://www.youtube.com/watch?v=xkeNEZ-G-Rw.
Higginbotham, Evelyn Brooks. *Righteous Discontent: The Women's Movement in the Black Baptist Church, 1880–1920.* Harvard University Press, 1994.
Hill Collins, Patricia. *Black Feminist Thought: Knowledge, Consciousness, and the Politics of Empowerment.* Rev. 10th anniversary ed. Routledge, 2000.
Hurt, Byron, dir. *Hip-Hop: Beyond Beats and Rhymes.* PBS documentary, 2007. https://www.pbs.org/independentlens/documentaries/hiphop/.
Holiday, Billie. "Strange Fruit." Lyrics. Genius.com. Accessed October 29, 2024. https://genius.com/Billie-holiday-strange-fruit-lyrics.
hooks, bell. *Where We Stand: Class Matters.* Routledge, 2000.

Hopkins, Dwight N. *Being Human: Race, Culture, and Religion*. Fortress Press, 2005.

Hopkins, Dwight N. *Black Theology: Essays on Gender Perspectives*. Cascade Books, 2017.

Hwang, Fuu-Jiun, Richard H. Roth, Yu-Wei Wu, et al. "Motor Learning Selectively Strengthens Cortical and Striatal Synapses of Motor Engram Neurons." *Neuron* 110, no. 17 (September 7, 2022): 2790–2801.e5. https://doi.org/10.1016/j.neuron.2022.06.006.

Jennings, Willie James. *The Christian Imagination: Theology and the Origins of Race*. Yale University Press, 2010.

Johnson, Cedric C. *Race, Religion, and Resilience in the Neoliberal Age*. Palgrave Macmillan, 2015.

Kendi, Ibram X. *How to Be an Antiracist*. Updated ed. One World, 2023.

Keyes, Helen, Sarah Gradidge, Nicola Gibson, et al. "Attending Live Sporting Events Predicts Subjective Wellbeing and Reduces Loneliness." *Frontiers in Public Health* 10 (January 4, 2023). https://doi.org/10.3389/fpubh.2022.989706.

Kindelan, Katie. "Serena Williams Alleges 'Discrimination' in How Often She Is Tested for Drugs." ABC News, July 25, 2018. https://abcnews.go.com/GMA/Culture/serena-williams-alleges-discrimination-tested-drugs/story?id=56804801.

Knobloch-Westerwick, Silvia, J. C. Abdallah, and Andrew C. Billings. "The Football Boost? Testing Three Models on Impacts on Sports Spectators' Self-Esteem." *Communication & Sport* 8, no. 2 (April 1, 2020): 236–261. https://doi.org/10.1177/2167479519830359.

Kotler, Steven, Michael Mannino, Scott Kelso, and Richard Huskey. "First Few Seconds for Flow: A Comprehensive Proposal of the Neurobiology and Neurodynamics of State Onset." *Neuroscience & Biobehavioral Reviews* 143 (December 1, 2022): 104956. https://doi.org/10.1016/j.neubiorev.2022.104956.

Kross, Ethan. *Chatter: The Voice in Our Head, Why It Matters, and How to Harness It*. Reprint ed. Crown, 2022.

Kross, Ethan, Emma Bruehlman-Senecal, Jiyoung Park, et al. "Self-Talk as a Regulatory Mechanism: How You Do It Matters." *Journal of Personality and Social Psychology* 106, no. 2 (2014): 304–324. https://doi.org/10.1037/a0035173.

Lardone, Anna, Marianna Liparoti, Pierpaolo Sorrentino, et al. "Mindfulness Meditation Is Related to Long-Lasting Changes in Hippocampal Functional Topology During Resting State: A Magnetoencephalography Study." *Neural Plasticity* 2018 (2018): 5340717. https://doi.org/10.1155/2018/5340717.

Lee, Felecia, Rhonda Lewis, Jamilia Sly, Chakema Carmack, Shani Roberts, and Polly Basore. "Promoting Positive Youth Development by Examining the Career and Educational Aspirations of African American Males: Implications for Designing Educational Programs." *Journal of Prevention & Intervention in the Community* 39 (October 1, 2011): 299–309. https://doi.org/10.1080/10852352.2011.606402.

Li, Longxi, and Daniel M. Smith. "Neural Efficiency in Athletes: A Systematic Review." *Frontiers in Behavioral Neuroscience* 15 (August 5, 2021). https://doi.org/10.3389/fnbeh.2021.698555.

Linden, Dimitri van der, Mattie Tops, and Arnold B. Bakker. "The Neuroscience of the Flow State: Involvement of the Locus Coeruleus Norepinephrine System." *Frontiers in Psychology* 12 (April 14, 2021). https://doi.org/10.3389/fpsyg.2021.645498.

Madadi Asl, Mojtaba, Abdol-Hossein Vahabie, and Alireza Valizadeh. "Dopaminergic Modulation of Synaptic Plasticity, Its Role in Neuropsychiatric Disorders, and Its Computational Modeling." *Basic and Clinical Neuroscience* 10, no. 1 (2019): 1–12. https://doi.org/10.32598/bcn.9.10.125.

Marquez-Velarde, Guadalupe, Rachel Grashow, Christy Glass, et al. "The Paradox of Integration: Racial Composition of NFL Positions from 1960 to 2020." *Sociology of Race and Ethnicity* 9, no. 4 (October 2023): 451–469. https://doi.org/10.1177/23326492231182597.

"Marshawn Lynch/Cheated/USA Rugby/A Survivor's March." *60 Minutes Sports*, June 7, 2016. https://www.imdb.com/title/tt6573364/?ref_=ttep_ep6.

"Marshawn Lynch on Mental Health, Pete Carroll & More." I AM ATHLETE, February 20, 2023. https://www.iamathletetv.com/show/marshawn-lynch-lendale-white-on-their-mental-health-pete-carroll-more.

"Marshawn Lynch on the Origins of 'Beast Mode.'" CONAN on TBS, June 30, 2015. https://www.youtube.com/watch?v=tocg16sQkwk.

"Marshawn Lynch's Best Press Conference Moments." Accessed October 27, 2024. https://www.seahawks.com/video/marshawn-lynch-press-conference-best-moments.

McClure, Barbara J. *Emotions: Problems and Promise for Human Flourishing*. Baylor University Press, 2019.

McClure, Barbara J. *Moving Beyond Individualism in Pastoral Care and Counseling: Reflections on Theory, Theology and Practice*. Cascade Books, 2010.

McClure, Barbara J. "Pastoral Theology as the Art of Paying Attention: Widening the Horizons." *International Journal of Practical Theology* 12, no. 2 (October 2008): 189–210.

McNamee, Stephen J. *The Meritocracy Myth*. 5th ed. Rowman & Littlefield, 2023.

Mignolo, Walter. *The Darker Side of Western Modernity: Global Futures, Decolonial Options*. Duke University Press, 2011.

Moore, Louis. *We Will Win the Day: The Civil Rights Movement, the Black Athlete, and the Quest for Equality*. The University Press of Kentucky, 2021.

Morgan, Danielle Fuentes. *Laughing to Keep from Dying: African American Satire in the Twenty-First Century*. University of Illinois Press, 2020.

Neal, Mark Anthony. *Looking for Leroy: Illegible Black Masculinities*. New York University Press, 2013.

"NFL Media Access Policy." PFWA. Accessed April 30, 2024. https://www.profootballwriters.org/nfl-media-access-policy/.

Ocean, Frank. "Bad Religion." Lyrics. Genius.com. Accessed October 31, 2024. https://genius.com/Frank-ocean-bad-religion-lyrics.

Panksepp, Jaak. *Affective Neuroscience: The Foundations of Human and Animal Emotions*. Oxford University Press, 2004.

"Patrick Ewing's Former Coach Writes Script About Racism NBA Icon Endured." Audacy, March 30, 2023. https://www.audacy.com/cbssportsradio/sports/nba/mike-jarvis-writes-script-about-racism-patrick-ewing-endured.

Pels, Fabian, Jens Kleinert, and Florian Mennigen. "Group Flow: A Scoping Review of Definitions, Theoretical Approaches, Measures and Findings." *PLOS ONE* 13, no. 12 (December 31, 2018): e0210117. https://doi.org/10.1371/journal.pone.0210117.

Pronger, Brian. "Outta My Endzone: Sport and the Territorial Anus." *Journal of Sport and Social Issues* 23, no. 4 (November 1, 1999): 373–389. https://doi.org/10.1177/0193723599234002.

Redick, JJ, and Tommy Alter. "Stephen Curry." Apple podcasts, November 22, 2022. https://podcasts.apple.com/us/podcast/stephen-curry/id1525281746?i=1000587042299.

Reiss, Mike. "Tom Brady on Louisville QB Lamar Jackson: 'He's a Beast!'" ESPN.com, April 12, 2018. https://www.espn.com/blog/boston/new-england-patriots/post/_/id/4812827/tom-brady-on-louisville-qb-lamar-jackson-hes-a-beast.

Rhoden, William C. *Forty Million Dollar Slaves: The Rise, Fall, and Redemption of the Black Athlete.* Reprint ed. Broadway Books, 2007.

Roberts, Mark S. *The Mark of the Beast: Animality and Human Oppression.* Purdue University Press, 2008.

Rogers-Vaughn, Bruce. *Caring for Souls in a Neoliberal Age.* Palgrave Macmillan, 2016.

Rogoff, Barbara. *The Cultural Nature of Human Development.* Oxford University Press, 2003.

Rosen, David, Yongtaek Oh, Christine Chesebrough, Fengqing (Zoe) Zhang, and John Kounios. "Creative Flow as Optimized Processing: Evidence from Brain Oscillations During Jazz Improvisations by Expert and Non-Expert Musicians." *Neuropsychologia* 196 (April 15, 2024): 108824. https://doi.org/10.1016/j.neuropsychologia.2024.108824.

Scisciola, Lucia, Rosaria Anna Fontanella, Surina, Vittoria Cataldo, Giuseppe Paolisso, and Michelangela Barbieri. "Sarcopenia and Cognitive Function: Role of Myokines in Muscle Brain Cross-Talk." *Life* 11, no. 2 (February 23, 2021): 173. https://doi.org/10.3390/life11020173.

Shehata, Mohammad, Miao Cheng, Angus Leung, et al. "Team Flow Is a Unique Brain State Associated with Enhanced Information Integration and Interbrain Synchrony." *eNeuro* 8, no. 5 (September 1, 2021). https://doi.org/10.1523/ENEURO.0133-21.2021.

Smith, Archie. *The Relational Self: Ethics & Therapy from a Black Church Perspective.* Abingdon, 1982.

Solis-Moreira, Jocelyn. "5 Ways Cheering for Your Favorite World Cup Team Improves Your Health." *Popular Science*, December 2, 2022. https://www.popsci.com/health/world-cup-sports-cheering-mental-health/.

Speranza, Luisa, Umberto di Porzio, Davide Viggiano, Antonio de Donato, and Floriana Volpicelli. "Dopamine: The Neuromodulator of Long-Term Synaptic Plasticity, Reward and Movement Control." *Cells* 10, no. 4 (March 26, 2021): 735. https://doi.org/10.3390/cells10040735.

Statista. "NBA Players by Ethnicity 2023." Accessed October 29, 2024. https://www.statista.com/statistics/1167867/nba-players-ethnicity/.

Statista. "Share of NFL Players by Race 2023." Accessed October 29, 2024. https://www.statista.com/statistics/1167935/racial-diversity-nfl-players/.

"Stephen Curry (ft. Golden State Warriors): 2014–15 MVP Acceptance Speech." Speech delivered at the NBA Season Awards, May 4, 2015. https://genius.com/Stephen-curry-2014-15-mvp-acceptance-speech-annotated.

"Stephen Curry Draft Report: Actions Speak Louder Than Words." CoachUp Presents, September 22, 2015. https://www.youtube.com/watch?v=WLb8AwuZ7N8.

Townes, Emilie Maureen. *Womanist Ethics and the Cultural Production of Evil*. Palgrave Macmillan, 2006.

Tsuji, Taishi, Satoru Kanamori, Ryota Watanabe, et al. "Watching Sports and Depressive Symptoms Among Older Adults: A Cross-Sectional Study from the JAGES 2019 Survey." *Scientific Reports* 11, no. 1 (May 19, 2021): 10612. https://doi.org/10.1038/s41598-021-89994-8.

Turner, Jennifer D. "Freedom to Aspire: Black Children's Career Dreams, Perceived Aspirational Supports, and Africentric Values." *Race Ethnicity and Education* 25, no. 1 (January 2, 2022): 128–153. https://doi.org/10.1080/13613324.2020.1718074.

Vila, Jaime. "Social Support and Longevity: Meta-Analysis-Based Evidence and Psychobiological Mechanisms." *Frontiers in Psychology* 12 (September 13, 2021). https://doi.org/10.3389/fpsyg.2021.717164.

Wagner, Ryan, Karie Zach, Yuka Kobayashi, and Andrew W. Gottschalk. "Race and Concussion: An Emerging Relationship." *Ochsner Journal* 20, no. 4 (2020): 348–349. https://doi.org/10.31486/toj.20.0145.

Walker-Barnes, Chanequa. *Too Heavy a Yoke: Black Women and the Burden of Strength*. Cascade Books, 2014.

White, Rachel E., Emily O. Prager, Catherine Schaefer, Ethan Kross, Angela L. Duckworth, and Stephanie M. Carlson. "The 'Batman Effect': Improving Perseverance in Young Children." *Child Development* 88, no. 5 (2017): 1563–1571. https://doi.org/10.1111/cdev.12695.

Williams, Delores S. *Sisters in the Wilderness: The Challenge of Womanist God*. Anniversary ed. Orbis Books, 2013.

INDEX

Agent Smith, 112
Alexander, Michelle, 64n11
Ali, Muhammed, 101
Angelou, Maya, 153
Antetokounmpo, Giannis, 6. *See also*, Greek Freak

Baldwin, James, 59, 119n36
"beast," 2n1, 3–12, 14–17, 25, 27, 29, 33–35, 37–38, 44, 46–47, 49, 51, 53–54, 72, 75, 89, 106, 121, 133, 140–41, 151. *See also*, caricature
beast mode, 2–3, 7–8, 31, 49, 57
   as embodied brilliance, 141–44
   the beatitudes of, 166
Beethoven, 86, 144
Beyoncé, 86
Biles, Simone, 152
Bowman, Sarah, 98–99
Brady, Tom, 5–7n8
Bruce Bruce, xi
Butler, Judith, 111n26
Butler, Philip, 52–53, 56, 72–75, 82, 117–18, 120, 126–27, 131

caricature, xiii–xxi, 2, 4, 8, 12, 25, 44, 47, 50, 54, 72

Carlos, John, 21
Chauvin, Derek, xiv, 16, 27
Chireau, Yvonne P., 160
Cleveland, Christena, 150, 156
code switching, 108–12, 114, 138, 160
Coleman, Monica, 119–20, 126, 153, 155, 163
Collins, Patricia Hill, 108
Cone, James, 50–51, 119
contingent divinity, 156, 162
Cooper, Amy, 15–16, 27, 83
Cooper, Christian, 15–16
Copeland, M. Shawn, 54–55, 74–75, 80, 91
Craig, Tyler, xi
crux (of creativity), xx
   and code switching, 110
   and imago DNA, 141
   and inspiration, 138–39, 141
   as opposed to "soul," 79–81
   of Black athletes, 170
   of Black being, 157–58
   of culture, 103
Curry, Steph, xx, 59–63, 66–67, 70, 72, 85–86, 89, 115, 116, 120, 137, 139, 147–48, 151, 153–54, 168

Davis, Angela, 1
Douglas, Kelly Brown, 42, 45, 51, 157
Driver, Adam, 7
DuBois, W.E.B., xii, 112
Dyson, Michael Eric, 69

Einstein, Albert, 86
Ellison II, Gregory C., 14, 107
embodied brilliance, xxi, 49, 115, 131, 133, 148, 157
 of "beast mode," 141
 of Black athletes, 2, 4, 55, 88, 137, 141, 151–52, 170–71
 of Black people, 99
 of Black women, 155–156
 of Marshawn Lynch, 29, 57
 of "Prime Time," 95
energetic intimacy, 134, 137–39, 141
(e)strange(d) fruit(fulness), 49–51
Ewing, Patrick, 12n19–20, 17

flow, 59, 85, 142–44, 150
 group, 128–29
Floyd, George, xiv, xviii, 16, 80, 120

Gauff, Coco, 152
Gibson, Althea, 152
Greek Freak, 6–7
Green Sr., Gary ("Coach Green"), xii, xiv, xv

Higginbotham, Evelyn Brooks, 108–9
Hill, David, xiv
Hill, Jim, xiv
Holliday, Billie, 50
hooks, bell, 69

Hopkins, Dwight, 9, 45, 56, 85, 130, 153
Hurston, Zora Neale, 119n36

imago DNA, 141, 158, 162
Ingraham, Laura, 21
intelligence(s), 5, 56, 59, 85, 87–89, 148
 as biotechnology of becoming, 55
 athleticism as, 148
 blend of, 56, 62
 cognitive, 4
 embodied, 112
 of Simone Biles, 152

Jacoby, David, 6
James, LeBron, 11–12, 17, 21, 70, 101
Jennings, Willie James, 38–42, 45, 157
Jesus, 56, 104, 121, 129, 140, 148, 153, 157–59, 161
Jobs, Steve, 86
Johnson, Cedric, 23–24, 109–10
Johnson, E. Patrick, 111
Johnson, Katherine, 86
Johnson, Larry, 18

Kaepernick, Colin, 21, 25, 66, 152
Kendi, Ibram X., 37
Kerr, Steve, 61, 89, 154
King Jr., Martin Luther, 133
King Kong, 11–12n21
Kotler, Steven, 142
Kross, Ethan, 99–101

Lamar, Kendrick, 91
Lee, Spike, 7

Index

Lynch, Marshawn, xx, 2–3, 7–9, 16, 17, 27, 29–34, 38, 48–49, 52, 56–57, 66–67, 70, 120, 141–44, 147, 151, 153, 154
lynching, 1–2, 9, 13, 36, 46, 50–51, 106

magic, 123, 158, 164
  embodied, 123–24
  intellectual magic of athleticism, 148
  of belief, 123–25
  of flow, 143
  of muscle memory, 86, 120
  of myokinesis, 113
Martin, Trayvon, xviii, 43
Mathis, Robert, 2
Mayock, Mike, 19–20, 67
McClure, Barbara J., 77–79
Moore, Louis, 20–21
Morgan, Danielle Fuentes, 145–46
Moses, 121
muscle memory, xv, 72, 81–85, 89, 103, 105, 115, 117, 120, 140, 144, 168, 171
  as culture, 103
  as embodied magic, 123. *See also*, magic
  as intellectual magic, 148. *See also*, magic
  of ancestral spirituality, 160
  of cultural upbringing, 161
  of hypermasculinity, 149
  of mental imagery, 167
  of racist beliefs, 169
  of racialized mistreatment, 15
  of white supremacy, 144
myokinesis, 112–13

Neal, Mark Anthony, 12–14
Neo, 112
neoliberal, 64, 67, 69
  age, 109–10
  capitalism, 2, 21–23, 150
  governance, 23–24
  neoliberalism, 22–23, 25, 67–68, 106, 147–48
  rationality, 63–64, 67–69, 71, 75–77, 79
NFL Combine, 19–20n31, 93–94
NFL Draft, 18–19, 155

Ocean, Frank, 159, 161
O'Neal, Shaquille, 61–63, 101

Panksepp, Jaak, 134n1
Pearson, Dave, 154
play space(s), 72, 103–4, 134, 137, 146, 163
Prime ("Prime Time"), xx, 93–95, 101, 112, 114–15, 121–23, 125, 130–31, 148, 152, 155

Raible, Steve, 3, 16, 27, 133, 137
(r)evolutionary
  action, 170
  belief in oneself as a Black man, 125
  brilliance of Black embodiment, 51
  contributions of Black men, 33
  contributions of Steph Curry, defined, 62, 89
  nature of womanist standpoints, 155
  possibilities, 158

significance of Black athletic achievements, 56
Rhoden, William C., 64
Rittimann, Ron, xv
Rose, Jalen, 6

Sanders, Deion, xx, 31, 93–95, 101, 112, 115, 121–23, 125–26, 130, 147–48, 151, 153, 155
satire, 145–47, 149, 151, 153, 155–56. *See also*, satirical
satirical, 157
   advantage of feminine wisdom, 151–53
   blind spot of patriarchy, 148–50
   disruptions, 147
   performances, 146
   play, 144–45
   play of African spirituality, 156–62
   wit of Black women, 153–56.
     See also, ***with***
Sharpe, Shannon, 30n3, 94n5
Smith Jr., Archie, 76–77, 79
Smith, Tommie, 21
Sommore, xi
spirituality, xi, 85, 117, 129, 131, 133, 153, 158, 160, 162, 168
   African, 155–56, 158–60, 163

embodied, 117, 127, 131, 158, 162, 164, 167
neuro, 117, 124, 146
of Energy, 162, 164
of sport, 141

The Book of Acts, 129
The Gospel of Matthew, 129
Townes, Emilie, 26, 34, 38, 104–6, 113–15, 122
Trump, Donald, 21, 124, 128–29
Turner, Jennifer D., 71

Walker, Alice, 86
Walker-Barnes, Chanequa, 150
Washington, Denzel, 116, 168
Washington, John David, 7
white supremacy, xii–xiii, xviii–xxi, 8, 17, 25, 35–38, 42–43, 46, 52–56, 71–72, 75, 79, 83–84, 109, 140, 144, 147–51, 155–56, 158, 169
Williams, Delores, 155
Williams, Serena, 151–52
wit, 85, 144, 149
   of Black women, 151–56
with, 153–56
Woodbine, Onaje X. O., 84

Zimmerman, George, 43